The Holocaust and Genocides in Europe

The Holocaust and Genocides in Europe

Benjamin Lieberman

BLOOMSBURY

LONDON • NEW DELHI • NEW YORK • SYDNEY

Bloomsbury Academic

An imprint of Bloomsbury Publishing Plc

50 Bedford Square
London
WC1B 3DP
UK

175 Fifth Avenue
New York
NY 10010
USA

www.bloomsbury.com

First published 2013

British Library Cataloguing-in-Publication Data
A catalogue record for this book is available from the British Library.

ISBN: HB: 978-1-4411-1447-1
PB: 978-1-4411-9478-7
PDF: 978-1-4411-4655-7
ePub: 978-1-4411-1080-0

Typeset by Newgen Imaging Systems Pvt, Ltd, Chennai, India
Printed and bound in Great Britain

CONTENTS

LIST OF ILLUSTRATIONS

Introduction: The Holocaust and the genocides in Europe

Today Auschwitz Birkenau is a museum and memorial at the town of Oświęcim in southern Poland. During the Second World War close to 1 million European Jews were murdered at Auschwitz, along with tens of thousands of other victims, including Poles, Gypsies, Soviet prisoners of war, and prisoners of many nationalities. Today, visitors take guided tours to see the camp which housed prisoners set to forced labor as well as sites where the camp stuff engaged in murder and medical experiments and also the chief killing center. In 2011, the memorial recorded more than 1.4 million visitors.

The museum and memorial at the site of the former Auschwitz-Birkenau death camp is only one of many similar sites that commemorate the victims of acts of genocide and similar destruction across much of Europe. In Germany, it is possible to visit memorials at former camps including Dachau, the first of all the Nazi concentration camps, as well as former camps at Bergen-Belsen, Buchenwald, and Sachsenhausen. Outside of Germany, there are memorials at former camps at Mauthausen in Austria and at sites of former camps in countries, including the Czech Republic, the Netherlands, and Serbia.

Along with the memorials and museums that commemorate the Holocaust, other similar sites record the horrors of other European genocides of the twentieth century. Far to the east a memorial to a genocide that took place before the Holocaust stands along with a museum on a hill on the edge of Yerevan, the capital of the Republic of Armenia. A circle of slabs surrounds an eternal flame, and a nearby museum houses exhibits on genocide. Unlike the memorials at sites of the Holocaust, however, the genocide memorial and museum at Yerevan lie at some distance from the sites of the killings commemorated. Armenians fled during the First World War toward areas that at the time lay within the Russian Empire, but the actual genocide started mainly in Anatolia in territory that is now within the Republic of Turkey. A visitor to Turkey, however, will look in vain for any commemoration to this genocide because the Republic of Turkey does not recognize the Armenian Genocide.

In Europe's southeast, another memorial commemorates a much more recent massacre and act of genocide. A memorial and cemetery at Srebrenica-Potočari in the east of the small country of Bosnia-Herzegovina serves as the resting place for the remains of some of the approximately 8,000 Bosnian Muslim men and boys murdered in August 1995. The remains of victims are buried after being identified through DNA testing at a forensics lab in the Bosnian town of Tuzla.

From Armenia, to Poland, Germany, and Bosnia the many memorials to genocide across Europe testify to the extraordinary waves of violence that struck Europe in the twentieth century. With its many memorials, the Holocaust stands at the center of this history of genocide, but genocide had already taken place during the First World War in the lands of the Ottoman Empire in what is now Turkey as well as in adjacent regions. Moreover, genocide recurred almost through the end of the twentieth century in Europe as Srebrenica tragically demonstrated. From the start until the end of the twentieth century, Europe suffered from repeated outbreaks of genocide. European genocides destroyed and swept away entire communities and gave rise to the very concept of genocide as well as to the field of genocide studies. This book provides an introduction to this history of modern European mass destruction.

Genocides do not amount to the sum of all Europe's history, but the record of genocide shapes our perception of the overall place of Europe in history. Histories of the world often cast Europe as a center of progress, of the renaissance, the scientific revolution, the enlightenment, and social progress, but a history of the repeated outbreaks of genocide casts Europe in a very different light. Europe's history cannot be reduced to genocide, but genocide has left a permanent imprint on Europe's history. Indeed, this record of mass killing has even led to the use of the phrase Dark Continent to describe Europe's twentieth century.[1]

Definitions

During the midst of the Second World War, a legal scholar named Raphael Lemkin coined the term genocide. A Polish Jew, Lemkin from a young age became interested in violence and the destruction of groups and looked into many historical cases. The destruction of Armenians during the First World War troubled him. As a legal scholar he called for new laws against what he termed "acts of barbarity" and "acts of vandalism" before finally arriving at the term genocide, which he described in his book *Axis Rule in Occupied Europe* in 1944. Referring to the "destruction of a nation or of an ethnic group" Lemkin described how he combined "the ancient Greek word *genos* (race, tribe) and the Latin *cide* (killing). . . ."

Over the next several years the newly created United Nations discussed genocide and placed the concept in international law. In December 1946 the UN General Assembly declared genocide a crime under international law. Lemkin then took part along with other legal scholars in drawing up a draft convention on the prevention and punishment of genocide. In 1948, the United Nations adopted the final version of the Convention on the Prevention and Punishment of the Crime of Genocide. The convention made clear that genocide had already occurred, stating "that at all periods of history genocide has inflicted great losses on humanity. . . ." It then defined genocide as a series of acts "committed with intent to destroy, in whole or in part, a national, ethnic, racial or religious group, as such." The list of acts began with the most obvious method of genocide "Killing

ACTS OF GENOCIDE LISTED IN THE UN CONVENTION ON THE PREVENTION AND PUNISHMENT OF THE CRIME OF GENOCIDE

(a) Killing members of the group;
(b) Causing serious bodily or mental harm to members of the group;
(c) Deliberately inflicting on the group conditions of life calculated to bring about its physical destruction in whole or in part;
(d) Imposing measures intended to prevent births within the group;
(e) Forcibly transferring children of the group to another group.

members of the group." However, the Convention also extended beyond direct mass murder, listing other acts of genocide. These included placing groups under conditions that would bring about destruction, and preventing births, or transferring children.

The 1948 Genocide Convention anchored genocide in international law, but from the start the question of how best to define genocide prompted debate. Some of the acts of genocide listed in the original draft never made it into the final convention. Thus, earlier drafts referred to "cultural" genocide. The list of protected groups was also reduced. In draft form the convention aimed to "prevent the destruction of racial, national, linguistic, religious, or political groups of human beings." However, the Soviet Union opposed including political groups in the list of protected groups, and the final convention did not mention political groups. The definition of genocide under international law would influence later debates on whether to include campaigns of Soviet persecution as genocide. The convention also omitted mention of gender as a protected group, though there is language referring to births and to children. The convention also makes no mention of sexual orientation. Focusing on the acts of genocide and on the list of protected groups, numerous scholars have suggested alternate definitions. This literature has shaped the history and analysis of genocide, but the Genocide Convention still defines genocide under international law more than 50 years after its adoption by the UN General Assembly.

To describe and explain the multiple waves of genocide in twentieth-century Europe, this book at times also focuses on closely related acts of violence that in many cases overlapped with genocide. Ethnic cleansing, for example, refers, as a Commission of Experts formed by the UN Security Council in 1992 stated, to "rendering an area ethnically homogenous by using force or intimidation to remove persons of given groups from the area." Unlike genocide, ethnic cleansing has never been anchored in international law by any UN convention. Indeed, some scholars of genocide have argued that ethnic cleansing amounts only to another term for genocide, but more often it is seen as a closely related means for attacking groups. On the other hand, as the chapters in this book on the Armenian Genocide and on Yugoslavia will demonstrate, ethnic cleansing has at times merged with genocide. Ethnic cleansing and genocide converge when the means used to remove a group extend to acts of genocide.

Approaches

This book focuses on major cases of genocide in twentieth-century Europe, including the Armenian Genocide, the Holocaust, and acts of genocide in the former Yugoslavia. The book places genocide within a spectrum of violence directed against groups and also introduces closely related phenomena, including mass killing in the Soviet Union and ethnic cleansing. Scholars continue to debate how to relate the concept of genocide to terror in the Soviet Union, but to completely ignore mass killing in the USSR, especially under the Stalinist regime in the 1930s, would overlook both the key debates over how to understand genocide as well as the real parallels between Nazi Germany and the USSR.

The opening chapter outlines the origins and roots of twentieth-century European genocides. No single factor made genocide inevitable, but war, imperialism, and new ideologies and political movements shaped the paths that led toward genocide. A series of chapters then provides case studies on the Armenian Genocide, the Holocaust, mass killing in the Soviet Union, and genocide and ethnic cleansing in the wars for the former Yugoslavia.

For each major case, the book will describe the causes of genocide and explain how genocide was carried out. Genocide is most often understood in terms of the first act of genocide listed in the Genocide Convention or "killing members of the group," and the case studies will detail the killings at the death camps and at other sites. Along with such acts of mass killing, genocides in twentieth-century Europe also took place through other destructive methods. Because these are less familiar from representation of genocide in popular culture, it is vital to make clear the variety of acts of genocide. Drawing comparisons between major cases of genocide, the book will emphasize both common shared patterns in genocide and the distinct acts of genocide in the Armenian Genocide, the Holocaust, and in the former Yugoslavia.

Along with charting the methods of genocide, this book also focuses on the human actors in genocide, including perpetrators, victims, and bystanders. The goal here is to understand why and how Europeans took part in carrying out genocide, and how they responded to genocide. In the case of perpetrators, this text goes beyond detailing crimes to explore the motives for genocide. Each chapter on an individual genocide also illustrates the experiences and responses of victims, including their knowledge of the peril they faced, their efforts to survive, and the factors that influenced efforts at resistance. Between perpetrators and victims, the mass of people present in any genocide are usually bystanders. This book introduces the complex and varied experiences of bystanders, exploring what bystanders knew about genocide and how they responded. This section will outline, as well, how some bystanders shifted toward complicity or resistance. Recounting the experiences of perpetrators, victims, and bystanders repeatedly reveals the existence of a "gray zone" of genocide in which motives and roles could blur.

The book takes a regional approach on two levels. First, it explores genocide as a recurrent tragedy in modern European history and discusses common roots of European genocides. Europe itself is not an easily defined region as it is only the western edge of the much larger land mass of Eurasia. Thus the Soviet Union where death squads murdered Jews during the Holocaust was a European country that also extended into Asia, though German death squads killed Jews in European territories of the Soviet Union. This book counts as European genocides, not only genocides that took place exclusively within Europe, but also genocides that developed to a significant extent from developments and trends in European history. In the case of the Armenian Genocide, the majority of Armenians died in areas just outside of Europe, but this genocide was still for many reasons a European genocide. The state in which genocide took place had long been a European power, the ideologies and crisis that contributed to genocide had roots in Europe. In particular, the First World War, the war that helped to lead toward genocide, began as a European war.

Secondly, the book discusses genocide within particular regions of Europe. Genocide is often treated as a theme in the history of individual nations, but the massive body of research into genocide has yielded a picture of regional variation. Genocide did not just remake countries: it also drastically recast the ethnic and religious makeup of particular communities and regions. In some cases entire cultures were virtually wiped. The processes of genocide varied by region, and the roles or perpetrators and bystanders also varied at times by region.

Charting the history of genocide in Europe's twentieth century affords a vital chance to survey causes of genocide, patterns in genocide, and effects of genocide. Though Lemkin himself was deeply interested in prior atrocities and massacres in many regions, it was genocide in Europe that pivotally led to the emergence both of the field of genocide studies and to the anchoring of genocide in international law. The Genocide Convention pointed to the occurrence of genocide in all periods of history and genocides have taken place far beyond Europe, such as in Cambodia and Rwanda, but Europe's twentieth century still occupies a key place in the history of genocide. Without the genocides of twentieth-century Europe and genocides carried out by Europeans, it is doubtful that the twentieth century would have been identified as a century of genocide. The key place of Europe in generating genocides during the twentieth century also helps to explain why genocide is widely seen as both the height of barbarity and also as a product of modernity, a paradox that continues to shape reactions to genocide. A key challenge for the study of genocides lies in explaining how the most notorious of all crimes carried out against groups recurred repeatedly when Europe was also seen by many as a center for human progress.

This book concludes by reviewing the aftermaths of genocide and by placing the genocides of twentieth-century Europe in a global context. The book charts efforts to come to terms with the past and attempts to bring perpetrators to justice, and introduces the connections between genocide in Europe and genocides elsewhere around the globe. Genocides in Europe and elsewhere provide reason, finally, to look for useful lessons for detecting and preventing potential future genocides.

1

Origins of genocide and paths to genocide

Multiple causes produced the genocides that killed millions of people in twentieth-century Europe. The Holocaust, the single best-known of all the cases of genocide, demonstrates the challenge in tracing the paths that led toward genocide. Even after years of mounting threats, European Jews still found it difficult to fathom that Nazi Germany pursued nothing less than their complete destruction. And even after reports of mass murder had reached the allies, including Britain and the United States during the Second World War, many of the soldiers who liberated camps at the war's end and the journalists who accompanied them often saw genocide as unimaginable and unthinkable. To take a broader perspective, we know a great deal about why genocides take place but the reality of genocide still seems to defy explanation.

Each case of genocide stems from specific factors that this book will track in the individual case studies, but the recurrence of genocide and related forms of mass violence in Europe has also given rise to a search for more general roots of genocide. Because genocide employs extreme and massive violence, Europe's record of violence both at home and abroad has attracted scrutiny in the search for causes of genocide. In both locations, at home and abroad, Europeans created paths that led toward genocide.

Efforts to chart the origins of European genocides have led to identifying possible causes for genocide in the European record of conquest and violence outside the continent. Was it merely coincidence that a continent that gave rise to some of the most infamous of all genocides in the twentieth century had previously been so heavily involved in overseas imperialism? Europeans well recalled their recent imperial ventures in Africa and Asia. The philosopher Hannah Arendt, who left Germany in 1933, escaped the internment camp of Gurs in France in 1940, and made her way to the United States in 1941, memorably emphasized the role of imperialism in creating conditions for extreme violence carried out by totalitarian regimes in her book *Origins of Totalitarianism*.

Because genocide targets groups defined by identity, growing European obsession with classifying and categorizing identities stood out as another possible key precondition for an age of genocide. Preoccupation with marking identity took both political and scientific forms. Politics increasingly centered on forms of identity, including nationalism and race. Various forms of racial science, which posited the possibility of improving overall racial quality, gained a strong foothold within Europe, as well as in other industrializing countries by the early twentieth century.

Rapid and extreme changes in the structure and boundaries of European governments and states provided yet another possible route toward genocide. Neither a change in form of government nor in political boundaries leads inexorably to genocide, but there was a strong correlation in twentieth-century Europe between a changing political map, extreme shifts in forms of government and massive violence. During the twentieth century entire European countries vanished and new ones emerged in their place. Political boundaries were altered before and after the First World War, during and after the Second World War, and at the end of the Cold War. Forms of government also shifted radically, especially during the interwar years with the rise of new dictatorships and at the end of the Cold War with the collapse of many Communist states. Germany provides a striking example of this fluidity. In the late twentieth century it was possible to find Germans who had lived under five different political systems in a lifetime: the German Empire, the Weimar Republic, the Nazi Dictatorship, the Communist Germany Democratic Republic or East Germany, and finally the Federal Republic of Germany that was formerly known as West Germany.

The wars that repeatedly remade European boundaries escalated violence, radical nationalism, and racism, and created conditions in which multiple paths toward genocide converged. The connection to European war was obvious from the first mention of genocide. The legal scholar Raphael Lemkin, who coined the term genocide, took an interest in many areas of history, but he finally arrived at the actual term during the Second World War. Lemkin introduced the idea of genocide in extended form in his book *Axis Rule in Occupied Europe*, published in 1944. The Second World War therefore provided the backdrop for the first analysis of genocide. In similar fashion, war also coincided with other European genocides, whether in the Armenian Genocide during the First World War or in the ethnic cleansing and genocidal massacres in Bosnia in the 1990s.

This chapter will outline these possible routes toward genocide. We will chart the relationship between genocide and factors including war, imperialism, nationalism and racism, and forms of government and the rise and fall of states. These paths did not lead to inevitable outcomes and they did not emerge in isolation from each other. The same paths that led to genocide also branched out in very different directions. Some paths narrowed while others intersected creating greater potential for genocide.

Colonialism and imperialism

Given European involvement in carrying out violent campaigns and destruction at home and abroad it is surprising that it took so long for historians to begin to examine the possible connection between violence carried out by Europeans within and beyond Europe. Raphael Lemkin was well aware of campaigns of destruction in colonial ventures, but the emerging history of European genocide traditionally focused first and foremost on Europe, even though Europeans had at times carried out violent repression of resistance or pursued exploitation through means that predictably caused massive loss of life in their colonial empires.

Conquest of the Americas

The first wave of European overseas expansion that started with Columbus's voyages to the Americas quickly led to massive loss of life among native peoples. In the Caribbean Spanish conquistadors slaughtered and hunted down the native population to crush rebellion. The killings began on the island of Hispaniola and then spread to Cuba and to other islands as the Dominican Bartolomé de las Casas documented in his history, *A Short Account of the Destruction of the Indies.* He wrote that the "Spanish fell like ravening wolves upon the fold, or like tigers and savage lions who have not eaten meat for days."[1]

On the mainland of Central America Hernán Cortés employed massive violence during his conquest of Mexico: he carried out a massacre at the city of Cholula in 1519 and devastated the Aztec capital of Tenochtitlan in 1521. The later study of genocide frequently looked back to such attacks as possible acts of genocide, though the question of whether Spanish conquerors intended to wipe out native population and the role of diseases such as small pox led to debates about whether Spain actually committed genocide or whether the bulk of native deaths, especially beyond the Caribbean, occurred without any Spanish goal of destruction.

The scramble for Africa and the Congo

Genocides in twentieth-century Europe could not easily be directly traced to the initial conquest of the American centuries earlier, but European powers engaged in a new burst of imperialism in the late nineteenth century, taking territories in southeast Asia and above all in Africa. This phase of imperial expansion greatly increased contacts between Europeans and non-Europeans. In contrast, during the height of the Atlantic slave trade in the eighteenth century, European slave traders bought millions of captive Africans on the coast of West Africa, while seldom traveling any great distance inland. But in the nineteenth century Europeans capitalized on military and medical innovations to gain the capacity to move into much of Africa's interior. Where European travelers into the interior had once died in droves they gained some ability to counter tropical diseases such as malaria. European military power had previously evaporated quickly at any great distance from the coast, but by the nineteenth century new rifles and early machine guns gave Europeans increased military power. The writer and poet Hilaire Belloc summed up the new situation with the ironic poetic quip, "Whatever happens we have got the Maxim gun, and they have not." In truth, new rifles did yield power: the explorer and adventurer Henry Morton Stanley wrote long accounts of his exploits replete with details of multiple shootings. Of his travels in 1876 he wrote that "I could afford to lose weak, fearful, and unworthy men; but I could not afford to lose one gun."[2]

Many of the most extraordinary cases of violence and mass destruction in the imperial era occurred not in the immediate conquest of Africa or scramble for Africa, but afterwards when colonial rulers sought to exploit resources and crush rebellions. The grandeur associated with the idea of empire did not necessarily bring the wealth needed to pay for even the most minimal administration and military occupation. This problem was especially acute for Belgium's King Leopold who maneuvered to win control of the Congo Free State as a virtual personal fiefdom. He achieved all he had dreamed of with the creation of the Congo Free State under his rule in 1885, but then faced the prospect of financial ruin. At first the vast territory that far exceeded Belgium in size proved a drain: in an embarrassment the King was forced to turn to the Belgian parliament for a loan in 1888. However, Leopold's administration finally discovered a way to extract revenue from the Congo by amassing ivory, and colonial officials quickly resorted to intimidation and terror to speed and expand collection by Africans. In his novella The *Heart of Darkness*, Joseph Conrad, the writer who himself worked for a time in the Congo as a steamboat captain, alluded to the unsavory aspects of colonial exploitation through the voice of his main character Marlow: "The conquest of the earth, which mostly means the taking it away from those who have a different complexion or slightly flatter noses than ourselves, is not a pretty thing when you look into it too much."

Extracting rubber soon superseded ivory as a source for colonial wealth. With the invention of pneumatic tires by John Dunlop a new world market opened up for rubber, suddenly increasing the Congo's commercial potential: rubber became immensely valuable, but there were as yet no rubber plantations. Rubber collection in the rain forest, however, was slow, tedious, and often painful, so to maximize production at the minimum cost, Leopold's colonial regime turned to terror. Hostage taking, arson, and murder, as well as the practice of cutting off hands motivated natives to bring rubber to colonial agents. The violence also caused many to flee their homes. The resulting disruption further diminished food supply. The total death toll is difficult to estimate but may well have numbered in the millions.

ROGER CASEMENT AND THE CONGO

Visitors and missionaries slowly discovered the truth about the terror regime in the Congo, and began to bring the atrocities to public attention. One figure who collected information on violence in the Congo was Roger Casement, an Irishman who served in the British consular service. In 1903 he undertook an investigation of conditions in the Congo Free State that confirmed the emerging picture of inhumane treatment of the population and brought to light further details of terror. Casement met girls, boys, men and women, who had had hands cut off. He also learned that his very appearance was enough to prompt flight by some who feared that he came with government soldiers.

ENTRIES FROM ROGER CASEMENT'S DIARY

"June 5:   The country a desert, no natives left.
July 25:   I walked into villages and saw the nearest
             one—population dreadfully decreased—only 93
             people left out of many hundreds.
July 26:   Poor frail folk . . . —dust to dust ashes to
             ashes—where then are the kindly heart and
             pitiful thought—together vanished.
August 6:   Took copious notes from natives . . . They are
             cruelly flogged for being late with their baskets
             [of rubber]. . . . Very tired.
August 13:   A. came to say 5 people from Bikoro side
             with hands cut off had come as far as Myanga
             intending to show me.
August 22:   Bolongo quite dead. I remember it well in
             1887, Nov., full of people then; now 14 adults
             all told. . . ."[3]

Casement's report and others on the horrors of the Congo helped to sustain and strengthen a growing international movement. Writers from Mark Twain to Sir Arthur Conan Doyle inveighed against the cruelties committed in Leopold's Free State. Whether this carnage was genocide, depends in large part on how the definition is applied: the issues of intent and of identifying victims loomed large in later discussion. Exploiting resources, rather than the destruction of any particular group, was the first and foremost aim in the Free State. But if the term genocide may not apply exactly to all aspects of the terror in the Congo, to simply dismiss any connection to genocide overlooks an important outcome: the predictability of death. The methods employed to force natives to collect ivory and even more so rubber clearly led to increasingly high mortality: this fact was obvious to the observers who finally perceived the secret horrors of the Congo. Casement and others provided ample evidence of the practice described in clause c of Article 2 of the later UN genocide convention: "(c) Deliberately inflicting on the group conditions of life calculated to bring about its physical destruction in whole or in part. . . ."

German Southwest Africa

Aside from relentless exploitation, harsh suppression of organized resistance by natives formed another path to massive destruction. Within its African possessions, Germany resorted to overwhelming military force to suppress revolts in Southwest Africa or Namibia and in Tanganyika—now Tanzania. In German Southwest Africa competition for scarce resources, grazing land and water, brought African pastoralists and German settlers into conflict. The Germans and Africans, including the Herero and Nama peoples, wanted much the same things: land for grazing and water to nourish herds of animals. At the same time epidemic disease, Rinderpest, swept through herds of uninoculated cattle, killing off as many as 90 percent of the animals. These losses drove the Herero into debt as they sought to buy new animals to replace their dead cattle. In 1904 the Herero chief Samuel Maheroro shocked the German colonial administration and settler population when he staged an uprising that killed more than 100 settlers and traders. The German General von Trotha struck back and defeated the Herero in August 1904 at Waterberg, and pursued the Herero east into the desert.

Winning the upper hand, van Trotha cast his campaign as a war of extermination. He proclaimed in October 1904: "The Herero are no longer German subjects. They have murdered and plundered. . . . The Herero nation must leave the country. If it will not do so I shall condemn it by force. Inside German territory every Herero tribesman, armed or unarmed, with or without cattle, will be shot. No women or children will be allowed in the territory."[4] Von Trotha's campaign attracted critics in Germany, and he was recalled in 1905, but by that time as many as 70 percent or even more of the Herero had died, many as they fled to the east into the desert. Germany also beat back a separate uprising launched in October 1904 by the pastoralist Nama led by their elderly chief Hendrik Witbooi. The Nama employed guerrilla tactics, but were largely defeated by 1907.

German forces in Southwest Africa did not pursue some prior plan to purify the German colony but in their scale of killing, their destruction of population of some one-half of Nama and two-thirds of Herero, and in their use of camps, the methods employed to crush rebellion crossed over into genocide as it is often understood today. There is no single body with the responsibility or authority for identifying all cases of genocide, but increasingly the histories of genocide include the destruction of the Herero and Nama as early examples of twentieth-century genocides. Indeed, even before the creation of the term genocide, German military policy led Social Democrats and members of the Catholic Center Party to criticize General von Trotha.

CONCENTRATION CAMPS AND THE SHARK ISLAND CAMP

In their efforts to crush resistance by the Nama the Germans in Southwest Africa employed camps. By the time of the Herero and Nama uprisings, concentration camps were already known in Southern Africa: Britain had employed such camps as a means to cut off guerrilla forces from their popular base during the Boer War. Poor rations, inadequate shelter, and disease accounted for thousands of deaths against detained white and African civilians and prompted investigation and condemnation even in Britain. In Southwest Africa, German forces took the concept of the camp to a new extreme. Shark Island at Lüderitz on the coast of southwestern Namibia may serve as a symbol for the escalation of destruction. Unable to deport captured Nama to a more distant location, German commanders sent them to Shark Island. Without adequate housing or sanitation, prisoners on Shark Island fell ill: many contracted scurvy. As Germans discovered that internment there was increasingly tantamount to a death sentence some agreed to transfer prisoners elsewhere, but these plans failed: von Estorff, one German official who tried and failed to put an end to the deaths, stated, "for such hangmen's services I can neither detail my officers, nor can I accept responsibility . . ."[5] But the camp remained open for death: existing statistics suggested a death rate of over 100 percent per year for Nama—on average all Nama would die within a year, and so would many of those taken in to replace the dead.

In the colony of Tanganyika, Germany also used overwhelming destructive force to crush a rebellion. In 1905 a rebellion known as Maji Maji broke out against German rule in what is now southern Tanzania. Resistance drew on grievances of native Africans who resented compulsion to harvest cotton on new German cotton plantations. The Maji or medicine was thought to protect the warriors from the Germans' weapons. However, German forces in East Africa executed elders and burned villages and fields to break resistance, causing the deaths of some quarter of a million Africans. Though this example is much less frequently cited than the destruction of the Herero as an example of genocide, the campaign to break the Maji Maji rebellions similarly blurred lines between attacks on combatants and the destruction of civilian groups.

Settler society and aborigines in Australia

The actual European presence in most of Africa was small in numbers, but far larger settler societies emerged elsewhere, including in Australia. Britain established a penal colony at Sydney in 1788. In the nineteenth century settlers began to push beyond coastal outposts in search of land for grazing. Mining also further stimulated immigration. Where aborigines defended their terrain or raided animals, the white population and native forces in their pay retaliated with extreme violence, shooting the so-called blacks. As immigration continued the same pattern of conflict, Aboriginal resistance, and settler retaliation spread. The destruction was especially far ranging on the island of Tasmania south of the Australian mainland. Here the British introduction of sheep sparked competition for land and resources between settlers and natives. When Tasmanians struck against the settlers and their animals in the 1820s, British forces retaliated by sweeping natives out of the island and placing the survivors into captivity on a smaller island, where all so-called full-bloods died. This case is now frequently

ANTHONY TROLLOPE AND ABORIGINES IN AUSTRALIA

Anthony Trollope, the well-known novelist, was one of many Europeans to comment on the setbacks native peoples encountered when they came into prolonged compact with European civilization. In 1871 Trollope visited Australia where his son Frederic had become a grazier or farmer. Of the aborigines' uncertain fate he wrote, "We have taken away their land, have destroyed their food, made them subject to our laws, which are antagonistic to their habits and traditions, have endeavored to make them subject to our tastes, have massacred them when they defended themselves and their possessions after their fashion."[6] But Trollope, though sympathetic to the aborigines' plight, also described what he saw as an inevitable decline. In 1873 he expressed doubts about the possibility of teaching the "black man" in Australia. He predicted that "Their doom is to be exterminated; and the sooner that their doom can be accomplished—so that there be no cruelty—the better it will be for civilization." Such predictions that native populations would inevitably dwindle and expire became commonplace in the nineteenth century.

described as genocide, though Tasmanians of mixed ancestry were not completely eradicated.

From imperialism to genocide?

The fact that genocides in Europe followed soon after a period of extreme European violence against natives in the late imperial era suggests some kind of correlation, but establishing and outlining the exact connection between these periods of violence remains difficult. The case of the Belgian Congo dramatizes this problem. The horrors of the Congo came to epitomize the worst of imperial rule, but Belgium was not a genocidal regime within Europe. Indeed, there was no one-to-one correspondence between imperial rule in general and genocide in Europe itself. Britain and France, the leading European imperial states of the late nineteenth and early twentieth century, did not carry out genocide in twentieth-century Europe. Nor for that matter did the Netherlands, which still controlled a vast empire in southeast Asia in the Dutch East Indies (now Indonesia) nor Spain and Portugal, which still clung to pieces of their old imperial lands, though new research is now starting to list mass killing during the Spanish Civil War of the 1930s as a possible case of genocide. In general states in Western Europe were the chief imperial powers, but genocidal regimes of the twentieth century were clustered in Central and Eastern Europe.

Imperial encounters, though not an inevitable cause of destruction in Europe, nonetheless created paths that led toward genocide. Confrontation between Europeans and varied native populations and conflicts over resources contributed to the notion that some peoples were inferior and were destined to lose power and land and even to dwindle and disappear. Such thinking made tremendous loss of life seem natural and inevitable. As well as extolling the triumph of civilization, Western authors sometimes romanticized the stories of native decline.[7] But whether the destruction of native peoples was celebrated or mourned, Europeans at the start, of the twentieth century were increasingly familiar with the idea that some peoples might decline and eventually disappear altogether. Such images could disconnect cause and effect, and at an extreme, the experience of imperialism provided justification for genocide as a form of progress.

Colonial wars also eased the path to mass killing of noncombatants, another hallmark of genocide. Colonial powers found it easier to employ overwhelming destructive force against peoples regarded as inferior. Indeed, international law did not even cover war carried out against indigenous peoples in Africa and Asia. Removing even theoretical legal protections for both combatants and civilians, colonial war could escalate to the point of extermination, and even if colonial war did not reach this extreme point massive numbers of civilian deaths were seen as acceptable.[8]

Imperial and colonial antagonisms simultaneously sharpened a sense of race. The very act of seizing large tracts of the globe incorporated confidence in supposed racial supremacy. When they faced resistance, Europeans saw conflict with indigenous peoples in racial terms. Imperialism therefore provided a kind of school for European racism.

Politics and science of identity

The roots of Europe's century of genocide were complex because both European overseas imperialism and changes within Europe simultaneously created paths toward genocide. Within Europe, largely homegrown ideologies based on national and racial identity further increased the potential for violent action against groups. The champions of such ideologies idealized communities defined by their preferred form of identity—hero nations or master races, and in doing so they also created or at least accentuated boundaries with any groups defined as lying outside the nation or race. Neither nationalists nor racists automatically resorted to genocide, but the destruction of unwanted groups provided the most extreme and radical of all measures to seek to purify and perfect a given race or nation. Racial thinking also fused with science to provide justifications for discrimination and support for projects of racial improvement.

Nationalism

In the late eighteenth and well into the nineteenth century, the early nationalist movements in Europe called for liberation and self-determination, promising a future far removed at first glance from anything resembling genocide. Nationalists wanted to extol and recover the virtues, language, and history of their given nation, and when they lacked a state they demanded this too as the necessary site for national development. This shared agenda lent a cooperative quality to nationalism. Particularly in the early nineteenth century European nationalists imagined that they would all benefit from the same processes and saw themselves as marching together in solidarity and fraternity.

At the same time nationalism created possibilities for rivalry and competition. Nation-states pursuing similar interests competed with each other and with other states to create homelands. The connections between national struggle, nationalist competition, and war were obvious to Europeans who had only to look at the history of new nineteenth-century nation-states, including Italy and Germany. The unification of a German Empire came through wars with Denmark, Austria, and in 1870–1, France.

Beyond building potential for war between states, European nationalism also created greater readiness to attack people based on their identity. Nationalists increasingly lashed out at those they charged with blocking their aspirations, and they did not limit their animosity to political or military authorities. Those nationalists who hoped to create new nation-states in the Ottoman Empire, for example, described Turks as oppressors, speaking of a Turkish yoke. Castigating what he described as Turkish oppression, the Bulgarian nationalist poet Georgi Rakovski called for destruction in a poem entitled the Forest Traveler: "The Turkish Yoke, four centuries endured Let us smash heroically. . . ."[9] In turn, leaders or elites of a state such as the Ottoman Empire threatened by nationalist movements were increasingly likely to engineer or at least condone violent attacks against members of a restive nation. Rebellion and retaliation strengthened the idea of nationalism whether or not all or even most of the residents of a given region in fact possessed a strong or clear sense of national identity.

Nationalism carried a potential threat both to external and internal enemies. Historians today stress the fragility of national identity, and many nationalists themselves learned of the loose attachment to nation and deficient understanding of national symbols, history, or language on the part of many members of a prospective nation. Poorly educated rural populations proved especially difficult to school in nationalism. But if the persistence of traditions at odds with nationalism frustrated nationalists, they still believed that education, propaganda, military service, and other factors would eventually strengthen the national identity of even the most remote rural communities. In contrast, they perceived a much deeper and profound threat from groups that might not fit within their nation at all. A German, Greek, or Romanian with very weak affiliation to the idea of the nation might become more attached to a German, Greek, or Romanian nation or at least his or her sons or daughters might, but what of those whose identity ill fit the very nation in question? In an age of growing nationalism such populations faced a new level of suspicion and mistrust added on to any preexisting prejudices. In extreme cases, the growth of nationalism created not only nations but also traitors—groups accused of acting against the interests of the nation.

Racism and anti-Semitism

Obsession with race, along with nation, as a key form of identity further isolated, excluded, and, at an extreme, endangered groups deemed to lie outside the boundaries of a given race. As the example of anti-Semitism demonstrated, racism emerged in the nineteenth century as a new variant next to older forms of prejudice. Anti-Semitism or hostility toward Jews and discrimination against Jews can be traced far into the European past, long before the emergence of modern racism. Prejudice and discrimination against Jews can be traced back to Antiquity and also emerged in Christianity despite the fact that Jesus was a Jew.

The Jews of medieval Europe suffered period waves of violence. In many areas of Christian Europe, Jews figured as the most notable non-Christian group and were commonly depicted as enemies of the true faith. Outbreaks of violence struck Jews during the First Crusade in the late eleventh century. Zeal for holy war inspired attacks against Jews in towns in northern France and in towns on the Rhine and the Danube in 1096. A chronicler told of the massacre of the Jews of Mainz and of Jews who committed suicide, though some counts and bishops also sought to curb the violence of crusading bands. In the fourteenth century, the outbreak of the plague led to massacres of Jews along the Rhine—the victims were charged with having somehow caused the devastating sickness. Jews were also accused of engaging in ritual murder of Christians, a falsehood that recurred as a blood libel.

Excluded from many economic activities, Jews took up money lending, but the rise of new Italian banking houses made them more dispensable. England expelled Jews in 1290, and the French King expelled Jews in 1306. Jews later returned to both countries, but there was a general shift of Jewish population toward the east of Europe. In the east Jews developed the Yiddish language. Even where they remained, Jews lived in Europe as a people apart. In general, European Jews lived in segregated areas in medieval towns and cities. These became known as ghettos. The institution was formalized in Venice and spread to cities including Rome, Prague, and Frankfurt during the early modern era.

The enlightenment and the era of revolution brought contradictory trends for European Jews. On the one hand some gained emancipation. In the aftermath of the enlightenment legal prescriptions against Jews faded or were abolished in much of Europe, and Jews moved into many social, economic, and political spheres from which they had previously been excluded. Disabilities, or legal prohibitions against Jews, faded in Western Europe even as they survived in areas like Romania.

Even as many forms of discrimination decreased, Jews faced both economic resentments and a new variety of racial anti-Semitism. The new racism cast races as actors in historical struggle. In the 1850s Arthur de Gobineau's *Essay on the Inequality of Human Races* depicted three races. He saw the white race as superior to the yellow and black races and attributed corruption and the fall of civilizations to racial mixing. Houston Stuart Chamberlain further elaborated the themes of racism. In his book, *Foundation of the Nineteenth Century*, published in 1899, Chamberlain wrote of conflict between Aryans and Jews, a theme that Hitler would repeatedly draw on.

FROM FOUNDATIONS OF THE NINETEENTH CENTURY BY HOUSTON STEWART CHAMBERLAIN

"It is to the Teuton branch of the Aryan family that first place belongs, and the story of the Nineteenth Century is the story of the Teuton's triumph." . . .

"The races of mankind are markedly different in the nature and also in the extent of their gifts, and the Germanic races belong to the most highly gifted group, the group usually termed Aryans. . . . Physically and mentally, the Aryans are pre-eminent among all peoples; for that reason, they are by right, as the Stagirite [resident of the place of birth of Aristotle] expresses it, the lords of the world."

"Under the protection of Aryan tolerance the hearth was erected from which, for tens of centuries a curse to all that is noblest and an everlasting disgrace to Christianity, Semitic intolerance was to spread like a poison over the whole earth. Whoever wishes to give a clear answer to the question, Who is the Jew? Must never forget one fact, that the Jew . . . is the teacher of all intolerance, of all fanaticism in faith, and of all murder for the sake of religion . . ."[10]

Anti-Semitism in its modern racist form carried new threats. In most radical and extreme form the language of racism approached genocide: if a group by its very existence was essentially corrupting what remedy other than destruction could prevent such danger? However, such ideologies of hatred could only create potential for genocide as Hitler's own early life makes clear. In *Mein Kampf*, Hitler claimed that he first became aware of the dangers posed by Jews when living in Vienna where he lived from 1908 until 1913. It is difficult to corroborate his explanation of the growth of his own anti-Semitism from any independent source, but Vienna was a city with both Jews and local traditions of anti-Semitism. Karl Lueger, the city's popular Mayor who died in 1910 employed anti-Semitism to mobilize support and unify a political base. The most radical anti-Semitic politics were to be found in pamphlets and newspapers in Vienna. Nonetheless, the anti-Semitic politics and publicity in prewar Vienna gave no sign of leading to actual genocide.[11]

Once he became active in politics after the First World War, Hitler repeatedly claimed that superior races faced a threat from their racial inferiors. For Hitler the Aryan race was the preeminent and creative race. Indeed he asserted that all great cultural achievements of the present day were the fruits of Aryan labor and invention.

ARYAN CREATORS

Hitler, as in a speech to a Nazi assembly in January 1928, referred to the sight from a airplane on the world below to make the claim that all worthy creations came from Aryans.

"The culture in the world originates to 99 percent from Aryan peoples. We ascend to an altitude of 9,000 meters: we see the first airplane, everything about it and in it is Aryan. We go deeper below, so we see the cobweb of iron rods created by genuine Aryans. Aryans have made all that depends on it. We look as well over the wide sea: giant steamers draw their freight in the water; in this there is no invention that was not created by Aryans. In the large cities we see enormous apartment buildings, street car lines, elevated trains and subways, on the flat lands we find machines, all created by Aryans. The entire cultural development of the world goes back to Aryans. Other peoples have not participated in it. Aryans were the culture-bearers of the earth and are that still today. And if the Aryan dies then culture dies with him."[12]

Conversely, Jew, he claimed, only destroyed. History, from this perspective was a series of racial struggles, and the most important and fundamental racial clash was between so-called Aryans and Jews. "The constructive principle of Aryan humanity" Hitler claimed in *Mein Kampf*, the book he started writing while serving a grand total of nine months in prison for trying to overthrow the German government in 1923 "is thus displaced by the destructive principle of the Jews, They become the 'ferment of decomposition' among nations and races and, in a broad sense, the wreckers of human civilization."

Racial science

Hitler and other racists of the nineteenth and early twentieth centuries drew on the trappings of recent science. They were fond of tales of ancient German heroes, but they also cast racial struggle as a Darwinian struggle between superior and inferior races. Darwin was himself in no way responsible for the new racism, but racist writers jumped on Social Darwinism or the transfer of Darwinian language to attempt to describe society. For racists, social competition was racial.

Preoccupation with race also shaped science through the new field of eugenics. Sir Francis Galton, an eminent scientist of the Victorian era and a cousin of Darwin's, described eugenics as the "science of improving stock. . . ." Eugenics spread rapidly by the early twentieth century through Europe, North America, and Australia, among other regions, and gave rise to investigations of methods for encouraging desirable traits, the goal of positive eugenics, or discouraging those held to be undesirable, the approach of negative eugenics. Eugenicists carried out research to attempt to determine which traits were hereditary.

The approach in negative eugenics strongly resembled culling: individuals with characteristics defined as hereditary and highly undesirable faced action to prevent them from reproducing. This logic gave rise to both proposals and actual programs for compulsory sterilization. Though strongly associated with Nazi Germany such sterilization programs also took place elsewhere, including in several American states. With further radicalization in the Nazi case, the methods employed to cull the undesirable extended to mass murder as Chapter 4 will discuss.

Changing political boundaries and forms of government

Changes in forms of government and political boundaries that began during the nineteenth century and accelerated during the twentieth century magnified the radical effects of new ideologies. New European states began to emerge in the nineteenth century as the Ottoman Empire lost territories, and in the twentieth century Europeans experienced extraordinary political change. State borders and forms of governments entered into a period of flux. With the end of the First World War multiple empires collapsed, giving rise to a new map across much of Central and Eastern Europe. The interwar years brought a brief burst of democratization, but also a sharp turn toward varied forms of dictatorship and authoritarian or undemocratic regimes. During this period Nazi Germany and the Soviet Union stood at the extreme points of Fascist and Communist dictatorship. The end of the Second World War and the aftermath of the Cold War, in turn, propelled further shifts in forms of government. Such a history testified to repeated experiments with diverse forms of government ranging from democracies to varied authoritarian regimes and dictatorships.

Sharp shifts in political boundaries followed the end of both world wars and of the Cold War. The First World War ended with the collapse of large old dynastic empires, including Austria-Hungary, Russia, and the Ottoman Empire—the last survived the war in shattered form for a few years. In addition the much newer German Empire also came to an end as Germany became a Republic. The old dynastic empires of Central and Eastern Europe were succeeded by a series of new or recreated states in a belt that stretched between Germany to the Soviet Union and across old Austro-Hungarian and Ottoman lands. Baltic states gained independence; a renewed Poland emerged from regions formerly held by Germany, Russia, and Austria-Hungary. Austria itself, Czechoslovakia, and Hungary were successor states to Austria-Hungary, and some of the empire's old land went to Romania and to the newly created Kingdom of the Serbs, Croats, and Slovenes or Yugoslavia. The Ottoman Empire finally expired for good in 1923 to be succeeded by the Republic of Turkey as well as by other states in the Near East. A further burst of change followed the Second World War—on this occasion the major change came with a shift of boundaries toward the west as the victorious Soviet Union gained lands formerly held by Poland and Germany, among other states, and swallowed up Baltic states. Finally the end of the Cold War brought fragmentation across much of Eastern and Central Europe and the emergence of numerous new states that succeeded Yugoslavia or the successor states to the Soviet Union.

Mere change in political boundaries or in form of government did not create a one-way path to genocide but the remaking of European politics and boundaries increased the threat of radical action against particular groups. The shift from multiethnic dynastic empires to a new map of nation-states exacerbated and even created national and ethnic tensions. Living in smaller states that claimed to represent a single nation heightened the potential for hostility and discrimination. In a dynastic empire peoples from diverse ethnic, national, or religious groups shared a common bond as subjects of an imperial ruler, but in a nation-state they lived in principle in a country represented or dominated by a single nation. The old imperial lands of Central and Eastern Europe that stretched into Western Asia, however, were full of populations that did not fit easily into any map of new nation-states. Drawing new state boundaries invariably meant placing large numbers of people in states where they did not share the identity advanced by the nation associated with their new state. The new Poland, for example, was only narrowly a country of Poles: it also contained Ukrainians, Jews, and Germans, among other populations. Czechoslovakia as well had a large German minority. Ethnic or national rivalries, which previously flared up in larger empires, now took increasingly strong and explosive form in the smaller confines of nation-states.

At the same time, the rise of new dictatorships in a period of increasing obsession with marking and defining identity created further peril for groups that fell under any official suspicion. Dictatorships such as Nazi Germany and the Soviet Union concentrated and accentuated state power. They sought to create particular kinds of communities, in the Nazi case a racial national community and in the Soviet case a dictatorship of the Proletariat, while denouncing others, either racial or class enemies. Terror deployed by these dictatorships imperiled all who were declared to lie outside of the boundaries of the preferred form of identity. For Nazi Germany this meant new threats against all who were not Aryan or were held to weaken the national and racial community; whereas the Soviet Union took radical action against groups marked as class enemies. Categories of those subject to attack could also blend and blur in that purges of supposed class enemies acquired an ethnic dimension in the Soviet Union.

Two divergent political trends, the collapse and rise of states, intersected in Europe to increase the potential for genocide in the twentieth century. The collapse of old dynastic states exacerbated ethnic and religious tensions and fostered accusations of treason by loyalists looking for culprits to blame for defeats and setbacks. And when old states expired leaving a vacuum, competition over how to divide up old imperial lands increased chances for violence. On the other hand, the very rapid rise of new powerful states brought new schemes for classifying and categorizing populations and then encouraging or discouraging the presence of particular classes or groups of people.

War and Genocide

The major waves of warfare in Europe during the twentieth century repeatedly destabilized the continent, radicalized animosities, and created opportunities for carrying out genocide. The Armenian Genocide began during the First World War in 1915, as the Ottoman Empire fought on its eastern and western frontiers. In 1941 the Second World War reached a turning point: as the German army invaded the Soviet Union, special terror units called Einsatzgruppen massacred Jews in newly occupied territory and the killing expanded in 1942 with rapid mass murder in death camps. The Holocaust only ended with total German defeat. No subsequent armed conflict brought violence on the same scale, but new wars in Europe renewed memories and fears of genocide at the end of the Cold War. When war followed the breakup of Yugoslavia in the early 1990s, scenes of emaciated prisoners recalled the images of concentration camps of the Second World War and armed men carried out massacres that targeted victims for destruction based on their ethnic or religious identity.

War in itself, no matter how deadly, is not equivalent to genocide, but European warfare contributed to conditions for genocide in at least three ways. Total war or the attempt to completely mobilize resources and population of a society to wage war against an enemy's military, economy, and entire society accelerated the shift to genocide. War during Europe's twentieth century increased the overall level of violence, war blurred lines between combatants and civilians, and war encouraged allegations and charges of treason. This combination proved especially deadly when political movements and states lashed out entire groups accused of treason just as the overall level of violence was already escalating.

The First World War

The First World War combined all three of these destructive trends. In the first place, the war that started in 1914 escalated violence to new levels. Industrialization of war vastly increased killing power. The use of machine guns, and artillery created vast death zones. On the Western Front, the battlefields of France and Flanders, including Verdun, the Somme, Ypres, and others, became synonymous with carnage. These were battles unlike any others, lasting for months and inflicting hundreds of thousands of casualties. The Western Front was not unique for yielding scenes of death and shocking misery: soldiers serving Italy and Austria-Hungary suffered staggering losses along a front that crossed from the Adriatic Sea to Alpine snow fields. Other armies, Ottoman and Russia, faced their own grim experiences of crushing losses as did the British imperial forces that never managed to break out far beyond their landing zones at Gallipoli on the coast of Turkey in April 1915.

Recalled, after the Second World War, chiefly for the suffering of soldiers, the First World War also generated much broader destruction. Military campaigns at times singled out cultural targets such as when Germans burned the library at the University of Louvain in Belgium in August 1914. Intellectuals and academics also espoused war goals that went far beyond military aims: nationalist intellectuals spoke and wrote not simply of war but of war as a cultural as well as a military endeavor. Especially in Eastern Europe, massive losses afflicted civilian populations as well as combatants. Some 650,000 or more Serb civilians, for example, perished during the war.

The First World War brought devastation for both civilians and combatants, but the connection between loss of life and genocide was not direct. An enormous death toll in itself, even on the scale of some of the worst battles of the First World War, does not prove genocide, but the blurring of boundaries between combatants and civilians is one of the hallmarks of genocidal killing. Laws of war, such as the Hague Convention, built up a body of international law that distinguished between armed combatants and the civilian population. However, the European wars of the twentieth century not only exposed civilians to widespread devastation, but in many cases led to campaigns that targeted civilian populations as well as enemy combatants.

The First World War further increased the risk of genocide with the proliferation of claims of treason by particular groups. Such targeting of particular groups is a critical precondition of genocide, because genocide is not equivalent to destruction of all civilians but rather to the destruction of particular groups. War accentuated and created fissures and cleavages within European societies. At first, war appeared to foster unity: where European societies such as Germany had experienced sharply divided politics before 1914, the early stages of the Great War yielded claims of unity, solidarity across social classes, and strong support for the war credits that financed the struggle at the cost of launching the march toward uncontrolled inflation years later.

The excitement at war's start did not do away with personal anxiety or dread about the looming conflict, but demonstrations of war fervor were striking and highly public: one remarkable photograph captured a young Adolf Hitler in a large crowd in Munich on August 2, 1914 gathering in excitement at the news of the German declaration of war against Russia. Such popular fervor at news of war would not return in 1939 when the Second World War started.

As war dragged on and deaths and economic burdens mounted, the unity of early days faded, in many cases supplanted not only by war-weariness but by the breakdown of amity and the search for scapegoats and alleged traitors to blame for the setbacks of war. Where war started badly such divisions emerged quickly. In the Ottoman Empire, the Committee of Unity and Progress, a nationalist movement that had seized power on the eve of war, viewed Greeks, Assyrian Christians, and above all Armenians, as disloyal minorities ready to side with the country's enemies. In Russia, the military command in the west espoused deportations in the wake of defeat, pushing large numbers of Lithuanians, Latvians, and Poles east and in particular singling out Germans and Jews as disloyal. Russian officers evacuated Jews out of the war zone and with defeats in 1915 forced between 500,000 and a million Jews to move rapidly east. All the while Jews were subjected to pogroms or mob attacks, carried out by Russian forces, especially Cossacks, aided and abetted by local residents. Russia's Germans, for their part, suffered similar large-scale deportations away from the west.

In Germany war gave rise to a different form of anti-Semitism. German Jews served in large numbers in the German military during the war—indeed years later this fact made the expulsion of such Jewish veterans from the German nation during the Nazi era all the more shocking. Nonetheless, during the Great War itself, anti-Semitic agitation led the Ministry of War in 1916 to carry out a count or census of Jews in the army. The results failed to bear out any claims that Jews were traitors—they took part in the army in much the same proportions as any other Germans—but manifested a readiness to look for supposed traitors to the nation.

An escalating level of violence, blurring of lines between combatants and civilians, and the targeting of particular groups as traitors brought increased potential for genocide, but the full transition to genocide only occurred under regimes that combined and intensified these trends to the most radical conclusion. In general, genocidal potential was greatest on the eastern boundaries of Europe, and as Chapter 2 will explain just such a radical shift to genocide took place in Turkey during the First World War with the Armenian Genocide.

The Second World War

Just over two decades after the end of the Great War, a new world war led to even wider devastation and loss of life in Europe. Again war brought extraordinary violence, blurred the lines between civilians and combatants, and intensified persecution of alleged traitors. The swift pace of early German victories in the west with the invasions of Poland in 1939 and the Blitzkrieg victories of 1940 meant that there was no return to trench war on the Western Front or to the vast and typically futile and deadly offensives of the First World War. Instead of the months-long battles that caused so many deaths and injuries on the Western Front between 1914 and 1918, German mechanized units quickly pushed behind the front lines. However, this new war also exacted a devastating toll on combatants, especially in the prolonged and bitter fighting on the Eastern Front that started when Germany invaded the Soviet Union in June 1941 and ended only with the Battle of Berlin and German capitulation in early May 1945. Indeed, only with the war against the Soviet Union did Nazi Germany finally move toward total war, after having employed a series of quick lighting strikes and massive looting to sustain war to that point. In the Soviet Union alone entire cities were destroyed, tens of millions of civilians died, more than 5 million soldiers were taken as prisoners of war, and of those prisoners of war nearly 3 million died.

No war, no matter how deadly, is in and of itself automatically equivalent to genocide, but the Second World War opened up or expanded several potential routes to genocide. Even more so than in the First World War, the Second World War blurred lines between combatants and civilians. In particular, war in the east blended military, ideological, and political goals. Such war against entire peoples could more easily devolve into genocide than war seen as a conflict between militaries. Jotting down Hitler's remarks in a March 30, 1941 meeting with commanders, Colonel General Franz Halder wrote, "This is a war of extermination."[13] This statement offered a clue to the genocidal goals of the German war in the east. The war of extermination went far beyond any call to merely defeat the Soviet military with German orders that breached the laws of war. Orders to kill commissars (Soviet political officials) encouraged German soldiers to break laws of war and kill after combat had ended. Directives to round up and kill 50–100 so-called Communists in retaliation for every killing of a German soldier in occupied Serbia similarly expanded slaughter beyond the ranks of combatants.

Amidst the escalation of killing beyond military combatants and outside of any normal operations, the Second World War, like the First, intensified campaigns to punish and to eliminate traitor peoples. The combination of repeated killing and accusations of treason generated extraordinary genocidal potential. In Germany, Hitler began with the assumption that Jews had been to blame for the Great War and held in public in early 1939 that Jews would suffer a terrible punishment if they "should succeed in plunging the nations once more into world war. . . ." With this reversal of logic he blamed Jews for a conflict that he had himself launched, though in Hitler's vision of events, it seemed to be American entrance into the war after Japan's bombing of Pearl Harbor in December 1941 that truly made the conflict a world war.

Across much of Europe the war exacerbated and heightened ethnic, national, and religious divisions. The competition for power between the USSR and Nazi Germany created especially strong levels of resentment within Eastern European societies, especially after the Hitler-Stalin pact of August 1939, which led to a temporary division of power in Eastern Europe from the start of the war in September 1939 until the German invasion of the Soviet Union in Operation Barbarossa in June 1941. Which dictatorship—Soviet or German—posed the greatest threat divided opinion, at least before June 1941. Claims that particular groups collaborated or benefitted from occupation regimes justified calls for revenge. In areas occupied by the Soviet Union after the Hitler-Stalin pact it was common for nationalists to accuse Jews of joining in the Soviet regime, though the USSR included thousands of Jews among those deported as disloyal to the Soviet state in the period before the German invasion of the Soviet Union. Ironically, such deportation would actually save some from an even worse fate during the Holocaust.

The Soviet internal prison camp system was already vast before 1941, but during the war with Nazi Germany Stalin continued and extended his own tradition of singling out and punishing particular Soviet peoples on charges of disloyalty. During the Second World

War he shifted from a focus on class disloyalty to asserting that varied minorities in the Crimea and the Caucasus had sided with and supported the invading Germans.

As in the First World War, the full transition to genocide took place under radical regimes and political movements that pushed violence, attacks on civilians, and the targeting of alleged traitor peoples to the most extreme conclusions. The Nazi regime had already gained power before the war, but the Second World War further intensified genocidal potential by bringing radical political movements to power or at least by opening up new opportunities for such movements. Puppet states and Fascist movements championed racist and exclusionary policies. Placed in power after the German conquest and dismemberment of Yugoslavia the previously exiled leadership of a Croatian Fascist movement named the Ustasha gained the chance to kill and expel in pursuit of forging a pure Croatia. In Hungary, local Fascists under the name the Arrow Cross acquired increasing power in 1944 as Germany occupied the country. In mixed Polish-Ukrainian areas, the breakdown of civil authority and the murder of prior elites created fertile conditions for deadly warfare between Polish and Ukrainian irregulars or paramilitaries who fought their own war within the larger war.

Wars at the End of the Cold War

With the end of the Second World War most of Europe soon settled into a cold and sometimes tense peace, but with the end of the Cold War in the late 1980s and early 1990s, war again inflicted severe damage in several areas of Europe. In this case genocidal potential varied enormously by region. Despite fears to the contrary, the actual collapse of Communism regimes took place with comparatively few outbreaks of violence. In late 1989 the Communist regime in East Germany imploded, and Czechoslovakia experienced a "Velvet Revolution" with little violence. In Lithuania Soviet troops shot and killed protesters at a broadcast center in 1991, but this kind of violent crackdown proved the exception rather than the rule. The massive escalation of violence came not with the fall of Communist governments but when the political transition afterwards brought ethnic and religious power struggles. These cases brought together intense violence, a blurring of lines between combatants and civilians, and the targeting of particular groups.

The end of the Cold War generated just such patterns of warfare and violence in Yugoslavia as well as in much of the Transcaucasia region that up until 1991 made up the southern tier of the Soviet Union between the Black and Caspian Seas. In the early 1990s the shelling of towns and cities in Croatia and Bosnia within easy travel of European capitals proved especially shocking to public opinion. A period celebrated for a hoped-for transition to democracy and peace became known for the wreckage of homes, monuments, mosques, churches, and persistent shootings of civilians. In the Bosnian capital of Sarajevo residents endured and sometimes died from shelling carried out from the mountain sites above the town that had only a few years before served as venues for the Winter Olympic Games in 1984. On the Black Sea areas that had once served as desired vacation resorts in the Communist era became a war zone and refugees, or in many cases internally displaced persons, crowded into the capitals of the newly independent states south of the crest of the Caucasus.

Twentieth-century European wars created potential for genocide but also for very different outcomes. European wars took different forms, and the conduct of war varied by region. War by itself was not equivalent to genocide. Terrible destruction during total war did not necessarily lead to genocide and the effects of occupation by conquering armies extended all the way from humiliation and exploitation to mass murder. Nevertheless, the repeated association between war and genocide was more than mere coincidence. Warfare blurred lines between combatants and civilians opening up the possibility for wide-ranging attacks against targets defined more by their identity as members of particular groups than by any combatant status. War also splintered and radicalized societies, exacerbating suspicions of minorities in new or still embryonic potential nations. War gave opportunity to radical movements to seize power and simultaneously offered new opportunities to wage campaigns of destruction against those defined as either internal or external enemies.

Making connections: The German case

War, imperialism, the politics and science of identity, and the rapid shifting of political boundaries and systems all created potential paths toward genocide, but how did such paths intersect to actually lead to particular cases of genocide? In, other terms, what connects a potential cause of genocide to genocide? It is easier to show a correlation between genocide and any possible cause than to demonstrate an actual connection. The Holocaust, the single most famous case of genocide in twentieth-century European history, can provide a starting point for introducing the problem of making connections between possible causes of genocide and genocide itself.

In the case of the Holocaust, war by itself did not make genocide inevitable, but war was also indispensable for genocide. The massive violence on the Western Front that Hitler himself had experienced did not lead to genocide in the First World War, and rapid German victories through Blitzkrieg produced no immediate turn to genocide in 1940 in newly occupied areas of Western Europe. However, war also brought Nazi Germany to a new phase of mass destruction that far exceeded even the most discriminatory anti-Semitic polices of the prewar years. War provided more than mere opportunity to realize and execute radical genocidal plans: changing conditions of war both blocked and opened up new options for Nazi policy toward Jews. Holocaust history has increasingly analyzed the relationship between Nazi planning and events in the war. The Nazi leadership embarked on the Holocaust as a "Final Solution" to eliminating the Jews of Europe after the early years of the war both promoted extreme racist ambition and blocked alternative "solutions" to ridding Europe of Jews.

The possible connection between imperialism and genocide was extremely complex in the German case. Any connection from imperialism to genocide could not be simple and direct because of the German loss of all overseas colonies after the First World War— the Treaty of Versailles took away all German colonial possessions. However, there were still some possible links between previous German colonial destruction and genocide during the Second World War. The destruction carried out on camps such as Shark Island established a possible precedent for later concentration camps. There were also some family connections between the Nazi elite and the past colonial experience: namely the father of Hermann Goering, one of Hitler's chief deputies, had been the German Governor in Southwest Africa.[14] In addition, German use of language during the Second World War showed some recognition of the colonial past: Askari—a term Germans used to describe native auxiliaries in Eastern

Europe, was actually the same word earlier used to refer to their native soldiers in East Africa. More broadly, Nazi planners looking at the newly conquered eastern territories in the Second World War viewed the region as a new kind of German imperial realm.

The experience of colonial warfare built a precedent for using overwhelming destructive force and blurring the lines between military foes and entire peoples, but to what extent did German destruction of African peoples in colonial warfare create a path toward the Holocaust? To find some family or personal connections between Nazi leaders and earlier figures in the German colonial administration in Africa is hardly surprising—this does not mean, however, that key perpetrators of genocide during the Third Reich tended to have such connections. As far as intellectual influences go, Hitler regularly expressed interest in acquiring living space in the east. He spoke at times of Germany's new eastern empire in terms reminiscent of the colonial era, but he did not seem terribly interested in Germany's own African experience let alone in anything that had transpired in Southwest Africa. Imperialism, broadly speaking, influenced Hitler's aims for the future, but he envisioned expansion first and foremost in Europe itself rather than overseas.

HITLER ON COLONIES JUNE 1931 INTERVIEW WITH THE *TIMES OF LONDON*

In an interview with the *Times of London* a little more than a year and half before he became German Chancellor, Hitler distinguished between recovering colonies and some kind of program of colonization in Eastern Europe.

"In pursuance of this train of thought he states that the recovery of colonies is not a major German interest as he sees it. But Germany must export; the export of goods becomes increasingly difficult, and therefore she must export men. If she has no colonies she must look elsewhere and particularly towards the east. Herr Hitler does not specify this conception precisely, but his mind seems to take the Polish Corridor in its stride and to contemplate German colonization of an unlimited eastern area."[15]

The connection between racism and anti-Semitism and Nazi genocide is not in question but even here there was no simple connection between cause and effect. Anti-Semitism by itself did not lead inevitably to genocide as European history before the Holocaust demonstrated. In the nineteenth century German states experienced violent outbreaks against Jews, and there were anti-Semitic politicians and parties in the German Empire, but anti-Semitism was in no way restricted to Germany. In France, for example, the response to the conviction in 1894 of Captain Alfred Dreyfus, a French Jew, on charges of treason and later public controversy about Dreyfus's conviction, revealed powerful anti-Semitic currents in French society. After Dreyfus was sent to Devil's Island on the basis of a forged letter purporting to show treason, the novelist Emile Zola helped to bring the affair to public attention and Dreyfus was released in 1899, though only exonerated in 1906.

Especially when they looked to the east, German Jews had little reason to believe that they lived in the most anti-Semitic society in Europe. Jews suffered from far greater risk of violent attack in the Russian Empire. Jews endured pogroms in 1881 and 1882 after the assassination of Tsar Alexander II. Renewed outbreaks of pogroms took place in 1903 and in 1905 and 1906 during years of revolution and defeat in the Russo-Japanese War. Pogroms continued even after the collapse of the Russian Empire during the Russian Civil War of 1918–20, in regions including Ukraine: the death toll in these pogroms of the Russian Civil War era extended into the tens of thousands.

In the use of state and party institutions to discriminate against and then decimate Jews the Holocaust depended on state power. This point is so obvious, to the extent that the Holocaust has come to exemplify genocide, that a focus on the abuse of power overlooks the point that the collapse of state power can also contribute to genocide. A powerful state need also not be well organized: the Nazi state and party were rife with competition between rivals who vied for authority under Hitler and for the Fuhrer's favor even as they worked to advance his goals.

As the case of Germany and the Holocaust demonstrates, diverse causes led to genocide. War, imperialism, racism, and state power (and this is not an exhaustive list of every possible influence) all created possible routes to genocide without by themselves making genocide inevitable. Indeed, the interaction between imperialism, racism, and war created more radical conditions than did any of these factors on their own.

The case of Germany raises the further possibility that genocide can arise from a kind of learning process. Along with the destruction of the Herero and Nama in Southwest Africa another possible point of transmission to genocide can be traced to the First World War when Germany was the Ottoman Empire's most important ally at the time of the Armenian Genocide. German officers and other personnel were posted to Turkey, both to advise the military and to stiffen resistance to the allies, in particular at the Dardanelles Straits that separated Turkey's European and Asian territories. The issue of German responsibility for the genocide of Armenians has caused much debate, though stressing German culpability casts Turks themselves in an oddly passive role. One of the German diplomats posted to eastern Turkey during the Armenian Genocide, von Scheubner Richter became an early member of the Nazi Party, but he observed rather than planned the assault against Armenians. Von Scheubner Richter's career as a prominent Nazi was also very brief because he was shot and killed during the 1923 Beer Hall Putsch when Hitler tried and failed to seize power through a coup in Munich.

A possible influence of the Armenian Genocide on the Holocaust is often perceived in a remark of 1939 attributed to Hitler on the fate of the Armenians: "Who after all today speaks of the destruction of the Armenians?" Though providing no hint of a motive, this remark suggests that Hitler thought the long-term costs of genocide could be low. Any such belief did not carry over to the way in which Germany pursued mass destruction: increasingly the perpetrators of the Holocaust sought to maintain secrecy, by shifting the bulk of killing to death camps. Hitler did not appear, as far as can be determined from his writings, comments, and speeches, to be particularly interested in Armenians. He was aware of their fate, but appeared to spend little time or energy thinking about their actual destruction.

As the German case indicates there were multiple paths to genocide. Even the case of the Holocaust cannot be traced to the rise of a single ideology such as extreme anti-Semitism. Instead, varied factors including ideology, dictatorship, and war interacted to lead to genocide. General structural changes within Europe also increased the risks of genocide without making any single genocide inevitable. Genocides in twentieth-century Europe most often occurred during war and were closely associated with both the massive expansion and the breakdown of states.

European experiences outside of Europe created further indirect paths to genocide. There was no direct correlation between imperial expansion in the nineteenth century and genocide inside of Europe in the twentieth century, but imperial violence strengthened racism, interest in acquiring empires within Europe, and a conviction that some peoples were expendable and could be erased.

Study questions

- What was the correlation between war and genocide in twentieth-century Europe?
- How did imperialism lead to genocide and to acts of killing related to genocide by Europeans outside of Europe?
- How close or distant was the connection between imperial violence against native peoples outside of Europe and genocide within Europe in the twentieth century?
- How did racism and nationalism increase the potential for genocide?
- How did changes in forms of governments and in state boundaries increase the risks of violence and even genocide?
- Why is it difficult to attribute genocide solely to racism or to any other single factor?

Suggestions for further reading

Las Casas, Bartolomé de and Nigel Griffin, *A Short Account of the Destruction of the Indies* (London: Penguin, 1992).

Hochschild, Adam, *King Leopold's Ghost: A Story of Greed, Terror, and Heroism in Colonial Africa* (Boston: Houghton Mifflin, 1999).

Kiernan, Ben, *Blood and Soil: A World History of Genocide and Extermination from Sparta to Darfur* (New Haven: Yale University Press, 2007).

Laqueur, Walter, *The Changing Face of Anti-Semitism: From Ancient Times to the Present Day* (Oxford: Oxford University Press, 2006).

Weitz, Erich D., *A Century of Genocide: Utopias of Race and Nation* (Princeton: Princeton University Press, 2005).

2

Armenian Genocide

On the night of Saturday April 24, the Armenians of Constantinople, the chief city of the Ottoman Empire, were still resting after their celebration of Easter. The Ottoman Empire was at war, but Constantinople's Armenians, at least according to an Armenian priest named Grigoris Balakian, did not seem to have an accurate picture of events. Shortly after the outbreak of the First World War Balakian left Berlin, where he had been studying theology, and returned to Constantinople. There he found a local Armenian community that seemed to neither understand what was happening to Armenians in Ottoman provinces nor to grasp the actual course of the war. At Easter 1915, Armenians, he recalled were "preoccupied with concerts, dances, and parties, they were lost in mirth and exultation, each day expecting to hear of the capture of Constantinople by the European powers."

That Saturday night Balakian was taken up in a police sweep. He found himself, along with eight others, taken away in a small steam launch guarded by police officers. Arrival at the central prison brought further shock, the steady arrival of more and more Armenians similarly seized and taken away that same night. "It was as if all the prominent Armenian public figures—assemblymen, representatives, revolutionaries, editors, teachers, doctors, pharmacists, dentists, merchants, bankers, and others in the capital city—had made an appointment to meet in these dim prison cells. Some even appeared in their nightclothes and slippers." From there they were taken to a train station and dispatched into Asia Minor. At a train station near Ankara almost 75 of the Armenians were separated from the rest of the group, and taken away: Balakian would learn that many of them were later murdered. Balakian himself was sent with another group to an armory at Chankiri in central Turkey—many from that group as well would ultimately be murdered. Many Armenians from the surrounding countryside and towns in the region were deported and killed, but Balakian was able to stay at Chankiri. He did not explicitly say so, but it almost seems that the authorities had lost interest in his case. Indeed, in late August he was told that he was free to leave for anywhere except Constantinople, though his comrades who tried to make good on this offer were killed outside town.

Finally in early February 1916, the remnant of Armenians at Chankiri was deported and dispatched for exile in the region of Der Zor to the south in the Syrian Desert. As they left town most Turks seemed happy to see them leave, but one elderly woman at a vegetable garden, struck a very different tone, "they're taking these innocent people away to murder them; the enemy to come in turn, will treat us this way in the future. . . . Look here, those who remain alive won't enjoy the spoils. . . . may God be with you my children. . . ." They traveled over narrow mountain paths, passed across ground strewn with dead bodies. Balakian described "decomposed human skeletons and even more skulls. . . ." Asking the accompanying police captain who had ordered the massacre of the Armenians, Balakian learned that "The orders came from the Ittihad Central committee and the Interior Ministry in Constantinople."[1] The small column continued to travel south and east almost to the edge of what is now Syria until Balakian managed to escape. He managed to assume a variety of identities and survived until the end of the war.

Balakian's ordeal revealed many of the key elements of the Armenian Genocide. Balakian was fortunate to live through the roundup of Armenian leaders on April 24, the day later used to mark the Armenian Genocide Remembrance Day. Many of the other prominent Armenians seized that day were murdered. As a survivor, Balakian learned of the fate of most other Armenians. He came to dread the very name of Der Zor, seeing it as synonymous with deportation and a long journey south to the desert that usually ended with death. He also discovered who was most responsible for the slaughter: the Turkish nationalist grouping known as the Ittihadists (Unionists), so named for their organization the Committee of Unity and Progress, and the leadership of the Ministry of the Interior.

As an eyewitness and survivor of genocide, Balakian also raised unsettling questions about both victims and perpetrators. To this day, the Armenian Genocide is often denied, most often with the argument that Turkish authorities acted against Armenians out of self-defense. Balakian categorically rejected the notion that Ottoman Armenians threatened Turkey, but he also portrayed a very complex reality in which Armenians abroad and in Constantinople angered Turks. He recalled for, example, that Armenian newspapers in the capital "extolled the victories of the Entente powers, both spurious and actual." This was a case of genocide carried out by a vengeful political movement in a highly fractured society.

Toward Genocide

Ottoman roots

We know that mass slaughter of Armenians began in the summer of 1915, but close to a century later there is still no consensus about the exact origins of genocide. The explanations for this genocide fall into two major groups: long and short term. The long-term interpretation sees the Armenian Genocide as the logical conclusion of many years of growing hatred of Armenians in the Ottoman Empire. The short-term interpretation, in contrast, finds the key causes of genocide in radicalization of Turkish anti-Armenian policy during the First World War.

Long-term explanations begin by focusing on the distinct religious identity of Armenians and on the challenges they faced living as Christians in the Ottoman Empire. Like Bishop Balakian the large majority of Ottoman Armenians belonged to an independent Armenian church. The Armenian Christian Church, sometimes referred to as Gregorian after the Saint who had brought Christianity to Armenia, dated back to the early fourth century AD, and Armenians remained Christians into the early twentieth century, though by this time a minority of Armenians had become Protestants and a smaller number still had become Catholics. During the course of Armenian history there were Armenian kingdoms, but more often Armenians lived as subjects of larger empires—many had lived in the Byzantine Empire, and with the final defeat of the Byzantine Empire in 1453 they came to live under Ottoman rule.

Armenians, like Christians in general, faced some disadvantages in the Ottoman Empire under the rule of Muslims. Non-Islamic peoples of the empire traditionally endured certain slights and symbols of submission. These included prescriptions on riding horses, and limits on legal standing in cases that involved Muslims, though some such restrictions such as rules calling for distinctive clothing faded in the nineteenth century. From the start of the genocide, some observers attributed the massacres of Armenians to a long-term pattern of scorn and disdain for Christians.

Rule under a Muslim Empire did not, however, force religious uniformity or conversion. Armenians counted among the followers of prophecies recognized in the Quran or as people of the book—a category known as the Dhimmi or Zimmi. They therefore belonged to an accepted religious community within the Ottoman Empire, as did Orthodox Christians and Jews. As a Millet, as such religious communities came to be known, Armenians possessed their own religious leadership—the Armenian patriarch. Many Armenians also prospered and gained positions of influence during the Ottoman era.

Although religious differences did not lead inexorably to genocide, Ottoman Armenians suffered new forms of persecution in the late Ottoman era. Foreign intervention in Ottoman affairs and the emergence of nationalism introduced new sources of instability during the nineteenth century. In a society organized around religious communities or millets, some of the Sultan's subjects began to identify themselves by their national identity. Nationalism took root only very slowly among the masses of peasants, but made quicker progress among students, teachers, and professionals. Their nationalism posed a threat to a large imperial state that did not represent any particular nation. Uprisings, motivated at least in part by nationalism, eroded Ottoman power in Europe during the nineteenth century. These possessions, known by the name Turkey in Europe, diminished as parts of Serbia, Greece, and Bulgaria broke away.

Rebels fighting for varied motives and forces loyal to the Ottoman state waged extraordinarily violent wars. Irregular forces carried out sweeping reprisals against civilians that left burned villages, massacres, and streams of refugees. The famous British liberal leader William Gladstone in 1876 condemned "Bulgarian horrors" carried out against Bulgarians after an uprising while Muslims compiled their own accounts of atrocities. The memories of massacre and flight propelled future political radicalization and created a sense of an empire under siege during the late nineteenth century into the early twentieth century.

During the nineteenth century European powers pressed for reforms and sought to gain material advantage from Ottoman weakness. Competition in the eastern Mediterranean and Black Sea as well as concern for Ottoman Christian subjects gave reason for foreign powers such as Britain to press for reforms during a period termed Tanzimat. The Tanzimat period in the Ottoman Empire began in 1839 with an Edict that moved toward a society of equality before the law. However, conservative reaction and the stifling of a new constitution in 1877 by Sultan Abdul Hamid II left a mix of old and new legal concepts and systems.

Nationalism, reform, and Great Power intervention created particular potential and risks for Ottoman Armenians. With the spread of nationalism, Armenians formed new political parties, including the Hunchaks and Dashnaks (Armenian Revolutionary Federation or ARF). These Armenian parties formed initially in Geneva and in Russia, but soon gained a presence in the Ottoman Empire as well. They pursued social reform, greater autonomy, and self-determination for Armenians, and in the Hunchak case even independence. Armenian political activists also hoped to capitalize on foreign intervention on behalf of Ottoman Christians. However, this strategy not only overstated the degree to which European powers might press the Ottoman authorities on behalf of the Sultan's Armenian subjects but also identified Ottoman Armenians with states sometimes seen as hostile to the Empire. Moreover, Armenians, in contrast to at least some of the Empire's other peoples, were particularly exposed in that there was no foreign state that represented Armenians. The Ottoman Empire, for example, contained many Greeks as well as Armenians, but there was no Armenian equivalent to the Kingdom of Greece that emerged in the nineteenth century. Beyond Ottoman borders, Armenians lived as well in the Russian and Persian Empires, but neither were Armenian states.

In the 1890s, Abdul Hamid II, the last powerful Ottoman Sultan, presided over a violent campaign of massacres of Armenians. In 1894, Armenians of the eastern Anatolian highland region around Sassoun or Sasun, angered by taxes and Kurdish raids, carried out an uprising. The Ottoman military responded with harsh reprisals, destroying entire villages. In turn Armenians held a demonstration march on the Sultan's government in Constantinople in 1895, protesting the violence in Sasun and calling for a reorganization of Armenian provinces under a European governor. The rally ended with an altercation between protesters and gendarmes and the beating of Armenians, some to death, in the streets. Violence spread and escalated in the fall of 1895, especially in towns in the Empire's east. Witnesses told of mob attacks that burned and destroyed shops and left many Armenians dead. The cycle of protest and violent reprisals continued into 1896. In all deaths amounted to at least tens of thousands and may have reached a few hundred thousand. For his part, Abdul Hamid earned much international scorn: images in the foreign press showed the Sultan dripping with blood.

VAN 1896

The eastern city of Van near the Ottoman eastern border with Russia was a key site for Armenian resistance and for violence against Armenians both during the Abdul Hamid massacres and later during the First World War. Through 1895 Van and the city's Armenians largely escaped the violent attacks suffered by Armenians in other towns. However, by early 1896, the region surrounding Van was the scene of scattered killings and rumors and news of massacres elsewhere spread fear. Armenians also told of facing attacks by Kurds. In 1896 a clash that involved Turkish gendarmes, soldiers, and an unidentified group led to attack on Armenians of Van. In June 1896 Hamidian forces of the Sultan urged on mob attacks on Armenian neighborhoods that destroyed property and killed hundreds. Armenians defended themselves in the Garden City where most lived adjacent to the walled city of Van. Armenians organized by Armenian political parties fought off a military assault until they agreed to leave after receiving a safe passage to nearby Persia—instead they were slaughtered.

In a simple interpretation of the causes of the Armenian Genocide, the Abdul Hamid massacres could be seen as a prelude to a subsequent more massive campaign of violence that escalated to genocide during the First World War, but it is not possible to draw a direct line between the two eras of violence. Sultan Abdul Hamid lost the throne in 1909, several years before the onset of genocide. Indeed, key domestic opponents of the Sultan would carry out the genocide after they had overthrown Abdul Hamid. The killings of the 1890s influenced later ethnic and religious relations and revealed the very real potential for escalating violence without leading inexorably to genocide.

The rise of the Young Turks

The political ferment in the late Ottoman Empire also gave rise to the movement known as the Young Turks that would count among its members the key perpetrators of the Armenian Genocide. The same nationalist ideas that caught hold among sectors of Bulgarian, Greek, and Armenian opinion also won a following among Turks. The modern Turkish nationalist movement, known most broadly as the Young Turks, emerged in 1889 at the Imperial Medical School with a political movement that became known as the Committee of Unity and Progress or CUP (CUP's members were also termed Unionists or Ittihadists). Like other nascent nationalist movements, the Young Turks won strongest support among educated and professional circles as well as army officers, though not all nationalist pioneers fit this exact profile. Talat, who played a central role in the CUP government during the First World War, worked as a telegraph operator. Official repression failed to quash the movement for good: some members of CUP continued to organize from within the Empire while others became active in exile in Geneva and Paris.

On the surface, the Young Turks did not appear intent on persecuting Armenians. Young Turk groups aimed for political reform, for limits on the Sultan's authority, and for restoration of the long-suspended constitution of 1876. Such goals to a significant degree coincided with those of Armenian political parties, but Young Turk gains promised both opportunity and peril for Ottoman Armenians. By attacking the foundations of imperial authority,

Young Turks could either more fully incorporate Armenians in Ottoman society or exclude Armenians from a future society. One possible route to a future society lay in forging an Ottoman identity that would unite diverse peoples of the Empire, including Turks and Armenians among many others. Indeed, some Turkish nationalists negotiated and cooperated with Armenians in the early 1900s. However, others envisioned a new society united by membership in a Turkish nation that in principle had no place for Armenians.

In 1908 the Committee of Unity and Progress led revolution against the Sultan, and in 1909 the CUP responded to attempts at counterrevolution by deposing Abdul Hamid II. The 1908 revolution at first showed the potential appeal of reform to unite diverse ethnic, national, and religious groups within the Ottoman Empire. The revolution started in Macedonia where diverse communities in the mixed city of Salonica showed enthusiasm for the uprising. At the same time, key figures within the CUP, such as the sociologist Ziya Gokalp, espoused Turkish unity and identified groups such as Armenians as damaging to Turks and their interests.

The cycle of counterrevolution and revolution also brought renewed large-scale massacres of Armenians in 1909, this time along the Mediterranean Coast. Local residents joined in pogroms against Armenians, killing thousands at the city of Adana and in the coastal region called Cilicia. Armenians faced an onslaught from the foes of revolution, though some claimed that Unionists had also joined in the attacks. Such charges revealed the complex state of late Ottoman politics, for the Unionists in principle opposed any counterrevolution.

Radicalization

Though massacres under Sultan Abdul Hamid II revealed that Armenians had become a people at risk in the late Ottoman Empire, there are two key problems with drawing a direct connection between the late Ottoman massacres and genocide: the first lies in the fact that the government that oversaw killing in the 1890s was swept from power before the First World War and the second in the different scale of killing. Abdul Hamid II became infamous for Armenian massacres, but the Committee of Unity and Progress was very different in orientation and goals from the Ottoman Empire's prior rulers. The genocide that the CUP carried out could be seen as an escalation of previous massacres, but even after the Abdul Hamid era massacres and the killings at Adana, Armenians, as well as many Muslims, still experienced genocide as a radical rupture or break with the past. Much like Jews in the 1930s who may have thought that they already knew the worst manifestations of anti-Semitism, Ottoman Armenian could have thought that they were already familiar with the worst-case scenario. That Armenians could suffer persecution and even massive violence in the Ottoman Empire was clear by 1909, but there was still little sense of the scale of deportations and killings that would devastate Armenians during the First World War. Revolution, reform, external pressure, and new nationalist movements contributed to crisis, but that combination had as yet not led to genocide.

Long-term trends placed Armenians at growing risk and created precedents for violence, but a rapid process of radicalization also led to mass killing in the Armenian Genocide. Political radicalization continued and indeed accelerated in the period leading up to the First World War. A key turning point came with the Balkan Wars that preceded the First World War. Overlooked later because of the magnitude of the Great War that followed, the First Balkan War in 1912–13 was a massive defeat for the Ottoman Empire. In the fall of 1912 Balkan states, including Bulgaria, Greece, Serbia, and Montenegro went to war against the Ottoman Empire. The Balkan allies quickly pushed Ottoman forces out of all but a sliver of Turkey in Europe, leaving little of the once vast Ottoman European domain. Dispute over the spoils of war among the victors produced a Second Balkan War in June 1913. Turkey seized advantage of the new war in which Greece and Serbia defeated Bulgaria, to regain some territory in Thrace from Bulgaria. However, the cumulative effect of the Balkan Wars was still catastrophic for the Ottoman Empire.

The First Balkan War, in particular, brought humiliation for Turkey. Ottoman forces mounted stiff resistance in some cases, defending the approaches to Constantinople against the Bulgarian army in the last stage of the war. However, the overwhelming impression left by Ottoman forces in 1912 was of an army that could no longer fight, let alone defend its country. For the most part the Balkan allies' gains came easily. In much of Macedonia ill-equipped, and poorly motivated Ottoman troops melted away before advancing Serb, Bulgarian, and Greek forces.

Defeat in the First Balkan War caused retreat not just of soldiers but also of hundreds of thousands of Muslims civilians. Muslims fled in fear of both Balkan armies and of bands of irregulars who carried out a terror campaign in many rural districts and in towns. Arson, massacres, and rumors persuaded Muslims to hurriedly pack and leave for remaining Ottoman territory. Clogging roads, packed into and on top of overburdened trains, the civilians made their way toward Constantinople. The refugees, former residents of Turkey in Europe, were a visible reminder of the humiliation of an Empire that could no longer protect their homes. In addition, they severely taxed the resources of an overburdened state suffering from shock. Homeless refugees were reduced to living out in the open—some even took shelter in graveyards. The arrival of refugees also accelerated a long-term shift in which Muslims made up an increasing proportion of the population in the remaining Ottoman lands.

In the midst of crisis the CUP struck against the Ottoman government. A dispute over new borders and the question of whether the Ottoman Empire would retain the city of Edirne or Adrianople on its western border in Thrace helped to precipitate action. Revolutionaries including Colonel Enver and Talat arrived at the center of the Ottoman government at the Sublime Porte, so known for a gate, and demanded the resignation of the Grand Vezir, the Sultan's chief political minister. In the ensuing tumult the Minister of War was killed. With the coup CUP moved ever close to seizing control of the Ottoman government, and by the start of the First World War, Enver, Talat, and their associates were the true rulers of Turkey in all but name.

The Balkan Wars created both general and specific peril for Armenians. Defeat convinced Turkish nationalists that they were best by both internal and external enemies, and some identified Armenians as a traitor people who turned against the empire in its hour of need. Claims of Armenian treason focused primarily on the activities of Armenians who volunteered to fight for the Balkan Allies during the First Balkan War. As Leon Trotsky, the Russian revolutionary who was then working as a journalist, reported, there were Armenians who accompanied the Macedonian Legion that fought for Bulgaria during the First War and carried out a terror campaign against civilians. "All the same," one told Trotsky, "some of us did carve the Turks. . . . Well, it has to be said, all of us remembered the pogroms in Armenia."[2] The actions of these volunteers did not demonstrate that Armenians undermined or in general obstructed the Ottoman war effort: Armenians also served in the Ottoman Army in greater numbers than ever before under a new policy that extended partial conscription to the Armenian population. However, the facts of the case mattered less than the growing conviction within the Committee of Unity and Progress that Armenians could not be trusted and favored Turkey's enemies.

CUP policy toward Christians and Armenians, in particular, continued to take more radical form during the period between the Balkan Wars and the start of the First World War. The CUP leadership concluded that remaining Ottoman territory would never be secure unless the percentage of Christians did not amount to more than 5 or 10 percent in any region. Indeed, CUP also extended this principle to consider resettlement of non-Turkish Muslims. Viewing the future with growing anxiety, the CUP leadership reacted against pressure for Armenian reforms. Negotiations with the European powers on the future of the Ottoman East led to an agreement between the Ottoman Empire and Russia in February 1914 that called for regrouping eastern provinces into two large provinces, each with its own foreign inspector.[3] Such reform programs that took into account Armenian goals struck CUP as representing a threat to the territorial integrity and security of the state and further intensified distrust of Ottoman Armenians. On the eve of the First World War, Turkish nationalists were already primed to see a connection between foreign intervention in Ottoman lands and Armenians.

The First World War further radicalized the Committee of Union and Progress. Over the summer and early fall of 1914 Turkey moved to enter the First World War on the side of the Central Powers, Germany and Austria-Hungary. Leading Young Turks had already formed close ties with Germany. Enver Pasha the newly appointed Minister of War had spent several years as a military attaché in Berlin. (Enver and Talat were often referred to with the Ottoman title of Pasha.) In August 1914, the Turkish purchase of two German battleships signaled the close ties between Germany and Turkey. Britain tried in vain to maintain Turkish neutrality, but on October 29 Turkey entered the war by bombarding the Russian Black Sea coast.

The approach of war exposed divisions between the Young Turks and the leading Armenian political parties, including the Armenian Revolutionary Federation (ARF) or Dashnaks. In August 1914 the Dashnaks held a congress at Erzerum in eastern Anatolia to determine their policy toward a war, which the Ottoman Empire had yet to join. A delegation from the Committee of Union and Progress went to the Erzerum and called on the Armenian political parties of Turkey to form bands to fight Russia in the Caucasus; however, the Dashnaks rejected the proposal. This refusal strengthened the belief of leading Young Turks, such as Dr Bahaeddin Sakir, that Ottoman Armenians could not be trusted in a war with Russia.

The war's first months brought great hardship for Ottoman Armenians living in the east near the borders of Russia and the Persia. Armed bands began to attack Armenian villages along the eastern border even before Turkey entered the First World War, and the attacks continued and intensified through the last months of 1914. Armenians in the region surrounding Erzerum complained of attacks by irregulars. The chief initiative for the attacks lay with a Special Organization (Teskilati Mahsusa) led by Dr Mehmed Nazim and Dr Sakir. From an operations base in Erzerum in Turkey's east, the Special Organization formed bands made of irregular forces, including tribal fighters, convicts released from prison, and Muslim refugees from the Balkans and the Caucasus.

From the end of December 1914 through April 1915 a final sequence of crises radicalized Turkish nationalism and deepened animosity against Armenians among the leaders of the Young Turks' Committee of Union and Progress. The key trend in these months was a shift in Turkey's fortunes in war. A series of military setbacks and threats shattered Turkish confidence in victory and amplified all the fears of disaster built up during the years of defeats before the First World War. As in the First Balkan War and the Aegean diplomatic crisis that followed the Greek move into the Aegean islands during the First Balkan War, members of Ottoman Christian communities received much of the blame for the success of an external foe. However, the connection between alleged internal traitors and foreign enemies struck Turks as far more dangerous in 1915 than in preceding years. Turkey's military situation was more precarious than ever before in that the final destruction of the Empire now seemed possible. After years of territorial loss and arrival of Muslim refugees, Turks were more willing than ever before to think the worst of a Christian Millet or community.

The first turning point in Turkey's war was a disastrous defeat on the Eastern Front against Russia. In December 1914, Minister of War Enver advanced with some 90,000 troops in the Ottoman Third Army toward Russian positions in the Caucasus. His German allies advised him to hold back, but he hoped to regain former Ottoman provinces lost to Russia in 1878. The Third Army initially advanced rapidly: Turkish forces pushed beyond the Russian border and one detachment entered Azerbaijan to the south and took Tabriz. However, cold and snow took a toll on the Third Army before it engaged Russian forces on December 29th at the town of Sarikamis at the end of the Russian rail line west of Kars. Over the next several days the Third Army suffered a total defeat. More than three quarters of the Third Army's soldiers were lost in the campaign and in the retreat west. By the end of January 1915, Turkish forces also gave up Tabriz.

The Battle of Sarikamis marked a key breaking point in Turkish-Armenian relations. It awakened fears that Turkey faced destruction and provoked a search for scapegoats. Enver retained a leading place within the Young Turk leadership, and the country's political leaders and military instead placed much of the blame for the disaster on Armenians, even though Armenians had served with the Third Army on the Eastern Front. Nonetheless, the defeat reinforced a conspiracy theory in which Armenian volunteers stabbed Turkey in the back and ensured Russian victory. In particular, this explanation of defeat singled out Karekin Pastermadjian a former Ottoman Member of Parliament, also known as Armen Garo, who fought as a volunteer with Russian troops in the Caucasus.

On the western edge of the Empire, Allied efforts to breach the Dardanelles, the waterway connecting the Aegean Sea and the Sea of Marmara, further intensified the aura of crisis in early 1915. Henry Morgenthau, the US Ambassador recalled the panic of days when Turkish leaders feared an imminent naval assault on Constantinople. He described the preparation of special trains to evacuate the government, though noting that Enver, among the Young Turk leaders, remained confident of victory. The Allied warships never reached Constantinople, but in April British and French imperial forces carried out at a landing at Gallipoli. Ottoman forces, including a division commanded by General Mustafa Kemal, who would later become known by the name Ataturk as the leader of Turkish Nationalists after the war, and German military advisors kept the Allies penned up on the beachheads until they abandoned the costly operation, but in spring 1915 the landing confirmed Turkish nationalists' own belief that they lived in an ever-victimized country facing the threat of imminent dissolution. Following setbacks in war with Russia, western military intervention intensified both the long-standing Turkish nationalist distrust of foreign powers that sought to profit from Ottoman weakness and their suspicion of internal groups such as Armenians who shared an interest in reforming and reorganizing the Empire.

Political radicalization carried a growing danger to all groups identified with those enemies who the Young Turks saw as intent on destroying Turkey. As the Empire became increasingly Muslim, non-Muslim populations in general fell under increasing Turkish nationalist suspicion, but CUP's leaders singled out Armenians. They accused Armenians of a pattern of disloyalty and treason. In fact, recent reforms had brought Armenians into the Ottoman military and even after the battle of Sarikamis Enver told the Armenian patriarch that Armenian troops had served well during the campaign, but Turkish nationalists increasingly blamed Armenian volunteers for assisting Russia. Finally, in April 1915, an Armenian uprising at the eastern city of Van cemented the CUP image of Armenians as a traitor population. Armenians depicted the events at Van as a local response to a governor they did not trust, but for CUP's inner leadership the conflict at Van amplified their determination to take radical action against Ottoman Armenians.

WHAT HAPPENED AT VAN?

Van was a city with mixed population in eastern Anatolia close to the Ottoman Russian border. Counts of the religious and ethnic breakdown of the city and region of Van produced wild discrepancies, but by any measure the city had a large Armenian population of approximately 40,000 at the start of the First World War. The population also included other Christians, as well as Muslims, and Kurds also lived in the surrounding region. Tension had already built in this region just to the west of the front during the fall of 1914 and the winter of 1915, and looting and killings carried out by varied armed bands spread in the aftermath of Sarikamis. A showdown between local Armenians and Turkish authorities approached with the appointment of Djevdet Bey, Enver's brother-in-law, as Vali or Governor. Djevdet demanded that Van supply Armenian men for mobilization, but after the murder of prominent Armenians and attacks on Armenian villagers, the city's Armenians saw the demand as a pretext for massacre and refused to comply. The battle for Van began on April 20 and lasted until the arrival of Russia forces precipitated Turkish withdrawal on May 16. A later Turkish counter-offensive retook the city, leading to a general flight of Armenians. A life-and-death struggle for combatants, Van gained significance as a symbol either of Armenian heroism or betrayal. Clarence Ussher, an American physician and missionary at Van described the city's Armenians as defending themselves against the threat of extermination. Of Djevdet Bey's demands, he wrote "Armenians ... felt certain he intended to put the four thousand to death."[4] On the other hand, the Young Turks asserted that Van represented a general tendency toward treason. "But if they ally themselves with our enemies," Enver later told Ambassador Morgenthau, "as they did in the Van district, they will have to be destroyed."[5]

Planning: Temporary deportation law as end point or starting point

No single document outlined a decision to rid the Ottoman Empire of most Armenians. The cabinet, acting during a period when the Parliament was suspended passed a temporary deportation law in the last days of May 1915. This allowed local military and political authorities to deport suspect groups. A statement from the Minister of the Interior sent to the Grand Vezier on May 26, 1915 clarified the intent of these measures, explaining the need to deport Armenians so that the issue is "brought to an end in a comprehensive and absolute way."[6]

The significance of the deportation law remains in dispute. The language was ominous, but when did deportation come to serve as nothing more than a mechanism for genocide? Even as a key step toward genocide the deportation law could have served as either an end point or as an intermediate, but still not absolutely final step. As an end point deportation would mark the culmination for ongoing discussions within the CUP leadership, but as an intermediate step, the deportation law spurred rapid expansion of ever-more sweeping deportations. In the first interpretation, the deportation law merely confirmed decisions already made at the earliest in late March or April—in this narrative, the temporary law provided legal justification for a policy previously approved by the upper echelons of the CUP. Alternately, in the second interpretation, the deportation law brought the inner circle of the Young Turks to the cusp of a decision that they would finalize over the following weeks, swiftly expanding deportation to sweep up Armenians across most of the Ottoman Empire.

Genocide

Assault against Armenian soldiers and leaders

The Young Turks' assault against Ottoman Armenians escalated during 1915 through a series of phases. Early phases targeted particular groups, usually men, including soldiers and elites or local or national leaders. Deportations then targeted particular regions such as Cilicia. In the next phase, a broader campaign of destruction brought removal of Armenian men, women, and children through methods that led to mass extermination.

The prelude to genocide began with a program of isolating, exploiting, and in many cases killing Armenian soldiers in the Ottoman army. This decision followed soon after the Ottoman defeat at Sarikamis. Although Minister Enver praised Armenian soldiers in the Ottoman military, he still ordered the army in early 1915 to take away weapons from Armenian soldiers in the east. Detached from their units, they were set to hard labor, digging ditches and building roads. Reports soon emerged of the shooting and massacre of the disarmed soldiers. As Dr Clarence Ussher noted, "When the makers of roads had finished their work, their Turkish officers, first circulating a report that they were in revolt, had groups of them surrounded and shot down."[7] The deaths numbered in the thousands and tens of thousands. This attack fell short of genocide only in that the victims, men and soldiers, did not clearly fall into any of the categories later identified in the UN Genocide Convention, but it had the quality of a genocidal attack targeting men or of what scholars would late describe as "gendercide." The assault against Armenian soldiers also signaled the final failure of any attempt to forge a broad new national identity in Turkey that would cross religious and ethnic lines. Finally, disarming and killing Armenian soldiers reduced the Armenian capacity to resist deportations later in 1915.

Even in this phase, however, the assault against Armenians was inconsistent. Disarmed Armenian soldiers suffered abuse and death, and their mistreatment possessed great symbolic importance. However, the policy did not necessarily apply to all Armenian soldiers—some continued to serve in the Ottoman armies on the Western Front in the fighting at Gallipoli.

The next phase on the assault against Ottoman Armenians came with roundups of prominent Armenians in cities and towns across the Empire. Attacks carried out by the Special Organization against Armenian local elites in border regions near Persia and Russia in 1914 foreshadowed the broader campaign in 1915. As Grigoris Balakian experienced, this phase started on the night of April 24–25 with a sweep that gathered up Armenian notables and leaders in Constantinople. Local authorities, including police, seized some 250 prominent Armenians. One of those taken into captivity was the poet Siamanto (Adom Yarjanian) who in the poems, *Blood News from My Friend,* had described the Adana massacres of 1909. Siamanto left for the United States in 1909 but fatefully returned in 1911. After his arrest on the night of April 24, 1915, he was deported to the interior and murdered.

ARRESTS IN HARPUT

The town of Harput or Kharpert in central Anatolia was one of many where Turkish authorities arrested local Armenian notables in the Spring of 1915 following the similar roundup in Constantinople. Henry Riggs, a third-generation American missionary in Turkey who had been born in Sivas and spent the bulk of his life living outside the United States in Turkey and Lebanon, told of the events of May 1915. A professor was arrested on May 1. "Within a few days, a considerable number of other arrests were made of men in similarly prominent position." The detained, some 40 to 50, were then tortured, some to death. "One man was hung up by his arms for 24 hours and the hairs of his beard plucked out." Others were branded with irons, all with the purpose, Riggs gathered "ostensibly to extort from the victims information about the seditious plot of the Armenians." Confessions extracted by torture in turn provided justification for a broader assault against Armenians Riggs, himself, suggested that the actual goal was to drive a wedge between local Muslims and Christians: "The real purpose of the action of the authorities, however, was probably not to secure any information, but to produce an effect on the minds of both Moslems and Christians, an effort in which they were highly successful."[8]

The pattern of roundups of prominent local Armenians soon spread. The arrests struck cities and towns in central and eastern Anatolia, including Harput, Erzerum, and Diarbekir, communities close to the Black Sea, such as Sivas and Marsovan, and towns elsewhere such as Izmid. Henry Wood of the AP described a common pattern. Police typically began the roundups at midnight—they "swooped down on the homes of all Armenians whose names had been put on the proscribed list sent out from Constantinople." They then carried out searches for "papers" and took the men away.[9] The repeated action amounted to a campaign to decapitate Armenian leadership. The murder of many of those detained extended the gendercide that had begun with the massacres of disarmed Armenian soldiers.

Deportations

The campaign against Armenians soon extended to deportations. Indeed, these began even before the Temporary Deportation Law of late May. In the region of Cilicia on the southeastern coast of Anatolia along the Mediterranean Turkish authorities deported Armenians from the region of Zeitoun (Zeytoun). This region had a history of resistance, and some Armenian deserters fought with government forces in March 1915, and then took refuge in a monastery. This was hardly a general uprising: the Armenians who took up arms did not gain widespread local support for their action even among Armenians. However, the Ottoman military and in particular Djemal Pasha, of the CUP opted to move Armenians out of the area. Turkish fears of possible British operations near Alexandretta (Iskenderun) sustained a nationalist policy of continuing deportations from Cilicia, under which Armenians were sent toward Konia and toward Aleppo in Syria and into the surrounding desert. The timing of these early deportations is vital in the debates over the planning for genocide. The early deportations can be seen as evidence of an early decision to eliminate the Ottoman Armenians. However, the fact that these early deportations from Cilicia did not yet extend to Armenians' other areas provides evidence to support the idea that the CUP leadership had not yet quite reached the point of making a final decision to launch a full-scale genocidal assault.

In June and July the deportations expanded rapidly, sweeping up ever larger numbers of Armenians in wider areas of Anatolia. In May and June as deportations continued in Cilicia, they also struck Armenians in the far east of Anatolia. Armenians, mainly women, children, and the elderly crowded into the town of Bitlis near Lake Van, but in June Bitlis was cleared of Armenians, after many of the men had been massacred. In general, groups of notables or local leaders were expelled in advance from towns and cities in eastern and central Anatolia in June, and by the end of June deportation orders increasingly encompassed entire Armenian communities. In the eastern town of Erzerum, for example, some 500 were deported on June 16 before further groups left on June 19–20, and June 26.

The deportations continued all summer long. Over the course of July and August most Armenians of central and eastern Anatolia and the Black Sea region were driven from their homes, and by August deportations also spread to smaller Armenian communities in central and western Turkey. Indeed by October 27, the deportations extended all the way to Edirne/Adrianople in Thrace on Turkey's far western border.

FIGURE 2.1 *Family of deportees on the road (Taurus pass).*

The deportations followed a common pattern (Figure 2.1). Armenians received very short notice, sometimes as little as a few days or even hours to arrange their affairs, though actual deportation was sometimes delayed for days or even weeks. Those assigned to depart had to leave houses, possessions, fields, animals, house-wares, and tools. Deportation in practice therefore amounted to economic confiscation. Men and women were often separated with many men massacred at the start or just after deportation. In some cases Armenians were supplied with food, but more often they left hungry.

Armenians sometimes started out with oxcarts. Some packed belongings on mules or donkeys. But most often they simply walked with whatever they could carry, including not only meager possession left to them but children. In western Turkey deportations also took place by train. Armenians were pressed into tightly packed rail cars and taken south and east along the Anatolian railway to towns in central Turkey, such as Konya. There tens of thousands were forced out into makeshift camps in surrounding fields, before being pushed further south on foot toward the desert.

From ethnic cleansing to genocide

The Armenian Genocide was both ethnic cleansing and genocide. As a campaign to drive a particular group defined by their identity out of an entire region it was ethnic cleansing. At the same time in this case ethnic cleansing amounted to genocide because the means employed to drive out Armenians also led predictably to their mass destruction.

The killing started early during deportations with massacres of Armenian men and boys. These murders built on the assaults of the spring which had targeted Armenian soldiers and local leaders. In many instances, Armenian were rounded up just before deportation and then taken away by gendarmes, never to be seen again. These enforced disappearances, to use a term created in the late twentieth century, also eased the work of rounding up and forcing out any surviving Armenians by reducing the chances of resistance.

Those Armenians not murdered at the outset were sent south on death marches. Armed bands and marauding tribesmen attacked, robbed, and slaughtered the columns of refugees. Doctor Ida Stapleton, an American physician and missionary, learned from a letter from one Armenian woman, that after two nights on the road, "a motley crowd of Kurds, Turks, soldier police began to attack the caravan with guns, swords, scythes, clubs, fists . . . All the men were killed outright except one."[10] Armenians arriving in Harput from Erzerum in early July similarly told the American Consul Leslie Davis that "all the men of the party had been butchered by Kurds . . . while the women had been robbed of everything they carried."[11] The killings left columns comprised mainly of women, and children.

On the Black Sea coast, some Armenians were killed in the sea itself. Armenians were told that they were being transported by sea, but were instead thrown overboard. Alternately, barges laden with Armenians were sunk. Meanwhile, those Armenians deported over land from the Black Sea region faced potentially the longest route of all. The journey south could last as long as three months, extended for detours to add to the level of exhaustion.

With a few exceptions there was little immediate effort to hide or disguise the killing. Travelers and observers all over the Ottoman Empire saw dead bodies. Corpses lined roads, lakes, and rivers. Travelers along the roads reported seeing corpses along the sides. Meanwhile, for weeks on end corpses floated south along the Euphrates.

LAKE GOLCUK

Lake Golcuk or Lake Hazar, a large lake in central Turkey to the southeast of Harput in better times had been a pleasant spot to visit for an excursion. The contingent of American missionaries and teachers in the city associated the lake with recreation. However, in 1915 it became one of many dumping grounds for disposing of the corpses of murdered Armenians. In September 1915 the American Consul Leslie Davis traveled back to Lake Golcuk. He saw dead bodies all along his route, many only covered in shallow graves, but that still did not prepare him fully or what he saw at the lake itself. "In most of the valleys," Davis wrote, "there were dead bodies and from the tops of the cliffs which extended between them we saw hundreds of bodies and many bones in the water."[12] Davis returned in October with the American missionary physician Dr Atkinson. Again and again at the valleys around the lake, Davis saw piles of hundreds of corpses, and one valley had at least 2,000. Atkinson set the number of dead around the lake at 5,000–10,000.

Armenians who escaped massacre made their way south until they entered the deserts of Syria and Mesopotamia. Armenians en route were desperate for bread, water, and shelter. Even when Armenians received some rations at the start of their journey, the supply of food rapidly dwindled to amounts far below the minimum necessary for survival, let alone for the arduous work of trekking across a rugged landscape. Armenians begged for food and were sometimes reduced to trying to eat grass, dead animals, or even seeds from animal dung. Exposure to the desert heat further depleted Armenians who in some cases tried to create make-shift shelter out of materials like goat hair. Their footwear stolen en route, many had to get by without shoes. All the while Armenians were repeatedly robbed and raped.

Columns of refugees who arrived in Syria and Jordan were so depleted by their journey that the Armenians continued to die in large numbers. Because so many men had already been murdered, those who reached the desert were mainly women, children and the elderly:

once in desert towns like Aleppo or Der Zor many died daily from exhaustion and disease. So desperate were the Armenians that women and children could easily be purchased. Indeed, some tried to give away their children to someone who might be able to feed them.

A final phase of destruction came in 1916 in the Armenian refugee camps along the Euphrates River. Armenians who had already survived deprivation died from famine and disease. Others were slaughtered. The death toll from this second phase of genocide amounted to many tens of thousands, and possibly to as many as 100,000–200,000 Armenians were slaughtered at this time. In all the number of deaths during 1915 and 1916 amounted to more than 1 million and may have reached as high as 1.5 million.

GENOCIDE FROM A GERMAN PERSPECTIVE

The fact that Germany was Turkey's ally and stationed military personnel in Turkey has long led to scrutiny of German knowledge and even possible participation in genocide. At the very least, Germans became aware of the genocide, whatever sympathies they possessed for the Ottoman Empire and its military cause. On June 17, 1915, the German Ambassador Baron von Wangenheim wrote to the Chancellor, stating that "The expulsion of the Armenian population from their homes in the East Anatolian provinces and their relocation in other areas is being carried out ruthlessly." Moreover, Wangenheim had come to doubt that these deportations were being carried out for military reasons. He added that the Minister of the Interior, Talat, had informed another German diplomat that Turkey was "intent on taking advantage of the World War in order to make a clean sweep of internal enemies— the indigenous Christians—without being hindered in doing so by diplomatic intervention from other countries." As the area affected by deportations expanded, Dr Mordtmann of the German Embassy noted on June 30 that "This can no longer be justified by military considerations; rather, it is a matter of destroying the Armenians, as Talaat Bey told me several weeks ago." By July 7, Wangenheim saw the campaign much the same way. "This situation and the way in which the relocation is being carried out," he informed Germany's Chancellor, "shows that the government is indeed pursuing its purpose of eradicating the Armenian race from the Turkish Empire."[13]

That the deportations under these conditions would lead and were leading to mass destruction was no secret. It has been claimed, though with decreasing frequency, that the destruction of Ottoman Armenians was not genocide because Turkish authorities intended to supply the deported civilians with the necessary supplies to keep them alive. However, observers across Turkey saw the deportations as tantamount to destruction. Far to the north in the ancient town of Trebizond, the Austrian consul wrote about what a deportation to distant Mosul would mean under the conditions that were already becoming known. Such a journey was "a death sentence" he told the Austrian embassy. One would have to look back far into the past to find such a "violent attempt at the annihilation of a people."[14] From Harput, Leslie Davis reached much the same conclusions. Few of the Armenians sent south would make it all the way to Mesopotamia: "Much of the way was over the desert . . . it was summer. . . . It was certain that most of them would perish on the way."[15] Indeed, Turkish Nationalists knew this full well. At Harput a Young Turk Member of Parliament, told Henry Riggs: "The Armenians know what massacre is, and think they can bear that. But let them wait and see what deportation is. . . . They will soon learn how much worse it is than massacre."[16]

Regions of genocide: Erzerum, Constantinople, Dersim

Amidst massive destruction, the unfolding of genocide also varied according to region. The slaughter accelerated most rapidly and reached greatest intensity in towns and cities in core Armenian regions of eastern Anatolia. One such town was Erzerum located on the eastern edge of the Anatolian plateau. An Armenian bank director was shot in February, but otherwise Erzerum's Armenians were largely untouched by any violence or persecution until May.

Limited deportations began in May: Armenians were driven out of villages to the north of Erzerum as irregulars carried out murders and rapes. In June deportations began to affect the Armenians of Erzerum. Late that month Erzerum's Armenians received a general deportation order. The deported were soon massacred, many in the Kemakh gorge—also the site for slaughter of Armenians deported from the town of Erzindjan. Armenians who survived those killings were then pushed south into the desert, a journey during which many died along the way. This outcome of widespread deportation and murder was typical for the major Armenian population centers of Anatolia.

In the Armenian Genocide, as in many other genocides, outcomes varied by region. Amidst the general misery and suffering there were local differences in the level of threat faced by Armenians. As deportation and massacres eradicated Armenians in central and eastern Anatolia comparatively remote areas such as Dersim offered both peril and the possibility of greater safety. Dersim was a mountainous and remote area in eastern Anatolia, and even as late as the First World War, Turkish authorities struggled to exert authority in heavily Kurdish regions like Dersim. Many of the Dersim Kurds were Alevi and practiced a syncretic form of Islam. Kurdish chieftains had often exacted heavy financial burdens on Armenians, and Kurds took part in attacks on the refugee columns. But in 1915, the Dersim Kurds also provided a safe haven of sorts for Armenians, though they sometimes collected money for their aid.

The regional variation in the outcomes of the Armenian Genocide was surprisingly most pronounced both in remote areas like Dersim and in the largest urban centers of western Turkey. Amidst pervasive deportation and massacres, Armenians generally escaped death in the large cities of the western Empire, Constantinople and Smyrna. Perhaps because so much of the debate over the Armenian Genocide has focused on identifying genocide, the main causes for this regional variation are still not fully explained. Greater German pressure, divisions within the Turkish government, and the presence of more foreign observers may have accounted for that difference between the fate of Armenians in the largest western cities and the destruction of their counterparts in Cilicia, in Central and Eastern Anatolia, and even in some smaller western towns and cities. In Smyrna, the regional German commander, General von Sanders, also opposed deportations. However, Armenians were not totally spared in Constantinople where deportations targeted Armenian men who had left their families in the provinces and come to work in the Ottoman capital.

Perpetrators

The leadership of the Committee of Unity and Progress made up the inner core of perpetrators responsible for the Armenian Genocide. In particular the Minister of the Interior Talat and the Minister of War Enver set the agenda for extermination. Djemal, one of the leaders of the 1908 revolution and 1912 coup, also held multiple important posts as Minister of the Navy and as commander in Damascus and military governor in Syria. Both Talat and Enver, when pressed by US Ambassador Henry Morgenthau, defended the decision to destroy Ottoman Armenians. Talat set out the Ittihadists' rationale during an August 1915 conversation with Morgenthau. Armenians, he asserted, "enriched themselves at the expense of the Turks." They were "determined to domineer over us and to establish a separate state," and, he charged, "they have openly encouraged our enemies. They have assisted the Russians in the Caucasus and our failure there is largely explained by their actions. We have therefore come to the irrevocable decision that we shall make them powerless before this war is ended." When Morgenthau suggested to Enver that perhaps the Committee was not aware of massacres, Enver took full responsibility. "I am entirely willing to accept the responsibility myself for everything that has taken place," he declared, "The Cabinet itself has ordered the deportations. I am convinced that we are completely justified in doing this owing to the hostile attitude of the Armenians toward the Ottoman Government. . . ."[17]

The Interior Ministry and CUP organized the genocide via a complex process in which unofficial communication by party channels sometimes superseded official government directives. Thus, the Ittihadists communicated through their own party apparatus. A friend of Grigoris Balakian's among the Armenians at Chankiri happened to see an example of this kind of internal communication while visiting a local party secretary who briefly walked out of the room during a meeting, leaving a document on a table which read, "Without mercy and without pity, kill all from the one-month-old to the ninety-year-old, but see to it that this massacre is not conducted in the towns and in the presence of people." Coded telegrams and oral directives supplemented actual written orders. The Lieutenant Governor of Chankiri read such a telegram to an Armenian who had happened to be his professor. This text from the Minister of the Interior read: "TELEGRAPH US IMMEDIATELY AS TO HOW MANY ARMENIANS HAVE ALREADY DIED AND HOW MANY ARE LEFT ALIVE-TALAAT."[18] Messages delivered with the CUP party apparatus were also sent to local party secretaries.

Within the CUP Dr Sakir and Dr Nazim were instrumental in organizing killing. They oversaw action by a Special Organization (Teskilat-I Mahsusa), which carried out attacks against specific groups, including Armenians. This grew out of armed bands, employed during the Balkan Wars and also continued a pattern of decades in which units separate from the military had carried out many of the most violent attacks against civilians during wars of the late Ottoman period. In eastern Anatolia, Dr Sakir led the Special Organization out of Erzerum. The Organization both undertook operations in warfare along the Russian and Persian border, sometimes carrying out raids beyond Ottoman territory, and also targeted undesirable groups within Ottoman borders. The CUP increased direct control over the armed bands in May by detaching the Special Organization from the Ministry of War and placing command directly under Dr Sakir.

The Special Organization recruited personnel from several sources. These included Kurds, Muslim refugees from the Balkans and the Caucasus, and convicts released from prison. Kurdish chieftains in some regions were already accustomed to using threats and force to exact payments from local Armenians. Refugees, for their part, who felt victimized by the loss of their homes, could be deployed against Armenians in pursuit of vengeance, even though Ottoman Armenians had not cost them previous homelands. Many who entered the Special Organization were criminals. The verdict for the Harput Trial conducted by a Turkish military tribunal after the First World War found that Sakir under the title " 'Head of the

Special Organization' . . . assumed the leadership of the ensemble of convicts who were set up and formed out of a group of criminals released from prison. . . ." The key goal was to kill Armenians, or as the Harput verdict put it, Sakir "took into his service individuals from this section of the Special Organization, which had been formed for the purpose of destroying and annihilating the Armenians."[19]

The ranks of perpetrators extended beyond the circles of either the Special Organization or other similar local irregular forces. Police frequently took part in rounding up Armenians, and also in some cases escorted them during deportation and joined in killing. In principle the military did not lead the destruction of Ottoman Armenians, but military units at times were drawn into the genocide. The military, including units of the Third Army, took part in massacres of Armenians in Eastern Anatolia, and there were also financial links between the Information Service of the General Staff and the Special Organization.

Notably, General Mustafa Kemal who became the leader of the Turkish Nationalists after the First World War and became known as Kemal Ataturk did not take part in rounding up or killing Armenians. During the peak of the genocide in 1915 he oversaw the successful defense of Gallipoli against the British landing and was only later posted to the front in the east in 1916.

A PERPETRATOR'S TALE: CAPTAIN SHUKRI

Obtaining a direct glimpse into perpetrators' understanding of their own participation in killing is always difficult given the human inclination to avoid such topics—accounts by survivors can be difficult to find but invariably outnumber accounts by perpetrators. However, Grigoris Balakian had the opportunity to talk at length to one perpetrator, Captain Shukri of the police soldiers, during the early stages of deportation from Chankiri in 1916. As Shukri and police soldiers accompanied this small group of remaining Armenians out of Chankiri, Balakian frequently rode alongside the captain.

He attributed Shukri's readiness to talk to the boredom of a long journey and the tendency to seek out another fellow rider for conversation. As they passed by corpses, Shukri gave an estimate of numbers killed in that region: "about 86,000 Armenians were massacred" including some from other provinces but were killed in the Yozgat area. Captain Shukri also attributed the order to kill directly to CUP. Asked whose orders he was following he answered, "The orders came from the Ittihad Central committee and the Interior Ministry in Constantinople," adding that a local official who came from Van had particular motive to follow the orders because his family had been killed, Shukri said, in Van by Armenians.[20] Shukri further explained that he and his men killed men before women, and collected gold, silver, and jewelry from Yozgat's Armenian women before taking them to be slaughtered. These comments pointed to the importance of central direction by CUP, a cycle of revenge, and the added incentive of personal gain as motives for perpetrators in the Armenian Genocide.

The ranks of perpetrators extended beyond the CUP, the Special Organization, varied armed bands, police, and in some case even the military, to include ordinary people. Turkish and Kurdish civilians did not initiate and drive the killing, but some nonetheless took part in attacks on Armenians. The very importance of irregular forces to the killing blurred the lines between special detachments of murderers and the rest of Turkish society. Captain Shukri, for example, told of a massacre outside Yozgat in which government officials enlisted the local populace on religious grounds, so that a mob, ready with crude weapons-hoes and the like—at hand waited to kill Armenians: "people grabbed whatever they could from their villages—axes, hatchets, scythes sickles, clubs, hoes, pickaxes, shovels—and they did the killing accordingly."[21]

Varied groups joined in carrying out the Armenian Genocide, but participation was not uniform. Even within the government, enthusiasm for the killings and deportations varied. Where some local governors pressed forward to remove Armenians others dragged their feet. Some were even dismissed for declining to take part, and a few accounts even referred to local officials killed. Thus, the German consul in Aleppo stated that "Not one, but rather several public officials were supposedly killed, because they did not act mercilessly against all Armenians in their district."[22]

Victims and survivors

In face of relentless assault any Armenian faced the likelihood of death. Survival in this, as in most other genocides, meant more than living through a single moment of immense danger. Most Armenians who lived through the genocide typically had to survive through many phases of killing; the Armenian Genocide brought swift death to many but was also a long drawn-out process that continued from initial massacres to attacks on refugees heading south, to exposure to the elements and famine. The threat of death extended for some to further attacks in early 1916 on camps near Der Zor. These killings also advanced the broader CUP goals on limiting the percentage of non-Muslims in any single region.[23]

Their precise religious affiliation slightly affected the chance of survival. Armenians were Christians, but by the early twentieth century they did not all belong to the Armenian Christian Church. These Armenians Christians were also known as Gregorian in honor of Saint Gregory who had originally brought Christianity to Armenia. In principle, Protestant and Catholic Armenians had a slightly better chance of survival because Turkey's chief allies, Germany and Austria-Hungary, were concerned for their own domestic reasons with the fate of Protestants and Catholics— Germany had a Protestant majority and a large Catholic minority; whereas Austria-Hungary was predominantly Catholic. Turkish officials periodically pledged protections for Protestant and Catholic Armenians but any such promises were observed very sporadically. Much like Gregorian Armenians, Protestant and Catholic Armenians were deported as well, though in some cases their journey south was delayed slightly. In September, the Austrian Ambassador noted Turkish failure to follow through on protections: Talat's assurances that Catholic and Protestant Armenians had nothing to fear "have so far proven untrue."

Once the genocide started, Armenians sought to escape death by all manner of means. They tried to find hiding places and rescue in their own towns, either by finding aid from Turks or from foreign neutrals, including American missionaries and diplomats, though these could not provide shelter for most. Armenians also tried to escape across mountain ranges to Russia or sought ports to the south from which they could leave the Ottoman lands far behind. Estimates varied but a few hundred thousand eventually reached Russian territory. Some passed, as well, as Turks or Muslims, and some actually became Muslims.

Gender influenced both genocide and efforts at survival. Armenians, whether women or men, faced a common threat of destruction but this genocide, more so than the Holocaust, had strong qualities as a gendercide, targeting first men and then women. Groups of refugees that struggled into towns in the Syrian desert after the death of most Armenians en-route or escaped east to the Caucasus were made up disproportionately of women. Relief workers themselves observed that widows made up a high proportion of all surviving adults and that adult men made up a small proportion of the refugees.

Armenian women were frequently raped but also taken into the homes of Turkish or Kurdish men. They suffered both physical and psychological trauma. One relief worker named Mary Caroline Holmes who worked at Urfa after the First World War observed, "There was scarcely a girl in the orphanage over twelve years of age who had not been a wife to some Moslem, and not a few from ten years of age!"[24] Many suffered from disease. At the same time, while being taken into a Muslim home could simply continue exploitation and abuse it was sometimes a path to survival, and relations between Muslim men and Armenian women varied greatly. Some, as converts to Islam, found new lives in Muslim households and passed into the Turkish population. Their stories remain mostly hidden, but some Turkish citizens have discovered the stories of grandmothers or great-grandmothers with an Armenian past. Though this can only have been the experience of a minority of Armenian women, this still marked a real distinction from the experience of Jews in the Holocaust who could not openly be taken into a German or Aryan family.

Along with women, some Armenian children were also taken into Muslim families. Indeed, it was not unknown for desperate mothers to seek to sell their children en route south or from camps. Such children as converts similarly passed into the general Turkish populations. Children who survived against long odds also made up a disproportionate share of refugees in relief camps. Many were orphaned and became dependent on foreign relief. The city of Alexandropol or Gyumri in the small Armenian Republic that was quickly incorporated into the Soviet Union was home to vast orphanages with many thousands of orphans.

The highly organized attacks against Armenian leaders, massacres of men, and disarming of soldiers all worked to reduce the chances that Armenians would stage uprisings. Indeed, given the enormous obstacles that any such resistance faced, it is ironic that the theme of Armenian resistance so often featured in CUP justifications for the assault against Armenians. Nonetheless, Armenians did manage to organize armed resistance in several instances, such as in the well-known conflict at Van and in the action by deserters at Zeitoun. Armenians also carried out organized armed resistance to seek to prevent deportation at Musa Dagh in Cilicia and at Urfa. Armenians from several villages took refuge at Musa Dagh, a mountain on the coast of Cilicia, and managed to hold out until they were rescued by a passing French warship. Franz Werfel, an Austrian Jewish author later wrote a novel about the resistance and rescue entitled *The Forty Days of Musa Dagh*. Published in 1933, the book was widely read before and during the Second World War—and was read by Jews in ghettos during the Second World War.

Resistance more often came without rescue. In Urfa, the former Edessa, in southeastern Turkey, a few thousand Armenian men staged an uprising in October 1915. Here, a German military aid, Colonel Wolfskeel turned his guns on the Armenian district to help crush resistance. Armenians taken at Urfa were killed and in some cases forced to march back and forth across a stretch of desert. In another case of resistance Armenians also tried to hold out in the fortress of Sebinkarahisar on the Black Sea in June 1915, but were defeated by July.

Bystanders

Among bystanders, responses to the unfolding genocide varied. The very swiftness of Armenian deportation placed bystanders before a tempting array of goods. When Armenians tried to sell their goods, furnishings, tools, and possessions, their neighbors had the chance to gain almost anything they desired at a fraction of its normal cost. In the days before deportation the streets filled with goods, and Turks and other non-Armenians could be easily spotted picking up cut-rate bargains. In Harput the American consul Leslie Davis observed that "The streets were full of Turkish women, as well as men, who were seeking bargains."[25] Bystanders also ransacked recently emptied houses, though Armenians' homes fell disproportionately to those with good political connections. The bargain hunting extended to the caravans of exiles as Armenians forced out onto the roads often found that they could not carry all that they had packed and had to discard their remaining possessions. At camps along the routes south bystanders from local communities again had the chance to profit from others' misery, buying the few things the refugees still possessed as well as young women and children. All these opportunities for gain, if they did not actually drive the deportations, gave motive to stand aside.

At the same time some Turks did not approve of the deportations. George White, a missionary who had spent decades in Turkey and observed the genocide unfolding in the northern town of Marsovan, found that "Many of the Turks slowly reached a conviction that what was done was wrong, but those who were not caught by one motive were apt to be ensnared by another, and so there was no general sentiment against the atrocities."[26] Even economic considerations could lead to regrets about the deportations. Though many profited from the economic destruction of Turkey's Armenians, the seizure of so many businesses also brought long-term economic costs, especially in the poorer regions of eastern Anatolia.

The role of bystanders blurred not only in the direction of moving toward complicity in Armenians' destruction, but also toward rescue. As they encountered Armenians desperate to avoid deportation and death some Turks, Kurds, and others provided refuge. Economic rewards still shaped the decision to aid Armenians: there was often a thin line between exploitation and rescue. However, some bystanders nonetheless provided protection for Armenians who otherwise would have died.

Along with residents of the Ottoman Empire, citizens of foreign states also observed the Armenian Genocide. Foreign missionaries, medical personnel, engineers, and educators were present during the expulsions and massacres. Indeed, one of the odd things about the long-standing campaign to deny the Armenian Genocide stems from the very fact that so many foreigners present in Turkey at the time wrote and spoke of the mass slaughter and that these observers came from different countries. The foreign residents could do little to avert catastrophe. At most, they could provide shelter at some risk to only a very small portion of Armenians. Many sympathized with the Armenians. Some came from Turkish allies, mainly Germany, but even those Germans who initially shared the prevalent view among the CUP leadership that Armenians had betrayed the state, nonetheless, came to see the campaign against Armenians as inhumane and destructive.

With all the reports emanating from Turkey, foreign powers learned of the assault against Armenians. On May 24, 1915 the governments of Britain, France, and Russia issued a joint declaration condemning the Turkish government for "crimes against humanity and civilization." If not every detail reached the public in other countries, the press reports were accurate as far as they went. Headlines in the *New York Times* from October and December 1915 respectively read, "800,000 Armenians Counted Destroyed," and "Million Armenians Killed or in Exile." In Germany information was less forthcoming but even there a report by the Protestant pastor Johannes Lepsius, a long-time advocate for Armenians, was passed along through Protestant churches after being banned by censors in 1916.

Once the genocide was underway, reports of the destruction led to little direct action by foreign governments. Within Turkey, US Ambassador Henry Morgenthau pressed the leaders of CUP as well as the ambassadors from Germany and Austria to curb the slaughter. His German and Austrian counterparts seem to have regarded him as something of a pest, though they gradually recognized the diplomatic risk posed by the perception that their countries were in any way responsible for the campaign against Ottoman Armenians. Lepsius, for his part, was sufficiently troubled by this record of lack of effort to protect Armenians that he edited out sections of diplomatic reports that indicated a German policy of inaction in a collection of documents that he published after the war. In one notable statement the German Consul in Erzerum wrote to the German Ambassador Hohenlohe-Langenburg, who had taken the top diplomatic post during Wangenheim's illness, "I was aware—and this also corresponded to the instructions that were passed on to me from Your Excellency—that we do not have a *right* to stand up for the innocent Armenians who have been expelled, nor do we have any kind of protective rights over them."[27] Lepsius, however, in the collection of diplomatic records that he published deleted the reference to any official instructions to preserve a passive stance in the face of suffering.

ARMIN WEGNER: WITNESS TO GENOCIDE

Amidst the comparative passivity of German diplomats and the close ties of some German officers to the Turkish military there were Germans who outlined and even opposed the unfolding genocide. Armin Wegner, a German nurse, stationed in Turkey, compiled much of the most striking photographic evidence of Armenian suffering and of the Armenian Genocide. Posted to the Ottoman Empire in 1915 he collected evidence of violence carried out against Armenians and also took photographs, which he managed to bring back to Germany. Following the war Wegner in 1919 wrote a letter to US president Woodrow Wilson urging him to act on behalf of Armenians. Wegner voiced his fear that Armenians would receive little attention at the Paris Peace Conference: "And so there is reason to fear that the importance of a small and extremely enfeebled nation may be obscured by the influential and selfish aims of the great European States. . . ." Wegner, already an accomplished poet, became a successful writer in the interwar years, but in 1933 he wrote a letter to the new German Chancellor, Hitler, opposing anti-Semitic policies and intimidation and harassment of Jews. "It is not only a question of the destiny of our Jewish brothers." Wegner wrote, "The very destiny of Germany is at stake! In the name of the people for whom I have the right and no less the duty to speak, as if they were of my own flesh and blood, as a German who has not been given the gift of speech to be a silent accomplice and whose heart is quivering with indignation, I address myself to you: Put a stop to all this!"[28] Wegner was seized by the Gestapo, tortured, and placed in several concentration camps during the 1930s but released in 1939. He was awarded the honor righteous among nations by Yad Vashem, the memorial to the Holocaust or Shoah in the state of Israel.

Private and nonprofit initiatives to aid survivors far outpaced any action at the official government level. In the United States the Armenian crisis gained widespread attention. The press reported that Armenians were being killed in vast numbers. Congregationalist, Baptist, Catholic Churches gathered funds, and the Rockefeller Foundation donated money as well. These and other religious, relief and charitable organizations, including Near East Relief extended much aid to survivors.

ARMENIAN RELIEF AS DESCRIBED IN THE *NEW YORK TIMES*, OCTOBER 22, 1916

"Give Millions Today to Save Armenians"

"50,000 Churches Throughout the Country Will Take up Collections"

"AID FOR SYRIANS ALSO"

"Anonymous Contributor Gives $43,000—One Dollar Sustains Family of 10 For a Week"

"In more than 50,000 churches and Sunday Schools throughout the United States collections will be taken today for the relief of the destitute war victims in Armenia and Syria. The proclamation recently issued by President Wilson set aside yesterday and today as 'Armenian and Syrian Relief Days' Yesterday every Armenian and Syrian in America was expected to begin a forty-eight-hour fast and to give the money which would otherwise have been spent on food to the funds for the relief of their suffering countrymen.

> To relieve the Christian Armenians, former Ambassador Henry Morgenthau has estimated that $3,000,000 is immediately needed, while another one million is required to afford the relief needed to the Syrian victims.
>
> . . . . Part of the receipts of the coming Harvard-Yale football game in the Yale Stadium will be donated to the fund, while the Reverend 'Billy' Sunday, who is holding a revival, is to take up a special collection in the Detroit Tabernacle. . . ."

Greeks and Assyrians

The Armenian Genocide was part of a broader campaign in which the Committee of Union and Progress sought to place an unchallenged Turkish imprint on Anatolia by cleansing and destroying groups they identified as enemies. Ethnic cleansing of Armenians found close parallels in Turkish deportations of Ottoman Greeks. Like Armenians, Greeks formed another large minority of uncertain loyalty in the eyes of the Ittihadists. Greeks lived in particular in the west of Anatolia in the city of Smyrna as well as in many other towns and villages. The Black Sea coast and littoral meanwhile was home to another Greek population, the Pontic Greeks, so named for the old name of the Black Sea—Pontus.

Greece and Turkey had long been on either tense or openly hostile terms. The modern Greek kingdom had emerged in rebellion against the Ottoman Empire in the early nineteenth century. More recently, the Ottoman Empire had defeated Greece in a short war in 1897, before losing ground to Greece during the First Balkan War. Greece and Turkey shared an interest in Bulgarian defeat in the Second Balkan war, but the two states competed to build up their naval forces in the Aegean during the immediate prelude to the Great War.

Persecution of Greeks began in Turkey in 1914 even before the First World War started. Facing intimidation, boycotts, and attacks by irregulars, Greeks began to flee some communities in western Turkey. Describing the growing fear, Ambassador Morgenthau wrote, "Whenever we passed the Greek consulate we could see a throng of excited Greeks besieging its doors in an effort to get passports to leave the country."[29] Armed bands and in particular Muslim refugees from the lost provinces of Turkey in Europe led the assault. Indeed, at this point such attacks on Greeks in the west closely resembled raids on Armenians in the east of Anatolia. A massacre of Greeks took place, for example, at the town of Phocaea (Foca). In Eastern Thrace, a region that after the loss of so many other lands was now on the Ottoman frontier, newly arrived Muslims acquired new homes in part by displacing Greeks.

With war, Turkish authorities removed Greeks from areas of the west. The rationale again closely mirrored that employed to deport Armenians: in both cases the CUP regime targeted a group suspected of disloyalty. Soon after the British landing at Gallipoli, Turkey removed selected Greek communities from the surrounding region. Greeks were also rapidly removed from islands in the Sea of Marmara. On the Black Sea Coast, charges that Greek armed bands supported Russia motivated deportations of Pontic Greeks to the interior in 1916. In 1917 Turkish forces once again deported thousands of Pontic Greeks away from villages along the Black Sea coast.

Ottoman Greeks shared much in common with Armenians during the Great War, but the CUP campaign against Greeks still fell short of the destruction meted out against Armenians. Many of the elements that led to genocide of Armenians were also in place for Ottoman Greeks, but the very fact that there was a Greek state placed constraints on CUP policy: Turkey had an interest in avoiding actions so radical that they might propel Greece, a neutral state, to enter the war. Indeed, a deeply divided Greek government did not join the war until 1917. As Greece moved toward entering the war, CUP undertook more aggressive actions against the Pontic Greeks.

Of all Ottoman minorities, the Assyrian Christians, also sometimes described as Nestorians, were in a position most similar to that of Armenians during the Great War. Assyrians made up another distinct Christian Church and lived in large numbers in northern Mesopotamia and in the Hakkari district situated in what is now the southeastern edge of Turkey to the south of Van. In principle the CUP leadership had less reason to strike at the smaller Assyrian population than at Armenians, but fighting on the border region in late 1914 and early 1915 saw localized ethnic cleansing of Assyrians carried out by irregulars or Kurds. The ethnic cleansing of

Assyrians gained state sanction and intensified in 1915. The killings angered the Assyrian Patriarch, who in May 1915 gave greater support to Russia than did any equivalent Armenian religious figure. CUP resolved to carry out ethnic cleansing of Assyrians. Talat at the end of June 1915 instructed, "We should not let them return to their homelands."[30] Massacres of men and deportations of women and children closely paralleled the campaign against Armenians, with the death toll of Assyrian Christians reaching approximately 300,000 or more.

Though the CUP regime often employed or relied on Kurds to strike at Armenians and Assyrians, Turkish authorities also deported Kurds from areas of eastern Anatolia in 1916 and 1917. Such action figured as a means to seek greater central control over regions where tribal rule was strong. Deportations of Kurds and resettlement of other Muslims in their place also fit into a broader national program of seeking to create a state dominated by one national group: Turks. These efforts foreshadowed growing tension between Turkish nationalism and Kurdish self-determination that would lead to many decades of conflict after the First World War in the Republic of Turkey.

The end of genocide

Genocide clearly peaked in 1915 and continued into 1916, but war in Turkey and in adjacent regions did not end at a single time. As Germany and Austria faced defeat in 1918, the CUP-led government resigned, and CUP's leaders fled shortly after an October armistice between the allies and Ottoman Empire. Genocide as an Ittihadist campaign to eliminate Ottoman Armenians or Assyrians was over, but warfare continued after the end of the First World War. On the Eastern Front, the collapse of the Russian Empire and the weaknesses of the Ottoman state created a kind of power vacuum in which varied forces and nascent states engaged in violent ethnic and religious wars. Visitors to Transcaucasia, the region just to the south of the highest mountain chain of the Caucasus, reported on fighting involving Armenians, Turks, and Azeris. Warfare in this region ended only in 1920 with the victory of the Bolsheviks in the Russian Civil War and the triumph in Turkey of the Turkish Nationalists led by Mustafa Kemal or Kemal Ataturk.

Under allied pressure, Turkey carried out trials of the CUP leadership. Indictments by a military tribunal charged the Ittihadist leaders in 1919 with "deportation and massacre." In 1919 a military tribunal found Talat and Enver guilty of massacre and sentenced them to death in absentia. Their sentences were never carried out, but Talat was assassinated in Berlin in 1921 by Soghomon Tehlirian, a young Armenian. Enver died fighting the Soviets in Central Asia in 1922.[31]

Despite the fact that he had shot Talat in view of witnesses, Tehlirian was acquitted. Survivors of genocide and expert witnesses, including Johannes Lepsius, told of the details of massacres. Tehlirian himself survived a massacre started by gendarme then joined by the local population. He testified to having seen his brother murdered with an axe and his sister raped. He came to surrounded by corpses and then found refuge with Kurds from Dersim. A dream in which he saw his mother, Tehlirian stated, gave him the determination to kill Talat. Expert witnesses described the psychological pressures affecting Tehlirian. There was another element: Tehlirian was also taking part in an effort by the Dashnaks or Armenian Revolution Federation to kill the perpetrators of genocide in an action termed Operation Nemesis.

Denial and genocide

The Armenian Genocide stands out among major genocides, not only of twentieth-century Europe but of world history, for the duration and intensity of debate over whether to even apply the term genocide. Denial of the Armenian Genocide has taken many forms. In most fundamental form, the case for denial maintains that there was no effort to destroy Ottoman Armenians. In this form, denial echoes many of the assertions made by the Ittihadists with deaths attributed not to an organized campaign to eliminate Ottoman Armenians but to the effects of a kind of civil war waged between Armenians and Turks. This scenario blurs the lines between civilians and combatants with deportations taken not as a sweeping measure to eradicate Armenian communities but as a justified and necessary response to military challenges. In modified form, this version of denial concedes suffering among Armenians but attributes the loss and deaths, not to a general campaign of genocide, but to local mistakes or incapacity to carry out deportations with scant resources in the midst of war. As a debate over numbers, this form of denial compares the death toll among Muslims and Armenians during the war to assert that Armenian suffering did not stand out in particular.

Attempts to reject the very concept of an Armenian Genocide also center on definitions and the reliability of sources. Such arguments note the suffering of deported Armenians but deny any intent to destroy Armenians in whole or in part, stressing also the exceptions made for Armenian communities of Constantinople and Smyrna. Arguments denying genocide have also attacked the reliability of accounts by Americans, and in particular American missionaries, on the grounds that those witnesses were predisposed to be sympathetic to Armenians.

The debate over the Armenian Genocide centers not simply on evidence, definitions, and interpretation, but on national identity. The Republic of Turkey has consistently and vociferously rejected the idea that there was an Armenian Genocide. Within Turkey, individuals have faced legal action for comments seen as recognizing the Armenian Genocide. Thus, the writer and winter of the Nobel Prize for literature Orhan Pamuk faced prosecution for his 2005 comments, "Thirty thousand Kurds have been killed here, and a million Armenians. And almost nobody dares to mention that. So I do." The charges were dropped on technical grounds. Focusing on an external audience, the Turkish Ministry of Foreign Affairs has publicized what they describe as "controversy between Turkey and Armenia about the events of 1915." Turkey has pushed back against recognition of this genocide by other countries. In the United States, for example, Turkey has warned against congressional resolutions recognizing the genocide under both Democratic and Republican administrations. French legislation to recognize the Armenian Genocide has also promoted Turkish rebukes. Such official efforts to dispute genocide are extremely unusual, especially after the collapse of the regimes charged with carrying out genocide.

US PRESIDENTS AND ARMENIAN GENOCIDE

Individual presidents and presidential candidates have spoken of genocide, but strategic considerations have blocked ultimate passage of such resolutions. In 2007, for example, President George W. Bush stated: "We all deeply regret the tragic suffering of the Armenian people that began in 1915. But this resolution is not the right response to these historic mass killings and its passage would do great harm to relations with a key ally in NATO, and to the war on terror." In 2010 President Obama in a statement issued on Armenian Genocide Remembrance day stated, "On this solemn day of remembrance, we pause to recall that 95 years ago one of the worst atrocities of the 20th century began. In that dark moment of history, 1.5 million Armenians were massacred or marched to their death in the final days of the Ottoman Empire." Obama referred to the "Meds Yeghern," an Armenian term for "Great Calamity," or "Great Tragedy," but neither Bush nor Obama used the exact term genocide.

Despite efforts by the Republic of Turkey to dispute the Armenian Genocide, the ongoing debate over the Armenian Genocide has reached a tipping point where both scholars and the interested public increasingly accept that this was indeed genocide. Increasingly comparative studies of genocide take the debate on genocide as concluded and treat the Armenian Genocide as one of the major genocides of twentieth-century Europe. Even in Turkey, where the use of the term genocide causes particular anxiety, scholars increasingly talk of far-ranging massacres carried out against Armenians during the First World War. The evidence of destruction is abundant and varied, and the key figures in the CUP proved strikingly loquacious in discussing their goals and fears and their determination to do away with the Armenian population. Though some eyewitnesses harbored ill feelings toward Turks or Muslims, a wide range of observers from different countries, including both neutrals and allies of Turkey described destruction as intentional and predictable.

"THE ARMENIAN GENOCIDE RESOLUTION UNANIMOUSLY PASSED BY THE ASSOCIATION OF GENOCIDE SCHOLARS OF NORTH AMERICA"

The Armenian Genocide Resolution was unanimously passed at the Association of Genocide Scholars' conference in Montreal on June 13, 1997.

RESOLUTION

"That this assembly of the Association of Genocide Scholars in its conference held in Montreal, June 11–13, 1997, reaffirms that the mass murder of over a million Armenians in Turkey in 1915 is a case of genocide which conforms to the statutes of the United Nations Convention on the Prevention and Punishment of Genocide. It further condemns the denial of the Armenian Genocide by the Turkish government and its official and unofficial agents and supporters."

Subsequent resolutions by the International Association of Genocide Scholars reaffirmed and extended this resolution.

The Armenian Genocide and European Genocide

To cite the earliest genocide of twentieth-century genocide is no easy task, but the Armenian Genocide was the first major genocide in twentieth-century Europe. The bulk of killing occurred in Anatolia, but this genocide was still an integral part of European history. The state in which genocide took place was still a European power. The destabilization the helped to propel genocide stemmed from European events such as the Balkan Wars and the First World War, and European trends also helped to build the ideologies that radicalized the Committee of Unity and Progress. In adopting nationalist ideas of purification and, to some degree, elements of racial thinking, the leadership of the CUP took part in a broader regional process of ideological change. These trends both inspired and alarmed the Young Turks—the breakup of the Ottoman Empire began in Europe. The continued collapse of Turkey in Europe in the First Balkan War and the attendant flow of refugees into Turkey further radicalized the Ittihadists.

The Armenian Genocide confirms the need to look both at both long-term and short-term causes to understand the path to genocide. It was far from coincidence that genocide targeted Armenians: they had suffered violent attacks and massacres in much of eastern Anatolia in the 1890s in some of the same towns and cities later struck by genocide in 1915, and they had more recently suffered massacres in Adana in 1909. After the ouster of Sultan Abdul Hamid II, the genocide of the First World War took place under a different political leadership under the Ittihadists, but the men of the Committee of Unity and Progress shared a conviction that Armenians colluded with those who wanted to continue the process of breaking down what was left of the Ottoman Empire in a Turkish core.

On the other hand, a much shorter-term process of radicalization was critical for leading to genocide. As recently as 1908 Armenian political leaders and some Ittihadists had shared some goals, and bringing Armenians into the Ottoman army signaled a move toward a more inclusive society. Between 1912 and 1915, however, a sequence of threats rapidly radicalized the Committee of Union and Progress. The Balkan Wars, the defeat at Sarikamis, the Allied attempt to break through the Dardanelles, the invasion at Gallipoli, and the uprising at Van cumulatively reinforced existing distrust of Armenians among the Ittihadists and overpowered the very tentative move toward greater cooperation that had emerged at the end of Abdul Hamid II's reign.

The Armenian Genocide exemplifies the point made in the UN Genocide Convention of 1948 that genocide had already taken place before the invention of the term or its use in international law. The Armenian Genocide saw the effort to destroy in whole or in part a group identified by its ethnicity, nationality, and religion. Multiple acts of genocide, as later listed in the Genocide Convention, created these destructive outcomes. The massacres repeatedly carried out against men, and the killings of Armenians in transit brought "killing of members of the group." Driving Armenians into deserts with scant food or water and little or no protection from attacks both of the Special Organization and marauding bands caused "serious bodily or mental harm" and also meant deliberately and predictably "inflicting on the group conditions of life calculated to bring about its physical destruction in whole or in part." Meanwhile the taking in of children given up by parents desperate to find anyone who could provide food, or left orphaned, compelled "transferring children of the group to another group."

The wide variety of acts of genocide carried out in the Armenian Genocide dispels the notion that genocide is carried out through any single method. Large numbers of Armenians, in particular men, were killed in massacres, but deportation convoys that amounted to death marches provided the chief killing method. Armenians as a group experienced genocide, but the history of the Armenian Genocide also shows that genocide at times targets men and women differently. The Armenian case also shows the role of a kind of forced assimilation—some Armenians, in particular women and children, could survive as long as they gave up their culture and identity. Indeed the CUP leadership encouraged a policy of placing Armenian children in Turkish and Muslim homes.[32] This form of genocide, briefly alluded to in the Genocide Convention in the case of children greatly interested Raphael Lemkin in his original writings on genocide.

Study questions

- What are the strengths and weaknesses of long-term explanations of the Armenian Genocide that trace the causes of the genocide to the history of the Ottoman Empire in the nineteenth century?
- How did a rapid process of radicalization that began with the revolution of 1908 and continued through the Balkan Wars and into the early years of the First World War lead to the Armenian Genocide?
- What were the chief phases of the Armenian Genocide?
- Who were the main perpetrators of the Armenian Genocide?
- How did bystanders respond to the Armenian Genocide?

- Why, despite disputes and outright denial of the idea of an Armenian Genocide, is the Armenian Genocide increasingly accepted as a genocide?

Further reading

Akçam, Taner, *A Shameful Act: The Armenian Genocide and the Question of Turkish Responsibility* (New York: Metropolitan Books, 2006).

Bloxham, Donald, *Great Game of Genocide: Imperialism, Nationalism, and the Destruction of the Ottoman Armenians* (Oxford: Oxford University Press, 2005).

Dadrian, Vahakn N., *The History of the Armenian Genocide: Ethnic Conflict from the Balkans to Anatolia to the Caucasus* (Providence, RI: Berghahn Books, 1995).

Miller, Donald and Lorna Touryan Miller, *Survivors: An Oral History of the Armenian Genocide* (Berkeley: University of California Press, 1993).

Suny, Ronald Grigor, ed., *A Question of Genocide: Armenians and Turks at the End of the Ottoman Empire* (New York: Oxford University Press, 2011).

3

Mass killing in the Soviet Union

The exact death toll remains disputed, but killing of civilians in the Soviet Union rivaled that in any other state in the twentieth century. The deaths came from multiple waves of terror as well as famine, but famine in the USSR was in large part the product of policy: Joseph Stain and the Soviet leadership exacerbated the effects of famine, dooming millions to death. The USSR also engaged in mass deportations and swept up wave after wave of prisoners into prison camps. Before the Second World War the number of prisoners in the vast Soviet prison and forced labor camps system, termed the Gulag, far exceeded the number held in German concentration camps. Large numbers of prisoners were executed or died of the predictable effects of malnutrition, disease, and hard labor in far flung prison camps in remote areas of the Arctic and the vast Soviet interior.

The massive killing of civilians in the Soviet Union is paradoxically both central and peripheral to the history of genocide in Europe during the twentieth century. Soviet killings of civilians were removed from genocide in large part through the process of defining genocide. The list of groups whose destruction amounts to genocide under the terms of the Genocide Convention does not include groups identified by political affiliation or class or economic status, the very categories used to justify much of the terror of the Stalinist era. This was no accident: the Soviets lobbied to exclude politics or class from the crime of genocide in the negotiations that led to the creation of the Genocide Convention. Excluding political groups from the list of protected groups served Soviet interests after the Soviet purges of groups such as Kulaks defined by political and economic criteria, but the Soviet Union was not alone in favoring this definition. Contemporary politic divisions also influenced early charges that the Soviet Union had carried out genocide. Raphael Lemkin himself cited Soviet genocide, referring both to what he saw as the destruction of cultures as well as famine, but in taking these positions, he also took part in early debates of the Cold War era.

Even the exclusion of key groups, however, did not fully distance Soviet crimes from genocide as defined in the Genocide Convention. Though Soviet campaigns of persecution ostensibly identified victims on the basis of class and politics, such class and political enemies in practice often overlapped with particular ethnic and national groups. To the extent that attacks on class enemies amounted to destruction of national, ethnic, or racial groups. Soviet crimes that met other elements of the Genocide Convention would then amount to genocide under international law.

Terror and Famine before the Second World War

The roots of the Gulag

From the early days of the Bolshevik Revolution of 1917 in which the Soviet Communist Party seized power, the new Communist regime deployed extreme violence to crush opposition and dissent. The terror methods that became synonymous with Soviet power had early roots: Lenin, the key Bolshevik leader, himself called for extreme measures to secure rule. He criticized Zinoviev, a key Bolshevik leader in Petrograd, for taking half measures after the assassination of another prominent Bolshevik, asserting, "It is necessary to applaud the energy and mass character of the terror against counterrevolutionaries." Zinoviev, in response, employed language of mass destruction. "We must carry along with us ninety million out of the one hundred million of Soviet Russia's population. As for the rest, we have nothing to say to them. They must be annihilated."[1] Lenin established a security organization called the Cheka which rapidly expanded. He called for terror to crush opposition and in particular Kulaks, a term used to refer to ostensibly wealthier peasants, though hangings, seizure of grain, and hostage taking. Security forces, including the Cheka, and the NKVD, the Commissariat of Internal Affairs, established camps to hold class enemies and carried out executions. Roundups also brought in bishops, priests, and monks. In his classic work on the Soviet prison camp system, the *Gulag Archipelago*, Aleksandr Solzhenitsyn wrote of the religious, "their silver locks gleamed in every cell and in every prisoner transport en route to the Solovetsky islands."[2] Revolutionary Tribunals known as Troikas made summary judgments. By 1921 the new Soviet state had established permanent camps in remote northern areas, including the Solovetsky islands, an archipelago in the White Sea in the far northwest of Russia. In all the new camp system held tens of thousands and as many as some 200,000 prisoners. Before the Second World War, this total exceeded the number held in German concentration camps.

Winning the power struggle to succeed Lenin who died in 1924, Stalin expanded the Soviet security and terror apparatus. The OGPU or Unified State Political Administration as the reorganized Cheka was known after 1923 became a permanent state security force dedicated to monitoring and defeating any possible opposition. Stalin focused on crushing supposed class enemies. By 1928 he supported action against so-called bourgeois experts, accusing them of sabotage. Engineers accused of conspiring with foreign powers to destroy machinery confessed at show trials. Such show trials in which the accused made spectacular confessions would remain a feature of Stalinist terror for many years.

Collectivization and Famine

Terror further intensified and expanded as Stalin aimed to modernize the Soviet Union at breakneck pace. The violence of the Stalinist era had both economic and ideological roots. The Soviet Communist Party saw itself as representing the Proletariat or working class, but the Bolshevik Revolution had taken place in an overwhelmingly rural country where peasants far outnumbered workers. To build the industrial base and the Proletariat, the Soviet leadership embarked on Five Year Plans, which presented industry with extraordinary targets for rapidly increasing production. Meanwhile, in the countryside the Soviet leadership instituted collectivization with dual purposes. Collective farming would not only remake property relations along socialist lines, but also gave the state greater power to accelerate grain exports to pay for the rapid construction of massive new industrial facilities.

With collectivization, the Soviet security forces engaged in all-out assault against Kulaks, said to be the wealthier peasants and local landowners. The actual ability to define and identity so-called Kulaks mattered less than the goal of transforming the Soviet countryside. Rural terror explained as a campaign against Kulaks pushed forward collectivization. Stalin on December 27, 1929, announced the "liquidation of Kulaks as a class," and the Communist Party in January 1930 followed through with "Measures for the Elimination of Kulak households. . . ." Here, the order closely foreshadowed genocide with the exception of the choice of a targeted group identified by class status.

To eliminate Kulaks, OGPU oversaw a campaign of sweeping deportations and terror. Troikas made up of police, party and state procurator representatives screened peasants to identify and select Kulaks who were then transported to prison camps and special settlements. The terror apparatus struck against Kulaks throughout the Soviet Union but acted with special severity in Ukraine: of the 1.7 million Kulaks dispatched to special settlements, 300,000 were Ukrainians. Those deported included both adults and children.

Forced labor, malnutrition, and disease in the camp system led inexorably to high death rates. Typhus afflicted nearly half of the prisoners crammed into the Solovetsky camp. Tens of thousands labored on a canal to connect the White and Baltic Seas, a feat celebrated in Soviet propaganda without reference to the deaths of the prisoners who worked on the project.

In 1931 the Soviet state pressed forward with collectivization. The dislocation combined with poor weather to produce a much worse harvest than that of the previous year. However, Soviet authorities made no concessions for the low yield but instead continued to draw grain out of agricultural regions, and in particular out of the Ukraine. By 1932 peasants across Ukraine lacked grain either to plant a new crop or to eat. In a memoir of the famine, a survivor who wrote under the name Miron Dolot recalled that by May Day of 1932, "Many of our schoolmates had already died, and many others were sick from starvation and could not participate in the celebration."[3]

Stalin's refusal to acknowledge the deteriorating conditions produced catastrophic results for the rural population. Despite mounting evidence of famine, Stalin responded with a combination of denial and anger. Local Communist Party reports told of desperation for food and starvation to the point where even the Ukrainian Communist Party asked for but did not receive food for Ukraine. Instead, Soviet authorities treated the hunger as evidence of malingering, intransigence, and treason. To ferret out food and prevent peasants from taking any grain for themselves, party activists set up watchtowers for spying on peasants who might seek to get into the fields to make off with the property of the state.

As famine spread across Ukraine, Soviet authorities not only continued high grain exactions but added new measures to take still more food out of Ukraine to punish and crush resistance, real or imagined, to collectivization. Collectives that failed to meet their grain targets were forced to pay special grain penalties, and peasants who did not hand over sufficient grain had to supply meat. These and other punitive measures further reduced the supply of food in already desperate conditions. Meanwhile, Soviet authorities continued to collect grain.

During the famine, Ukrainians died in the countryside and they died in cities and they died in search of food. Miron Dolot recalled the bodies along the road toward a nearby town, "Everywhere we looked dead and frozen bodies lay by the sides of the road."[4] Some lay dead in the fields where they had fallen while searching for food. Starving parents tried to give away their children or sent them to beg. They piled up at railway stations looking for a way to get out; however, the Soviet authorities blocked flight out of Ukraine and sought to push starving peasants out of cities. At the peak of the famine, some even resorted to cannibalism.

In Ukrainian history, the famine resulted in death by starvation or what was later termed the Holodomor. Estimates of the death toll were politicized from the start. When a census in 1937 turned up a large shortfall in projected population, the offending demographers were executed. Estimates of the number of deaths from hunger in Ukraine alone ranged from more than 2 million to close to 4 million.

GARETH JONES ON THE FAMINE

The Welsh journalist Gareth Jones provided some of the few contemporary accounts of the effects of famine compiled by a foreign observer:

Famine, far greater than the famine of 1921, is now visiting Russia. The hunger of twelve years ago was only prevalent in the Volga and in some other regions, but today the hunger has attacked the Ukraine, the North Caucasus, the Volga district, Central Asia, Siberia—indeed, every part of Russia. I have spoken to peasants or to eye-witnesses from every one of those districts and their story is the same. There is hardly any bread left, the peasants either exist on potatoes and cattle fodder, or, if they have none of these, die off.

In the three agricultural districts which I visited, namely, the Moscow region, the Central Black Earth district, and North Ukraine, there was no bread left in any village out of the total twenty villages to which I went. In almost every village peasants had died of hunger.

Even twenty miles away from Moscow there was no bread. When I travelled through these Moscow villages the inhabitants said: "It is terrible. We have no bread. We have to go all the way to Moscow for bread, and then they will only give us four pounds, for which we have to pay three roubles a kilo (i.e., nominally nearly 3s. a pound). How can a poor family live on that?"

A little further on the road a woman started crying when telling me of the hunger, and said: "They're killing us. We have no bread. We have no potatoes left. In this village there used to be 300 cows and now there are only 30. The horses have died. We shall starve." Many people, especially in the Ukraine, have been existing for a week or more on salt and water, but most of them on beet, which was once given to cattle.

Last year, the weather was ideal. Climatic conditions have in the past few years, blessed the Soviet Government. Then why the catastrophe? In the first place, the land has been taken away from 70 percent of the peasantry, and all incentive to work has disappeared. Anyone with the blood of Welsh farmers in his veins will understand what it means to a farmer or a peasant to have his own land taken away from him. Last year nearly all the crops of the peasants were violently seized, and the peasant was left almost nothing for himself. Under the Five Year Plan the Soviet Government aimed at setting up big collective farms, where the land would be owned in common and run by tractors. But the Russian peasant in one respect is no different from the Welsh farmer. He wants his own land, and if his land is taken away from him he will not work. The passive resistance of the peasant has been a stronger factor than all the speeches of Stalin.

In the second place, the cow was taken away from the peasant. Imagine what would happen in the Vale of Glamorgan or in Cardiganshire if the county councils took away the cows of the farmers! The cattle were to be owned in common, and cared for in common by the collective farms. Many of the cattle were seized and, put into vast State cattle factories.

The result of this policy was a widespread massacre of cattle by the peasants, who did not wish to sacrifice their property for nothing. Another result was that on these State cattle factories, which were entirely unprepared and had not enough sheds, innumerable live-stock died of exposure and epidemics. Horses died from lack of fodder. The live-stock of the Soviet Union has now been so depleted that not until 1945 can it reach the level of 1928. And that is, provided that all the plans for import of cattle succeed, provided there is no disease, and provided there is fodder. That date 1945 was given me by one of the most reliable foreign experts in Moscow.

In the third place, six or seven millions of the best farmers (i.e. the Kulaks) in Russia have been uprooted and have been exiled with a barbarity which is not realised in Britain. Although two years ago the Soviet Government claimed that the Kulak had been, destroyed, the savage drive against the better peasant continued with increased violence last winter. It was the aim of the Bolsheviks to destroy the Kulaks as a class, because they were "the capitalists of the village."

Weather and pests affected agricultural yields in Ukraine in the early 1930s but the famine in Ukraine was to a large degree a manufactured catastrophe. Soviet policies both contributed to and exacerbated the famine. Collectivization, the attacks on so-called Kulaks, and the seizure of food and animals to stop hoarding all intensified the crisis. Despite reports of disaster, Stalin and the Soviet leadership refused to take any action to increase food supply and instead implemented measures that took still more food away from a starving population. Up to a point, the famine can be described as an example of inhumane and radical social engineering carried out without intent to destroy a particular group listed on the Genocide Convention. On the other hand, key elements of the famine in Ukraine fell under genocide as later anchored in international law. Predictable death from starvation repeated at least in part one of the major methods used to kill Armenians off. Also while the initial campaign against Kulaks began by targeting enemies identified by class position, national, economic, and political categories overlapped as the Soviet leadership saw famine as evidence of Ukrainian national resistance to collectivization, and the policies that magnified the effects and the losses from famine focused on Ukraine in particular.

The famine or Holodomor both shared key elements of genocide and diverged from some of the cases of genocide in twentieth-century Europe. One problem with genocide studies is that comparisons can be seen, especially by those who have suffered severe assaults, as attempts to rank genocides on some kind of scale of evil. For those killed by human action the differences would be meaningless. However, genocide studies can also veer off in the direction of attempting to force equivalency in all respects between all different cases of genocide and mass killing. There was at least one significant difference between the famine in Ukraine and the Holocaust as well as the Armenian Genocide, not in the areas of intent or predictable death, but in what perpetrators were willing to accept at the end. The perpetrators of the Holocaust aimed for the destruction of European Jews, and the goals were nearly the same for Armenians, albeit with partial exceptions for a few urban communities as well as for converts. In the Soviet Union, in contrast, the Soviet leadership was willing to accept a pulverized, weakened, and devastated Ukrainian population without actually seeking to destroy the Ukrainian presence. Sending new settlers to

Ukraine altered but did not completely overturn the demographic balance in Ukraine.

The Great Purge

After the famine, Soviet terror continued to both diverge from and converge with genocide as understood in the later definition in international law. Stalin targeted vast numbers of supposed internal enemies during the Great Purge that peaked from 1936 to 1938. The purge began with attacks against old members of the Bolshevik Party. The assassination of Sergei Kirov, a prominent Communist leader and member of the Politburo, in December of 1934 served as the starting point for an intensifying and expanding search for traitors. The question of who was responsible for the murder has never been clarified, but Stalin took advantage of the assassination to further consolidate his own power. The NKVD, which succeeded OGPU, increased arrests for political offences, and the regime staged a series of show trials. Decades of service to Communism brought no protection for those who appeared at show trials. A 1936 show trial in Moscow, for example, brought the conviction and execution of 16 so-called Old Bolsheviks including Grigory Zinoviev and Lev Kamenev.

Expanding terror brought arrests of both political and military figures, including many commanders and officers of the Red Army. The hunt for traitors moved beyond the state to encourage an all-out search for traitors and conspirators within Soviet society. As the purge continued, Stalin's security apparatus executed hundreds of thousands of Soviet citizens and sent even more to the Gulag, swelling the already vast prison camp system to the point where it housed some 2 million inmates.

The Great Purge, at first glance, incorporated the destructive goal of genocide while again targeting a group not listed in the Genocide Convention. Stalin himself in 1937 pledged to destroy enemies, "We will mercilessly destroy anyone who by his deeds or his thoughts—yes, his thoughts!—threatens the unity of the socialist state. To the complete destruction of all enemies, themselves and their kin!" With his call for annihilation of enemies of the socialist state he identified victims chiefly in terms of politics and class, but his threat extended also to the relatives of the guilty. The campaign against class enemies included yet another round of destruction of Kulaks. Order 0047 instituted "repression of former Kulaks" along with "... other anti-Soviet elements." By 1938 the NKVD executed 386,798 in fulfilling Order 0047.[5] Troikas identified victims, exacted confessions, and shot the victims. The executions took place at scattered sites. The NKVD frequently shot prisoners in the basements of buildings, including NKVD offices. They killed elsewhere as well: in prisons and sometimes in churches and in labor camps. The bodies were then placed in pits, sometimes thousands at a time.

ALEKSANDR SOLZHENITSYN ON THE NUMBERS SHOT

In the Gulag Archipelago Solzhenitsyn conveyed the difficulty fathoming the vast numbers shot:

"Thus many were shot—thousands at first, then hundreds of thousands. We divide, we multiply, we sigh, we curse. But still and after all, these are just numbers. They overwhelm the mind and then are easily forgotten. And if someday the relatives of those who had been shot were to send one publisher photographs of the executed kin, and an album of those photographs were to be published in several volumes, then just be leafing through them and looking into the extinguished eyes we would learn much that would be valuable for the rest of our lives. Such reading, almost without words, would leave a deep mark on our hearts for all eternity."[6]

Despite the focus on class and political enemies, Soviet terror during the Great Purge again shared key features of genocide as later defined in international law in the targeting of victims. Terror was often haphazard for individuals swiftly executed or deported into the camp system to labor or die, but at the collective level terror was not random. Any arrest of a so-called Kulak could lead to quick death, but the chances for immediate execution soared among ethnic and national minorities. The renewed anti-Kulak campaign once again brought terror to Ukraine.

During the Great Purge Stalin also focused terror on population groups that resided both within and outside of the Soviet Union. Poles, for example, counted among the victims of the Great Purge.

Soviet authorities had long accused Poland of hostile intent. Any possible actual Polish military threat to the USSR had long receded, but during the Great Purge Soviet authorities lashed out against the activities of a supposed Polish Military Organization. Yezhov, who succeeded to direct the NKVD after the purge of his predecessor Yagoda in August 1937, issued Order 00485 for "total liquidation" of spies of the Polish Military Organization. All manner of ties to Polish culture or Catholicism could serve as evidence of guilt for Troikas who passed along recommendations for executions to the NKVD leadership. In 1938 the Troikas moved to summary justice and execution on the spot. Poles made up some 1/8 of victims of the Great Terror or Purge even though they accounted for 0.4 percent of overall Soviet population.[7]

In similar fashion to Poles, other ethnic minorities associated with states beyond Soviet borders also fell under suspicion during the purges. In the west, such minorities included Germans, Latvians, Estonians, and Finns, as well as Poles. Soviet authorities also shut down Latvian and Estonian cultural institutions. The vast wave of arrests in 1937 and 1938 included some 121,000 seized for membership in supposed nationalist counterrevolutionary organizations as well as alleged Polish, Japanese, German, Latvia, Finnish, Estonian, and Romanian spies.

Ethnic cleansing

Along with executions and arrests, Soviet terror brought deportations of officially suspect peoples and groups. The more these actions swept up entire populations, the more they converged with ethnic cleansing. (As in the case of genocide, the exact term ethnic cleansing did not yet exist, though contemporaries sometimes employed similar terms to refer to cleansing or purification of populations.) Even before the Second World War, Soviet authorities resorted to deportation to push ethnic Germans to the east. Ethnic Germans were registered with the Soviet Central Committee, and in November 1934, the Central Committee ordered the removal and deportation of "hostile anti-Soviet element from the German villages." Beginning in 1935, the Soviet Union sent some thousands of German families from Volhynia to Siberia. Between February 20 and March 10, 1935, Soviet authorities deported 41,650 people, more than half of them Germans and Poles, from Kiev and Vinnytsia in western and central

Ukraine to eastern Ukraine. After some further small deportations, Soviet authorities deported another 15,000 German and Polish households in January 1936, this time all the way to Kazakhstan. At the same time, Finns from the Leningrad region were also being sent east, several thousand in 1935 and 20,000 to Siberia in 1936.[8] The campaign against so-called enemy-nations extended as well to executions of thousands of supposed spies, including 16,573 accused of espionage for Latvia, 7,998 executed for the same offence in connection with Estonia, and 9,078 killed for their alleged work on behalf of Finland. The purges of suspect nations increased in 1937 and 1938. Even though total NKVD arrests fell from more than 936,000 in 1937 to more than 638,000 in 1938.[9]

Soviet authorities also deported suspect minorities from borders in the Far East, including Koreans as well as some Chinese. In early 1937 at Lenkoran on the Caspian Sea, the English traveler Fitzroy Maclean came across trucks "each filled with depressed-looking Turko-tartar peasants under the escort of NKVD frontier troops with fixed bayonets." In October, he encountered a similar scene at Altaisk, this time "Koreans, who with their families and belongings were on their way from the Far East to central Asia."[10] They made up but one contingent of some 171,781 Koreans, sent from their homes in the Soviet Far East to Kazakhstan and Uzbekistan by October 29.

By the start of the Second World War, the Soviet regime engaged in at least partial ethnic cleansing. As in the case of other phases of terror class enmity became a marker for ethnicity in carrying out deportations. Ethnic identity was critical in distinguishing those minorities that suffered deportation from many other ethnic minorities left in place during the 1930s.

Punished peoples during the Second World War

Soviet deportations of suspect minorities continued into the Second World War. The Hitler-Stalin pact of August 1939 temporarily served the interests of two powers otherwise divided by ideology. Weeks after Hitler invaded Poland in September 1939, the Soviet Union pushed into eastern Poland, and Poland remained divided until the German invasion of the Soviet Union in June 1941. The Soviet authorities also pushed their power to the west in other contested areas, retaking many regions formerly held by the Russian Empire. They moved in stages into the Baltic States and into the region of Bessarabia, which Romania had gained after the fall of the Russian Empire. Taking hold of disputed border zones, the Soviet regime extended the campaign of deporting suspect minorities. Those accused of anti-Soviet activities included local elites and in many cases Jews.

After the German invasion of the Soviet Union, deportations took a new turn, targeting ethnic minorities accused of having supported Germany. The most obvious targets were the Soviet Union's ethnic Germans. The First World War provided precedent for deporting Germans out of the war zone: in 1915 Russian military authorities had ordered ethnic Germans out of the Empire's western regions for the interior. In the Second World War, Soviet deportations moved to full-scale ethnic cleansing, driving Germans altogether out of regions including Volhynia, the Black Sea, and the Volga River, and the north Caucasus and into the world of labor camps and special settlements in Siberia, Central Asia, and the Urals. Many tens of thousands and perhaps up to 200,000–300,000 died.

The Stalinist regime deported both during the catastrophic defeats of the early phase of German invasion and during the long Soviet drive to push back German forces. With victories, the Soviet regime expanded deportations but shifted to target ethnic groups accused of having offered support for the German invaders. Here again, Soviet terror built on precedent. The Russian Empire had struggled for decades to pacify border zones along the shores of the Black Sea and in the Caucasus and adjacent regions during the nineteenth century and had resorted to deportations of peoples such as Circassians. During the Second World War, the Soviet Union struck at a long list of ethnic and religious groups along their southern borders. The removed included Muslims, including Chechens, Ingush, Karachai, Meskhetian Turks, Balkars, and Crimean Tatars as well as the Kalmyks who were Buddhists.

Germany in fact sought to win support from certain Soviet minorities, but the blanket punishment exaggerated the extent of collaboration and overlooked service to the Soviet military. A German officer recruited among the Kalmyks, for example, but Kalmyks also fought in the Red Army, and when Germany did enlist minorities they often did so among prisoners of war who otherwise faced the very real likelihood of death. This was the case among Crimean Tatars enlisted into German ranks from Soviet soldiers taken as prisoners, and other Tatars fought as partisans against German occupation. In Chechnya anti-Soviet guerrilla forces formed with the collapse of state power, but Germany did not support the cause of Chechen independence.[11]

Ethnic cleansing during the years of Soviet victory took place with unrivalled speed. The very first deportations, those of the Karachai, a Turkish group, set a standard for efficiency: most of the Karachai were rounded up for transport east on November 2, 1943. Deportations of Kalmyks began with similar speed with mass detention between December 26 and December 30. Swift deportations of Chechens, Ingush, Balkars, Meskhetian Turks, and Crimean Tatars followed in 1944 with populations quickly rounded up and then sent east to destinations in Kazakhstan, Kirgizstan, and Uzbekistan in Soviet Central Asia. Many did not even get the chance to struggle to survive in special settlements: the NKVD, for example, killed thousands of Chechens before the journey east.

Perpetrators, bystanders, and victims

The Soviet cases of ethnic cleansing and killing through famine exemplify policies of destruction carried out by a powerful state. While identifying the famine as genocide has caused debate, the Soviet case features prominently in theories that attribute mass killing to powerful modern states. The Soviet campaigns of terror clearly began from the highest reaches of the Soviet state and security apparatus.

With the support and approval of Lenin and Stalin, the Soviet internal security forces carried out purges, executions, and deportations. The Cheka, OGPU, and the NKVD in succession led these efforts. From the 1920s onward Troikas handed out sentences. In the 1930s Troikas comprised of representatives of the NKVD, the Communist Party, and the Prosecutor made decisions that determined life and death. NKVD agents, assisted on occasion, by troops of the Ministry of Internal Affairs, meanwhile, carried out the roundups and deportations of suspect minorities.

The caste of perpetrators was ever-changing as the Great Purge reach deep into the security apparatus itself. Genrikh Yagoda, for example, directed the NKVD from July 1934 until September 1936 and oversaw the executions of Zinoviev and Kamenev, but was himself toppled during the purge by Nikolai Yezhov. Yagoda was executed in March 1938 after boasting of his achievements in plea for mercy directed toward Stalin: "I appeal to you! For you I built two great canals!" However, Yezhov's hold on the NKVD was also short-lived. He was displaced by Beria by 1938 and executed in 1940. During the Second World War Lavrenty Beria directed deportations. Indeed he personally oversaw the rapid strike against Chechens in the Grozny in February 1944. Beria survived through the end of Stalin's life after which he was swiftly put on trial and executed in December 1953.

The instability at the top of the NKVD was symptomatic of a deeper process—thousands of NKVD agents were killed during the Great Purge. The victims included both high-ranking staff killed after the executions of Yezhov and Yagoda as well as ordinary agents. Here again executions carried out for ostensibly political reasons had another dimension: many fell to terror, but the purge took a particularly devastating toll on Jews within the NKVD. The Communist Party was in no way a specifically Jewish organization, but a disproportionate percentage of NKVD officers were Jews, at least until the late 1930s. After the Great Purge, however, the proportion of Jews within the NKVD's upper ranks plummeted and the agency became increasingly Russian, albeit, with a powerful presence of the Georgians close to Beria.[12]

Small numbers of NKVD men carried out the vast bulk of the shootings, but the boundaries between the core perpetrators and the mass of bystanders were fluid. The regime encouraged Soviet citizens to denounce their fellow citizens who belonged to hostile classes. Thus, Communist officials received such denunciations of Kulaks and of class enemies during the Great Purge. Ideology and the search for security encouraged such action: denouncing fellow Soviet citizens served the Communist cause, and informers, through their actions, could also hope to establish their own credentials as loyal Communists. Fear of denunciation, in turn, gave reason for extreme caution in confiding critical views of the state or Communist Party to anyone. Many also struggled to conceal an unfavorable past class identity.

NADEZHDA MANDELSTAM ON INFORMERS

Nadezhda Mandelstam was a writer and the wife of the famed Soviet poet Osip Mandelstam who was swept into the Gulag and died. Nadezhda Mandelstam described Soviet terror in her books, *Hope against Hope* and *Hope Abandoned*, which were published in the 1970s. Here she discusses informers and the fear that afflicted virtually anyone in Soviet society:

"All of this took place on a massive scale and affected even those who were not specifically followed. Every family was always going over its circle of acquaintances, trying to determine who were the provocateurs, the informers, and the traitors. After 1937 people stopped meeting with each other altogether. And with this the secret police were well on their way to achieving their goals. Apart from gathering a constant flow of information, they aimed to weaken the bonds between people, to create an alienated society, and they had drawn large numbers of people into their circle, calling them in from time to time, harassing them and swearing them to secrecy by means of signed statements. And all those crowds of the 'summoned' lived in eternal fear of being found out and were therefore just as interested as regular members of the police in the stability of the existing order and the inviolability of the archives where their names were on file."

There were also economic and personal reasons for bystanders to assist perpetrators. Denunciations offered the opportunity to settle scores or to win benefits. In the Soviet Union, where housing construction utterly failed to keep pace with rapid urbanization, apartments were scarce and crowded. Entire families lived in individual rooms of apartments while others made do with corners or spots in a hall. The irritation and resentments produced by conflict over space reinforced the campaigns against class enemies. Denunciation for political offense could provide the means to gain a better room or more space.

Bystanders diverged in their responses to exiled peoples settled in their midst. Survivors of deportation recalled being treated kindly by local populations, including Kazakhs and other Soviet citizens previously sent east, but they also told of hostile treatment, for example by Uzbeks, at least in the very early years of exile, though they also recalled improving relations.[13]

For victims, the blows delivered by the state security forces fell quickly. The memory of Old Bolsheviks held up for rebuke at show trials does not convey the typical speed and shock of the Soviet terror. The Troikas sped up the already rapid process of punishment as they dispensed with the fiction of seeking central approval for their sentences. Those deported as members of traitor populations similarly suffered the start of their punishment almost immediately after learning of their fate.

ACCOUNT BY TENZILA IBRAIMOVA OF CRIMEAN TATAR DEPORTATION

In this account, a Crimean Tatar woman described deportation:

"We were deported from the village of Adzhiatman . . . on May 18, 1944. The deportation was carried out with great brutality. At 3:00 in the morning, when the children were fast asleep, the soldiers came in and demanded that we gather ourselves together and leave in five minutes. We were not allowed to take any food or other things with us. We were treated so rudely that we thought we were going to be taken out and shot. Having been driven out of the village we were held for twenty-four hours without food: we were starving but not allowed to go fetch something to eat from home. The crying of the hungry children was continuous. My husband was fighting at the front, and I had the three children. Finally we were put in trucks and driven to Yevpatoria. There we were crowded like cattle into freight cars full to overflowing. The trains carried us for twenty-four days until we reached the station of Zerabulak in Samarkand region from which we were shipped to the Pravda Kolkhoz in Khatyrchinskii district."[14]

The purges and deportations brought those victims who were not immediately executed into the vast world of prison and labor camps and special settlements that Aleksandr Solzhenitsyn dubbed the Gulag Archipelago. Solzhenitsyn wrote of the ports of the Archipelago, which the ordinary prisoners or Zeks passed through. They entered the system in Transit Prisons, which in some cases housed tens of thousands. Exiles were sent to Special Settlements located in remote areas of the steppes or taiga.

The early years in Special Settlements brought further deprivation and many deaths. Members of exiled nations arrived at their new sites in weakened conditions only to find, in some cases, that they had to build their own settlements. Hunger and famine were common through the late 1940s. Mortality soared. Between 1944 and 1949 the death rate for resettled Balkars reached 49 percent and approximately 35 percent for Chechens and Ingush at Akmola on the Steppes of Kazakhstan.[15] Deportees died of malaria, dysentery, and yellow fever. They struggled to adapt to unfamiliar environments and climate while carrying out forced labor all day long. In southern Uzbekistan, for example, Crimean Tatars were set to forced labor in cotton fields.[16]

Though the deportations affected entire populations, the Soviet executions were directed mainly against men. The Troikas typically ordered execution of adult men. In the Gulag as well, the overwhelming majority of prisoners were men. Still, those women who were sent to the Gulag suffered harsh punishment and abuse. Through the Second World War some were sent to mixed camps.

Mass killing in the Soviet Union

After the killing had ended, the parallels as well as the differences between Soviet terror and the Holocaust gave rise to debate about the relationship between the many Soviet terror campaigns. Both Nazi Germany and the Soviet Union employed massive state power to carry out far-ranging plans of deportation and expulsion of unwanted populations and to imprison millions, and the policies of both regimes led to millions of deaths. Focusing on the state role in killing, the political scientist Rudolph Rummel employed the term "democide."[17]

On the other hand, even leaving aside the debate about whether to extend the list of victimized groups from the Genocide Convention, the Soviet Union did not pursue ethnic or racial purity and also did not seek extermination of entire populations in the manner that Nazi Germany pursued a "Final Solution" that would entirely eliminate all Jews from Europe. There is therefore no scholarly consensus on identifying the Soviet case as genocide: prominent historians and scholars of genocide have concluded that the Soviet Union did carry out genocide, but others have seen it as carrying out closely related policies and have employed other terms such as "mass killing."

BENJAMIN VALENTINO ON MASS KILLING

Mass killing is "defined here simply as the intentional killing of a massive number of noncombatants. Victims of mass killing may be members of any kind of group (ethnic, political, religious, etc.) as long as they are noncombatants and as long as their deaths were caused intentionally. Three aspects of the definition of mass killing warrant further elaboration."

1. "the mass killings must be intentional, which distinguishes it from deaths caused by natural disasters, outbreaks of disease, or the unintentional killing of civilians during war. This definition is not limited to 'direct' methods of killing such as execution, gassing and bombing. It includes deaths caused by starvation, exposure, or disease resulting from the intentional confiscation, destruction, or blockade of the necessities of life. It also includes deaths caused by starvation, exhaustion, exposure, or disease during forced relocation or forced labor."

2. "Unlike most scholarly definitions of genocide, mass killing does not specify that perpetrators must possess the intent to destroy an entire group or even a specific percentage of it."

3. "The definition focuses on the killing of noncombatants because it is violence directed against noncombatants that distinguishes mass killing from other forms of warfare and that most offends our moral sensibilities."[18]

Even as a form of mass killing, Soviet terror shared close similarities with acts of genocide. Through executions the NKVD and other security forces engaged in "killing members of the group." The conditions of forced labor and imprisonment frequently led not only to "serious bodily or mental harm," but also meant "Deliberately inflicting on the group conditions of life calculated to bring about its physical destruction in whole or in part...." By any reasonable standard, it was predictable that Soviet policy in Ukraine during the famine and in subjecting large numbers to harsh living conditions in remote prisons and work sites would lead to massive numbers of deaths.

THE SPANISH CIVIL WAR

Between 1936 and 1939, a violent Civil War in Spain coincided with the peak of purges in the Soviet Union. In Spain, rebels led by General Francisco Franco fought and eventually defeated Republicans. As in the case of the Soviet Union, many of those killed in Spain were targeted because of their political affiliation. The war is often recalled as a kind of training ground for the Second World War. Nazi Germany and the Soviet Union supported opposing sides, and in Germany's case formed a force called the Condor Legion that provided military assistance for the rebels, most infamously with the bombing of the town of Guernica in 1937. Many influential histories of genocide do not include the deaths that resulted from the Spanish Civil War; however, the historian Paul Preston has described what he terms a "Spanish Holocaust." "Behind the lines" during the war, ". . . nearly 200,000 men and women were murdered extra-judicially or executed after flimsy legal process." In using the term "Holocaust" Preston does not see equivalence to the Holocaust, but identifies "parallels." For example, the rebels drew on prior racist and anti-Semitic thinking that identified a conspiracy of Jews, Free Masons, and Bolsheviks. Both sides carried out killing, but "in the case of the military rebels, a programme of extermination was central to their planning and preparations."[19]

Study questions

- What were the main causes of Soviet terror?
- How did the Soviet authorities identify and select victims of terror?
- What was the role of the Soviet leadership in causing deaths from famine?
- How did bystanders react to the Great Purge of 1937–8?
- What were the main similarities between Soviet terror and the Holocaust? What were the main differences?
- To what extend does the term genocide apply to Soviet mass killing?

Further reading

Applebaum, Anne, *Gulag: A History* (New York: Doubleday, 2003).

Conquest, Robert, *Harvest of Sorrow* (Oxford: Oxford University Press, 1986).

Naimark, Norman M., *Stalin's Genocides* (Princeton: Princeton University Press, 2007).

Snyder, Timothy, *Bloodlands: Europe between Hitler and Stalin* (New York: Basic Books, 2010).

Solzhenitsyn, Alexander, Ralph Parker, Marvin L. Kalb, and A. Tvardovskii?, *One Day in the Life of Ivan Denisovich* (New York: Dutton, 1963).

4

The Holocaust

In July 1939 Dawid Sierakowiak, a Jewish boy from Poland enjoyed a last few weeks of freedom during a camping trip to the High Tatras mountains in southern Poland. In a diary he would keep until shortly before his death in 1943 he told of normal every-day pleasures and cares, such as his family's fear of his swimming. Along with other boys at the Jewish youth camp, he climbed, played ping pong, sang, and wrote and performed skits before returning home to the city of Lodz in late July. He would never leave the city again: his home-town would soon become his prison. On September 1 Germany invaded Poland and within a week occupied Lodz. With the Germans came looting, attacks on Jews, and forced labor. By November, Jews were ordered to wear a yellow patch. "We are returning to the Middle Ages," Dawid wrote.[1]

By early 1940 Dawid along with his young sister Nadzia, mother, father, and all the Jews of Lodz had been placed inside a ghetto. The occupation regime pushed them along with some 160,000 Jews into a small area of the city and divided them from the rest of the population with barbed wire. The Jews of Lodz lived to work: under the leadership of the ghetto elder, Chaim Rumkowski, the Jews of Lodz staffed a series of workshops. Inequity in access to desirable jobs and to scarce food angered Dawid who wrote caustically about the elder's penchant for doling out food to create a more compliant population. In October 1941, the arrival of Jews deported from Germany and Austria crammed still more Jews into the already over-crowded ghetto. Though angered by the concentration of power under Rumkowski, Dawid still struggled to maintain his hopes in a better future. As winter approached he wrote, "I'm certain that a wonderful, shining life is still waiting for us."[2]

Amidst shortages of food, rumors of imminent deportations sent shockwaves of fear through the ghetto's population in 1942. If life in the ghetto was hard, the alternatives seemed far worse. With employment as the condition for staying in Lodz, Jews sought jobs by every means so that they could continue to suffer disease and short rations rather than be removed. As Dawid put it in May 1942, "Death is striking left and right. A person becomes thin (an 'hourglass') and pale in the face, then comes the swelling, a few days in bed or in the hospital, and that's it. The person was living, the person is dead; we live and die like cattle."[3]

That there was worse to fear than "working and starving" Dawid soon learned. In September news came that the Germans were clearing patients out of ghetto hospitals, and the ghetto police than hunted down the sick. German demands for all children up to the age of 10, the elderly over 65, and anyone who was sick, unable to work, or without work, intensified the panic. Rumkowski explained that the deportations had to be carried out: "I must cut off the limbs in order to save the body," he is reported to have said. One of the victims was Dawid's mother.

No one from Dawid's family survived. In March 1943, his father, whom Dawid had come to resent for his greediness in taking scarce food, died. Dawid himself took a turn for the worse. In April, he wrote, "My state of mind is worsening every day. . . . Everyone in the ghetto is sick." He died of tuberculosis in August. His sister Nadzia held out longer until she, along with the remaining Jews in the ghetto, was deported to Auschwitz in 1944.

In Dawid's life and death in the Lodz Ghetto we see several key facets of the Holocaust. Most obvious and important was the simple fact that for the vast, overwhelming majority of Jews there was no way out, no escape. No amount of intelligence, bravery, creativity, or strength could ensure survival in the face of starvation, disease, and for those, who like Dawid's sister endured the longest, the gas chamber. There was no triumph of the human spirit of the sort that we sometimes so desperately seek to find in these tragic events.

A look back at Lodz also shows the complex relationship between perpetrators, bystanders, and victims as well as the difficulty in some cases of clearly defining categories of perpetrators and victims and placing all individuals into a single category. There were perpetrators—those responsible for death and killing. German occupying and security forces unquestionably held responsibility for the creation of the ghetto and the destruction of its inhabitants. But within the ghetto itself, as Dawid's diary outlined, the population fractured into those with relative privilege and those without. Boundaries between perpetrators and victims blurred in particular when it came to Rumkowski and his administration and police. Rumkowski defended himself, claiming that he made hard decisions to seek to save some, but Dawid saw the ghetto's leader and his police force as complicit in causing misery and breaking up families. Rumkowski, of course, after Dawid's death, would become a victim when he was deported and killed along with the last remnant of the Jews of Lodz.

In the history of the Lodz Ghetto we also see varied paths to death. Genocide is often seen as a single thing, but beneath that surface there was much regional and local variation even in the Holocaust. After much death and mass deportations in 1942, there were still tens of thousands of Jews in Lodz at a time when surrounding Jewish communities had been entirely extinguished. Lodz presented an extreme case of the contradictory German interests in exploiting Jews for work and killing them, though this was finally resolved through the liquidation of the ghetto when German authorities deported and murdered Nadzia Sierakowiak and the other Jews who had made it that far.

Paths toward the Holocaust

The Holocaust, an account such as Dawid Sierakowiak's reveals, did not start until deep into the Second World War. Confusion about when the Holocaust began is only one of many common misperceptions about this most famous or infamous case of genocide. However far back roots of genocide can be traced, actual mass destruction of European Jews did not begin with Hitler's accession to power in 1933, or with the Kristallnacht pogrom of 1938 when mobs of Nazi activists attacked, burned, and looted synagogues as well as remaining Jewish-owned stores. Nor did mass destruction of European Jews begin with the start of war itself and the German conquest of Poland in September 1939, though terror units targeted Polish elites at that time. Genocide did not start until the summer of 1941 when death squads known as Einsatzgruppen mowed down entire Jewish communities in the Soviet Union, and the mass murder in the death camps started only in 1942. This basic chronology of killing dispels another popular misconception about the Holocaust: the assumption that Hitler had always wanted to eliminate European Jews and simply waited until he had the chance to act on his murderous wishes. If that were true, why would Germany's leader or Führer have waited as long as he did? His radical and long-held anti-Semitism was clear, but the precise steps that translated hatred into action formed part of a long and complex chain that led to mass destruction of European Jews.

Decades of research into the precise causes of this emblematic genocide has focused on varied routes to killing. Ideological approaches look at the long-term development of anti-Semitism or, focusing on more immediate links to genocide, chart Hitler's intentions to seek to track how his hatred of Jews led to genocide. The history of Nazi Germany before the Holocaust has demonstrated the dedication of the Nazi regime to creating a racial state that not only excluded Jews from German society, but also pioneered methods for killing those deemed to present a threat to racial purity. Plans for building a racial empire beyond Germany featured both schemes for boosting the Aryan presence and programs for removing Jews.

It was long customary to divide up these approaches according to their emphasis on intentions or functions, but these approaches are increasingly complementary. There was not a single path to the Holocaust, but these different paths moved together to narrow the range of options in German policy toward European Jews, leading to the launching of the "Final Solution" to the "Jewish problem" or the fact that Jews existed. This "Final Solution" would become known as the Holocaust or the Shoah, a term employed more frequently in Israel.

Hitler's goals

To look to Hitler's goals and decisions to chart a route to the Holocaust makes sense in that Hitler as Führer was the pivotal figure in the Nazi state and possessed unrivalled power. Hitler's hatred of Jews formed a core of his political thinking. The search for the origins of that hatred typically leads to *Mein Kampf*, the book Hitler started during his very short term in prison after he failed to overthrow the German Government in 1923; however, Hitler's own explanations of the roots of his anti-Semitism cannot be corroborated by other sources. Indeed, there is no way to confirm exactly when or how Hitler became an anti-Semite. Hitler may have interested himself in anti-Semitism during his years in Vienna where he lived from 1908–13. The city's mayor Karl Lueger capitalized on political anti-Semitism, and the magazine *Ostara* which published racist and anti-Semitic articles could also have influenced the young Hitler. In *Mein Kampf*, Hitler later wrote about his negative views of Jews during the First World War. He asserted that he found Munich full of Jews in 1916 when he was posted to a battalion there after recovering from wounds. Such views echoed claims that led to a military census conducted by the Prussian Ministry of War to determine if Jews served in the military in proportion to their share in the overall population—in fact they did.

The precise origins of Hitler's anti-Semitism will likely always remain subject to debate, but it is clear that Hitler espoused anti-Semitism almost as soon as he became active in politics while living in Munich shortly after the First World War. In September 1919 he visited a meeting of the German Workers' Party or DAP, soon to be renamed the NSDAP or Nazi Party. Hitler soon proved to be the party's most effective speaker. In 1923 he sought to seize power in the failed Beer Hall Putsch, and while serving a very short prison sentence provided the most extended guide to his thought in *Mein Kampf* in which he wrote of eastern expansion and a racial struggle of Aryans against Jews.

After release from prison, Hitler shifted to a strategy of trying to gain power through elections. In 1930, as the global economic crisis struck, the NSDAP made an electoral breakthrough gaining more than 18 percent of the vote in Germany's crowded parliamentary field, and by 1932 the Nazi Party became Germany's largest single party, though neither it, nor any other party won a majority. Persistent attacks on Jews during the incessant campaigning of the early 1930s did not provide the chief incentive for votes for the NSDAP, but anti-Semitism appealed to the party's most enthusiastic supporters. And even Germans who supported the Nazis because of pledges of unity or reaction against the existing political system were willing to overlook vitriolic anti-Semitism in voting for the party. Nazi support appeared to stagnate in late 1932, but the party still provided a popular base that proved alluring to the arch-conservative politicians close to Germany's elderly President Hindenburg. Through 1932 Hindenburg turned to a series of authoritarian governments that lacked significant mass support. In early 1933, Hindenburg's confidantes persuaded the President to appoint Hitler Chancellor, assuming that they would be able to use the Nazis for their own ends: "We've hired him," one claimed.

Hitler detested Jews, but tracking the precise connection from Hitler's virulent statements to the actual start of the Holocaust has long challenged historians. Finding such a link is not so simple a matter as locating a single document in which Hitler ordered the extermination of Europe's Jews: there is no reason to expect that Hitler would have resorted to such a written order. In the Holocaust, as in the Armenian Genocide, official orders did not provide the critical justification for genocide.

Hitler's own most significant statement on the fate of Europe's Jews came in a speech he gave to the Reichstag in early 1939 which issued an ominous threat "If the international finance-Jewry inside and outside Europe should succeed in plunging the nations into a world war yet again," he declared, "then the outcome will not be the victory of Jewry, but rather the annihilation of the Jewish race in Europe!" This "prophecy" as Hitler referred to his own threat resurfaced periodically in Nazi propaganda, and Hitler returned to the theme in later speeches, typically at the end or beginning of a year. On January 30, 1941, for example, he reiterated his "prophecy" at a speech in Berlin to commemorate his appointment as Chancellor eight years earlier. He asserted, only misidentifying the speech in which he made his original public threat, "that if Jewry were to plunge the world into war, the role of Jewry would be finished in Europe. They may laugh about it today, as they laughed before about my prophecies. The coming months and years will prove that I prophesied rightly in this case too." A year later, he made almost exactly the same warning in a similar speech in Berlin. "I already stated . . . and I refrain from over-hasty prophecies—that this war will not come to an end as the Jews imagine with the extermination of the European-Aryan peoples, but that the result of this war will be the annihilation of Jewry."

Whether Hitler intended this warning as a general threat or as specific roadmap for the future remains open to debate: the Führer was fond of talk of annihilation, but in this case annihilation really did mean annihilation. He seemed fond of recalling his prophecy, and his threats struck Jews themselves as ominous. In February 1942, from within the Warsaw Ghetto the teacher Chaim Kaplan noted the Führer's speech "boasting that his prophecy was beginning to become true." Kaplan saw "proof that what we thought were rumors are in effect reports of actual occurrences." The Jewish Council and the Joint (American Jewish Joint Distribution Committee), a social service agency, confirmed a new Nazi policy of "death by extermination for entire Jewish communities."[4]

Jews, of course, could only guess about the connection between Hitler's statements and German policies, but even among perpetrators, much of the evidence only indicates what Hitler's chief lieutenants told others about the Führer's decisions and wishes. The Führer, they learned, approved of extermination, but the message came through highly placed intermediaries. Thus, Otto Bradfisch of the SS recounted an August 1941 conversation at Minsk in which he asked the SS leader Heinrich Himmler "who was taking responsibility for the mass extermination of the Jews. Himmler made this conversation the occasion for a speech, in which he told members of Einsatzkommando 8 . . . not to worry—the orders had been personally given by Hitler."[5]

The racial state

Well before the Holocaust, the Nazi regime recast German society along racial lines. The Nazi racial state awarded Aryans with benefits while systematically driving Jews out of German society. In power the Nazi regime rapidly consolidated power and instituted sweeping anti-Semitic policies. A boycott of Jewish shops in April 1933 was not a full success, but the Nazi dictatorship quickly banned Jews from numerous professions. Jews were removed from posts in the bureaucracy, judiciary, and universities. A key step came in 1935 with the Nuremberg laws, which removed Jews from the national or racial community. Jews were no longer citizens but became state subjects. Marriage or intimate relations between Jews and Aryans were also banned, though there was no policy of ending existing mixed marriages. The Berlin Olympics in 1936 briefly interrupted the tempo of intensifying anti-Semitism, but thereafter Hermann Goering pushed forward Aryanization or the takeover and seizure of Jewish businesses and assets. An endless list of discriminatory measures in matters large and small barred Jews from any number of activities of normal life: swimming, driving, and using a library among others. By 1939 German Jews were increasingly impoverished and isolated—they were placed, not into ghettos, but together into Jews' houses where they lived crowded together in apartments with other Jews and separated from Germans, except for those Germans in mixed marriages who followed a spouse into such a Jews' house.

Excluded from German society and driven out of the racial community, German Jews also faced the threat of violence. Jews learned to fear being dispatched to concentration camps, though these did not yet include the death camps created during the Second World War. Before the Second World War, Nazi anti-Semitism took most violent form with Kristallnacht—a kind of pogrom carried out in reprisal for the assassination of a German diplomat in France by a Polish Jew. Storm troopers and other "rioters" burned synagogues and Jewish-owned businesses and looked for Jews to attack. The mounting persecution and growing insecurity propelled many to seek a way out, but with their assets seized and many foreign countries closing their doors many Jews had no place to go. Others, such as the family of Anne Frank, which moved to the Netherlands at the start of the Nazi dictatorship in 1933 left only to find themselves living under German occupation during the Second World War.

THE *ST. LOUIS*

The voyage of the *St. Louis*, an ocean liner that sailed from Hamburg to Havana, in 1939 with 938 passengers, most of them German Jews, offered striking evidence of the extreme difficulty Jews encountered trying to get out of Germany. Most of the passengers had applied for US visas and ultimately sought entry into the United States. The *St. Louis* arrived in Havana on May 27, but Cuba allowed only a small number of the passengers to disembark. The ship sailed close by the United States, but was unable to land. Holding to a very restrictive immigration policy, the US government responded to appeals for entry only through a State Department telegram that informed passengers that they would have to wait on lists to "qualify for and obtain immigration visas." After the *St. Louis* returned to Europe, 288 of the passengers were allowed into Great Britain, but many other passengers who made their way into countries including France, Belgium, and the Netherlands ended up living under German occupation, and 254 died during the Holocaust. The entire sorry episode demonstrated the extreme difficulty that German Jews faced in finding a place to go even if they decided to leave Germany.

Within Germany itself, the task of purifying the Aryan racial community provided new methods for eliminating unwanted populations, though the Nazi Regime did not begin mass murder with Jews but with Germans. In the 1930s the Nazi Regime engaged in far-ranging sterilization of Germans held to have hereditary conditions that endangered the purity of the racial community. A 1933 Law for the Prevention of Progeny with Hereditary Diseases introduced sterilization, and a series of hereditary health courts, reviewed cases of Germans. In all hundreds of thousands were sterilized by courts that determined that they had schizophrenia, Huntington's chorea, manic-depression, or hereditary alcoholism, deafness, and blindness or that they were hereditarily "feeble minded."

Nazi eugenics policy was not without parallel elsewhere when it came to sterilization except for the massive scale of sterilizations carried out by German authorities, but the Nazi regime brought negative eugenics to a new racial form with a policy of extermination. Dr Karl Brandt, Hitler's accompanying physician, and Philipp Bouhler of Hitler's office as Chancellor began to develop a program for killing severely disabled Germans in 1938 when a family with the name of Knauer brought the case of their disabled baby to the Führer's attention. Permission was given to kill the baby, and Brandt and Bouhler extended their work, at Hitler's instructions, by planning for a general euthanasia program for disabled infants and children. In 1939 the Chancellery office expanded the program to include forced euthanasia of disabled adult Germans. Known as T4, a reference to the street address of the headquarters, the forced euthanasia program killed more than 70,000 Germans by gassing.

Despite issuing propaganda that stressed the cost of caring for the severely disabled and represented them as a drain on the racial community, the Nazi leadership did not make T4 public. Rumors of the killings, however, spread within the population. And in August 1941 Bishop Count Galen memorably spoke out against the program, warning, "If you establish and apply the principle that you can kill 'unproductive' fellow human beings then woe betide us when we become old and frail!"[6] The T4 program was soon concluded, though whether public pressure played a role or the program had already met its target remains a topic of debate. In any case, killings of the disabled continued in the concentration camp system.

A new Europe

Nazi agencies also moved toward developing plans for removing or eliminating European Jews as one in a series of interconnected policies for remaking the ethnic and racial map of Europe. Hitler aimed to create a racial empire beyond German borders. He spoke of his goals for a new Europe in October 1939, announcing before the Reichstag, of the need "to create a new ethnographic order; that is, to resettle the nationalities so that in the end, better lines of demarcation exist than is today the case." In practice, the work of creating the new order began in Poland's former west, land annexed to Germany. Hitler instructed Himmler to bring back Germans living abroad and told the SS leader to get rid of populations that would endanger Germans in Germany's new territories. Himmler and Heydrich united the work of moving German settlers and forcing out unwanted populations. Along with his position as leader of the SS, Himmler also headed an agency named the Reich Commission for the Strengthening of Germandom, more often termed the RKFDV, and Heydrich, head of the SD, was also leader of the Central Resettlement Office. As the Soviet Union pushed east in the period between the Hitler-Stalin pact of 1939 and the German invasion of the Soviet Union in June of 1941, Germans from regions that came under Soviet control, such as the Baltic and Bessarabia, provided a pool of settlers for the new German east. Making the East German, also took the form of forcing out Poles and Jews.

As Himmler and Heydrich sought to push Poles and Jews east, they met with opposition from German occupation and military authorities. A series of plans drove out hundreds of thousands of

Poles to make room for German settlers, but Hans Frank, the head of the General Government, the German occupation zone in central Poland, objected to accepting more Jews on the grounds that his occupation zone already possessed a large Jewish population. Military authorities, for their part, placed higher priority on other tasks than on moving civilian groups. Economic considerations also provided reason to keep Poles and even Jews in place as a labor supply. Nazi ideological goals, therefore simultaneously created immense pressure to move Jews as well as Poles, even as military and economic considerations provided reason to proceed more slowly. This contradiction and the ensuing tension, in turn, gave cause to seek still other "solutions" to the unwanted presence of Jews. And by seizing much of Poland, German authorities vastly expanded the numbers of Jews under their direct power.

In a movement with a racist and anti-Semitic core, the leaders and functionaries in the Nazi regime had strong incentives to advance the Führer's deeply held goals. They understood that Hitler desired a "solution" to the "Jewish question" or the fact that Jews existed in Europe. Planning to create a Europe without Jews, they advanced more than one means to the same end. Removal featured as a common approach, perhaps to Siberia or to the African island of Madagascar—a French colony. Interest in removing Jews to Madagascar peaked in the summer of 1940 when Himmler ordered a halt to deportations of Jews to the General Government, or German occupied zone, in Poland. Nazi proposals envisioned sending away as many as 4 million European Jews to this large island off the coast of Southeastern Africa. However, defeat in the Battle of Britain blocked further development of any plans to ship Jews en masse. Such schemes of mass-forced migration featured ethnic cleansing or forced removal of Jews, albeit, ethnic cleansing that could well have turned into genocide with the high number of deaths that such removal would likely have caused.

Much like Nazi planners, occupation authorities on the local and regional level found their own motives to look for "solutions" to the Jewish problem. Where food was short and all available resources were required for war, doing away with a group already identified as expendable provided a means to match supplies to the local population. In such instances, hatred of Jews and the search for "solutions" shaped a radical response to dire conditions and shortages: removing Jews would both advance Hitler's aims and free up additional resources for the remaining population. Killing Jews provided more food for others.

Toward the "Final Solution"

By 1941 the varied paths toward mass destruction converged until they all led in the same direction. Himmler's planners continued to draft ambitious schemes for moving millions of unwanted peoples, but even in annexed and occupied Poland German authorities squabbled over when and where to move Jews. By 1940 events in the war also ended the possibility of a distant maritime removal. Though victorious on land, German defeat in the Battle of Britain when the Luftwaffe failed to break the Royal Air Force maintained British naval power and revealed the notion of shipping Europe's Jews all the way to Madagascar to be a chimera. The "Final Solution" would be mass murder within Europe's core, rather than ethnic cleansing to some distant shore or remote frozen land. The size of the "Jewish Problem" at the same time grew ever larger as German forces seized land with more Jews. In Poland, occupying forces resorted to ghettoization as a temporary measure; in the Soviet Union they began simply to kill. Hitler, for his part, appeared to reaffirm the path toward mass destruction once Germany was actually in a world war. In June 1941 he invaded the Soviet Union, and in December, shortly after Japan bombed the American fleet at Pearl Harbor, he declared war on the United States.

Blaming Jews, for this world war, which himself had launched, Hitler appeared to reaffirm that the conditions for the destruction of European Jews had been met in a December 12, 1942 meeting with Nazi Party leaders. Recounting the Führer's comments in his day book, Goebbels wrote, "Regarding the Jewish Question, the Fuhrer is determined to clear the table. He warned the Jews that if they were to cause another world war, it would lead to their own destruction. Those were not empty words. Now the word war has come. The destruction of the Jews must be its necessary consequence." Hans Frank, the leader of the General Government, the occupation zone in central Poland, made much the same point, speaking several days later to his officials, reminding his audience, "The Fuhrer once put it this way: if the combined forces of Judaism should again succeed in unleashing a world war, that would mean the end of the Jews in Europe. . . ." Frank noted that he was also involved in plans to remove Jews east (though he had actually previously resisted Himmler's pressure for rapid removal) and brought up the economic incentives for regional occupation authorities to get rid of Jews: "For us too the Jews are incredibly destructive eaters." The Führer had predicted an end to Jews under conditions now met: removal was difficult, feeding Jews both costly and pointless. "But there are some things," Frank stated, "we can do, and one way or another these measures will successfully lead to a liquidation."[7]

This convergence between different "solutions" to the "Jewish Question" was even more obvious at the January 1942 Wannsee Conference. This meeting presided over by Reinhard Heydrich at a villa on the outskirts of Berlin dealt with several issues, including the status of mixed Jews and German Jews, but the participants now also presented varied paths to ridding Europe of Jews as simply different routes to the same outcome. Heydrich recounted several phases of expelling Jews from "every sphere of life" and from "the living space of the German people." Emigration of Jews had been carried out as the "only possible present solution." Conquests presented other options: "the evacuation of Jews to the east. . . ." However, this was still "provisional," though useful in gaining "practical experience" for "the future final solution of the Jewish question." Heydrich then listed the evacuations to take place from different countries, including Germany itself. The participants did not speak directly of murder, but Eichmann at his trial in Jerusalem testified that they had discussed killing and extermination: "they spoke about methods for killing, about liquidation, about extermination."

LUBLIN: EXPERIMENTS IN "SOLUTIONS"

The varied approaches to remaking Eastern Europe and eliminating Jews gave rise to a number of trial projects. The Holocaust ultimately killed and threatened Jews across Europe, but schemes for persecuting, removing, and killing Jews also emerged from Nazi efforts on a regional level. The Lublin reservation sometimes termed the Nisko reservation southeast of the Polish city of Lublin became a key site for developing "solutions" to the "Jewish problem." Soon after the Second World War began, Adolf Eichmann who was charged with Jewish emigration from Vienna and had also gained a staff in Prague, began to work on a plan to send Jews to the area southeast of Lublin. The first transports of Jews to the reservation took place in October 1939, but logistical problems and bureaucratic infighting soon curbed Eichmann's plans. By 1940 and 1941 Odilo Globocnik, an SS commander from Austria sought to make Lublin into a center for killing and resettlement. In 1940 he started to take land, if possible from Jews, with the aim of handing it over to German farmers, including SS settlers. In Globocnik's vision for Lublin, Germans would replace both Jews and Poles. In 1941 he pressed to build the Belzec death camp in the district.

Phases of the holocaust: From mobile killing to gassing

The meetings of late 1941 and early 1942 confirmed and redirected a genocidal campaign already responsible for the murder of more than a million Jews by the end of 1941. Invading the Soviet Union on June 22, 1941 Germany's war took a decisive turn with rapidly accelerating mass murder of Jews. In a first phase of killing, varied local militias, sometimes encouraged by Germans, began to murder Jews in some of the cities and towns which had fallen under Soviet domination since Hitler and Stalin had begun to divide up much of Europe's east in 1939. Killing squads known as Einsatzgruppen followed the German military and soon began to carry out massacres, mainly of men at first, on a far larger scale, and then shifted to killing of all Jews, men, women, and children during the summer of 1941.

Pogroms

Jews had previously suffered pogroms in areas of Eastern Europe. These mob attacks that targeted Jews took place in the Russian Empire in the 1880s and during and after the Russo-Japanese

War as well as in parts of Ukraine during the Russian Civil War of 1918–20. The start of the German invasion in 1941 brought yet another round of pogroms. While the results did not rise to the level of genocide they still killed many thousands. Most typically, the killers, if they offered any justification, claimed that they were punishing Jews for supporting Soviet occupation. Such assertions assigned Jews with a power over Communism that they did not possess and ignored the fact that Soviet authorities had deported Jews, among others, during purges. The claims of Jewish betrayal demonstrated the increasing fragmentation of sharply divided and fractured societies under occupation. Despite many acts of solidarity and even rescue, the members of the varied ethnic and religious groups of Eastern Europe, did not in many instances see themselves as part of a single nation and occupation and war expanded the divisions between varied ethnic and religious groups.

The town of Jedwabne in northeastern Poland, the city of Kaunas in Lithuania, and the city of Lviv (Lvov) in Ukraine counted among the sites hit by pogroms early on in the German invasion. At Jedwabne, as the historian Jan Gross documented, Poles massacred Jews. As one witness testified in 1949, "the Polish population bestially massacred the Jews, and Germans only stood to the side and took pictures. . . ."[8] Across the border in Lithuania, Lithuanian partisans killed Jews in towns and cities, including Kaunas: the dead numbered in the thousands. In the mixed city of Lviv in eastern Poland (in today's Ukraine) militias assisted by local residents, attacked and killed Jews. They claimed to be acting to revenge killings carried out by retreating Soviet NKVD, the Soviet state police. But Ukrainians also referred to older cycles of violence, speaking of Petliura days. Petliura had led a Ukrainian government implicated in pogroms during the Russian Civil War and had later been assassinated while living in exile in Paris in 1926—the assassin Sholom Schwartzbard, who had lost many relatives to pogroms, was acquitted.

Mobile killing

Even the thousands murdered in the pogrom wave would soon seem a small number of victims compared to the hundreds of thousands killed execution style by German death squads. Known by the vague name Einsatzgruppen (a term that amounted to something like operation or action group), these small units followed advancing

German forces east with the task of killing civilians. They murdered Communists officials, thereby doing their part to fulfill the German military's commissar order, which directed the shooting of any captured Soviet political officials or commissars, they killed, assorted others sometimes accused of committing offences, but most of all they killed Jews. Erich von dem Bach-Zelewski, an SS General charged with responsibility for anti-partisan operations, described the Einsatzgruppen's task to the International Military Tribunal at Nuremberg after the war: "The principal task of the Einsatzgruppen of the Security Police was the annihilation of the Jews, Gypsies, and political commissars." The death squads began by shooting male Jews by the dozens and soon by the hundreds. This brief phase of the Holocaust in early summer of 1941 had the character of a gendercide of male Jews.

Very soon the death squads moved from shooting Jewish men to murdering Jewish men, women, and children. A killing log compiled by an Einsatzkommando responsible for terror operations in Lithuania made the shift clear in entries for August. Whereas most entries broke down the number murdered by categories including ethnicity and gender, entries for August 26 and August 28 noted only "all Jews, Jewesses, and Jewish children" when describing the 1,911 and 1,078 Jews murdered respectively on those days in the Lithuanian cities of Kaisiadorys and Prienai. The shift from killing male Jews to murdering all Jews took place at a comparatively early point for this particular terror unit, but by early fall 1941 Einsatzgruppen pushing to the northeast, due east and to the southeast across conquered territories carried out the same basic work of sweeping through towns, villages, and cities to murder Jews.

The Holocaust is often recalled with just cause for the crimes carried out in the gas chambers of death camps, but the men in the Einsatzgruppen murdered by shooting over and over again. They typically entered a community, assembled Jews, if possible by using the ruse that Jews were to gather for resettlement elsewhere. They then took their victims to a suitable spot for mass murder. A depression or ravine, if one existed, offered an easy site for disposing of bodies, and if one did not exist they forced Jews to dig a pit. They completed their murderous task by shooting their victims. Repeating this process they killed more than 1 million Jews in the occupied Soviet Union. The Einsatzgruppen carried out massacres large and small depending on the number of Jews in any one area. In

Kiev, the largest city of Ukraine, the killers set out to murder more than 30,000 Jews. Soon after Germans occupied Kiev on September 19, Jews on September 27 and 28 saw posters, demanding that they gather for resettlement, and on September 29–30 Einsatzgruppe C, assisted by members of the police and military, shot more than 33,000 Jews who had not managed to get out of Kiev at a ravine called Babi Yar. A cemetery watchman, who observed the killings, described how the victims "found themselves on the narrow ground above the precipice . . . and on the opposite side there were the Germans' machine guns. The killed, wounded and half-alive people fell down and were smashed there. Then the next hundred were brought and everything repeated again."[9] Obviously very few survived: Dina Pronicheva, left for dead amidst the corpses, dug her way out of the pile of bodies.

For months the Einsatzgruppen pursued Jews. Many, along with other Soviet citizens, fled, but the collapse of Soviet military power left other Jews with no way out, and repeated sweeps of the death squads reduced the chances of escape. Amidst the widespread carnage, the rate of murder varied. In general the Einsatzgruppen completed their murderous task more rapidly in the north than in the south, but Jews nowhere were safe. In Odessa on the Black Sea, Einsatzkommandos helped Romanian troops murder Jews by the tens of thousands.

Shooting was also a chief method for murder of Jews in Serbia in 1941. Here the SD and the German military took leading roles. In Serbia the start of the Holocaust was closely linked to the struggle against partisans. In particular, German policy called for massive reprisals against partisan attacks with a ratio of executing 50 to 100 Communists for every German killed by partisan attacks. As in the Soviet Union, the categories of Jews and Communists overlapped for the killers. To round up and shoot Jews advanced both the anti-partisan campaign and the general work on a "solution" to the "Jewish problem" in occupied Yugoslavia. In the fall of 1941 the German military carried out mass executions of male Jews. General Franz Böhme, dispatched to Serbia in September 1941 to fulfill Hitler's instructions "to restore order with the severest measures," pursued this goal via expanded murder, targeting male Jews and Gypsies. The 717 Infantry Division, for example, filed periodic updates on the killing: in October the 717 Infantry Division reported the shooting of 1,736 men and 19 women in Kralejvo in central Serbia as punishment. Nearby villages were burned to the ground, and "all male residents shot." During the entire month the division recorded 5,073 "enemy losses," including 4,300 killed as punishment for German casualties. Through December 1941 German units altogether murdered 20–30,000 along with 3,562 identified as partisans, though any such designation was easy after the fact.[10]

Despite their ability to launch genocide of Jews in the occupied Soviet Union and Serbia, German authorities found mobile killing wanting in key respects. It was not that massacres were ineffective. Measured by the goal of reaching a "Final Solution," the pace of killing placed that end with in reach. The Einsatzgruppen, the SD, and the military and police who assisted murdered more than a million Jews in 1941, the overwhelming majority in only six months. Continued killing at this pace would have exceeded the total for each individual year of the Holocaust, save 1942, for sheer carnage. Even so, Himmler and the key figures in the elite Nazi terror organizations opted for a new killing method. The SS leader expressed concerns about the effect of the executions on his men. In testimony at Nuremberg Bach-Zelewski described Himmler's reaction to an execution carried out for him by Einatzruppe B as a demonstration at Minsk in August 1941. Himmler, according to Zelewski, found the experience stressful, even though he was only watching a very small number of the vast total of killings carried out that same year by SS men. Concerns about the burden on the SS gave reason to instruct Arthur Nebe, the commander of Einsatzgruppe B, to find another way to kill.

Along with concerns about the effects of near-daily killing on an elite force, the lack of secrecy of the massacres reinforced the logic for shifting to another method of murder. Killings of this sort and variety carried out in the open all over the occupied Soviet Union in communities large and small simply could not be kept secret, and news of the massacres soon started to filter out from remarks made by soldiers and security personnel on leave. Indeed, news stories about killings of large numbers of Jews in the east made it all the way to the foreign press and newspapers in Britain and the United States.

Even with the shift to new killing methods, massacres continued to add to the death toll of the Holocaust. From late 1941 through 1942, shootings continued in Ukraine and Belorussia after the start of killing in death camps. Killings during this phase, sometimes termed the second sweep, destroyed most remaining ghettos. Near Vilna German forces and their Lithuanian supporters regularly shot Jews at a site the Soviets had intended to use to store fuel at the town of Ponary outside the city. The sound of the shooting was plainly audible to bystanders and observers in the vicinity. The massacres continued periodically through 1944. A journalist named Kazimierz Sakowicz recorded the killings in a diary through 1943.

Death camps

In 1941, another killing method, gassing, lay close at hand. Germany had already assembled technical expertise in gassing through forced euthanasia programs, including T4. Personal accident furthermore made the use of carbon monoxide as a deadly agent abundantly clear to Arthur Nebe who had almost died after leaving his car running and falling asleep in his garage after coming home from a party. Test killings soon showed gassing to be the most effective alternative to shooting. Early prototypes employed gas vans, which distributed exhaust into a closed compartment, but even these, while deadly, suffered from certain defects when it came to fast and efficient killing: the struggles of the dying prisoners, often Soviet prisoners of war during the tests, could easily be heard, and the corpses then had to be disposed of.

From mobile gas vans, it was a small step to turn to fixed gas chambers, and work on creating gassing facilities started in occupied Poland during the Fall of 1941, though such planning by itself did not necessarily indicate when Himmler and his associates selected gassing as the prime killing method. In particular design work for Auschwitz incorporated crematoria with gas chambers.

The death camps developed out of a preexisting concentration camp system. From the very first year of Nazi rule in 1933 the regime created concentration camps. Dachau, the oldest, dated back to March 1933. Dachau as well as the other early camps featured chiefly as a destination for those viewed as undesirable by the new regime: many of the early inmates were Communists or Social Democrats. The camps also housed individuals from other groups targeted for persecution along with criminals and people identified as "asocial." The camps gained a sinister reputation as places to be avoided at all costs where one might well disappear, but the early concentration camp system remained far more limited in scale and in goals than its later form. Indeed, the Soviet Union housed far more prisoners in the Gulag during the 1930s. Before the Second World War, the total number of prisoners at any given time in the German concentration camp system vacillated from under 10,000 to upwards of 30,000. In 1938 there were waves of arrests of Jews with the Anschluss with Austria (the Germany annexation or Austria) and with Kristallnacht. Jews typically faced especially harsh treatment at these early concentration camps.

The goals and size of the camp system changed with war. While prisoners were killed, the camp system did not aim in its early years to exterminate entire groups, but the camp system quickly expanded in scale and in purpose during the Second World War. The SS created dozens of camps and sub-camps, far more than a hundred in all, though an exact count depends on which camps are identified as free-standing camps. Along with housing political prisoners the camps also served as sites for transit of prisoner populations and in some cases as sites for extracting slave labor. Within this vast empire of suffering and exploitation, the Nazi regime also created death camps—camps that aimed at mass destruction. The distinction with other camps lay not in the mere fact of killing, but in the design for rapid and repeated murder and the use to destroy entire groups in whole or in part. All camps were dangerous and often deadly; few were death camps.

The six death camps were all located in Poland. Belzec, Treblinka, Sobibor, and Majdanek lay in the occupied General Government while Auschwitz and Chelmno were on the far eastern edge of annexed western Poland. Even among the death camps there were significant variations. Auschwitz, the largest, was a death camp but more than a death camp. Auschwitz was actually a vast camp complex, a kind of macabre city comprised of an array of labor sites and main camp as well as an extermination center at Birkenau. The very fact that Auschwitz was both an efficient killing center and a labor camp complex accounts in part for its lasting notoriety. By numbers, the largest number of Jews were murdered at this camp, but as a labor camp complex Auschwitz was also the unwelcome home for a high proportion of all death camp survivors, though inmates at any camp, most definitely including Auschwitz faced long odds on survival. The Chelmno death camp to the north started operation in December 1941 and served chiefly as a killing site for Jews of annexed western Poland. Majdanek, like Auschwitz, served multiple functions, as a site for murder, forced labor, and for detention.

The remaining three camps, Belzec, Treblinka, and Sobibor were linked together as the killing centers for the Jews of the General Government of Poland, the largest single concentration of Jews under German rule, though Sobibor was also the final destination for some Jews from Western Europe. Where prisoners at Auschwitz worked on a variety of labor projects, including a vast never completed program to produce synthetic rubber, prisoners in almost all cases arrived at Belzec, Treblinka, and Sobibor to die. Constant selections to determine who could still work made the odds of survival at Auschwitz very long, but with the exception of small numbers selected to work directly on camp upkeep, Belzec, Treblinka, and Sobibor sent all others directly to the gas chambers. With no need for barracks to house or feed any large number of slave laborers, Treblinka, Belzec, and Sobibor were therefore very compact: Belzec measured less than 20 acres in area.

Camps made use of deception to seek to calm prisoners and ease the work of killing. Treblinka provided an extreme case. Arriving at Treblinka, Jews saw features to be expected at a normal train station. There were signs for buying tickets and for a waiting room. A fake schedule provided the times for the trains said to be leaving for other destinations. A false door referred to the imaginary stationmaster. The hands on the fake clock never moved. All was designed to calm arriving Jews during the short time before their murder.

Auschwitz was also distinct in the precise killing agent. Where other death camps typically killed prisoners with carbon monoxide, Rudolf Höss, Commandant of Auschwitz, opted for a different deadly gas. The chemical Zyklon B, a form of hydrogen cyanide, provided a rapid means for murder when the chemical fumigant stored in pellet form was dropped and released into the gas chamber. The killing agent was piloted in murders of Soviet prisoners of war and then employed to kill Jews.

The killing swiftly accelerated at the death camps during 1942. Massacres carried out through mass shootings never ceased entirely: Germans periodically turned to these tried and true killing methods to compensate for interruptions to transit or to search for Jews hiding in forests, but the death camps contributed to a spike in killing in 1942. In that year a vast killing operation carried out at Treblinka, Belzec, and Sobibor annihilated the overwhelming majority of all Jews of the General Government of Poland. The enterprise was named Operation Reinhard, possibly in honor of Reinhard Heydrich who died of wounds in June after an attack by Czech partisans in late May 1941. This killing spree murdered some 1.7 million Jews. Within months the staff at the Treblinka killing center, for example, murdered most of the Jews of Warsaw, up to that point the largest single Jewish community in Europe. Between July 23 and August 28 at the peak of the killing 245,000 Jews were deported from Warsaw and the Warsaw district to Treblinka and another 67,500 were deported from elsewhere in the General Government. Most deportations from the General Government had been completed by November 1942, with a small remnant of Jews left for the time being for forced labor.

With so many Jews from the largest Jewish communities already murdered, the killing could not continue at the same rate after 1942. The number of Jews murdered per year dropped simply because there were not as many Jews left in any single place to kill—those Polish Jews who survived at forced labor at Auschwitz counted among the prisoners who had survived the longest. However, mass destruction continued with the deportation and murder of Jews from throughout Europe. Deportations, for example, began from both France and the Netherlands in 1942 and continued until 1944 (Figure 4.1). Dutch Jews were sent to Auschwitz, Sobibor, and some were also sent to the transit camp of Theresienstadt or to the camp of Bergen Belsen in Germany. Deportations from Germany itself began in 1941, though at first some were merely warehoused in ghettos in the east, but most German Jews were deported by the end of 1942, and by June 1943 Germany was declared "Jew Free," though some remained in mixed marriages.

In 1944 the largest single Jewish community surviving up to that point, the Jews of Hungary, suffered deportation to Auschwitz. Up to 1944, Admiral Horthy who oversaw a conservative authoritarian government as Hungary's "regent" allied with Germany in the war but declined to deport Hungarian Jews. However, the breakdown of Horthy's alliance with Nazi Germany did away with any measure of protection of Hungary's Jews. When Horthy, recognizing that the Soviets were going to defeat Nazi Germany, tried to extricate

FIGURE 4.1 *Arrival of Jews at the Westerbork transit camp. The Netherlands, 1942.*

United States Holocaust Memorial Museum, courtesy of Trudi Gidan.

Hungary from the war, Germany occupied the country in March 1944, and when Horthy proclaimed a cease-fire in October 1944 the Germans promoted a coup by the Hungarian fascist movement, the Arrow Cross. During spring and early summer of 1944 Adolf Eichmann organized deportations of Hungarian Jews. The arrival of more than 400,000 swelled the population of Jews at Auschwitz one last time before selections decimated the camp's population yet again.

With the approach of the advancing Soviet army in the east the days of the death camps were numbered. Germans dismantled the Operation Reinhard death camps and tried to cover up the evidence, and an SS commando under Paul Blobel sought to further hide evidence of killing by digging up mass graves at sites such as Babi Yar and burning bodies, but the sheer scale of killing as well as the effort by desperate peasants to dig up anything of potential value made these efforts of no avail when it came to truly hiding the reality of genocide. Even without death camps, however, genocide continued into 1945 until Germany's total defeat.

ANNE FRANK'S LAST MONTHS

Toward the end of the war, prisoners were shifted between camps as in the tragic case of the killing of Anne Frank. After her family's hiding place was betrayed to German occupying authorities in the Netherlands in August of 1944, Anne Frank was taken to the Dutch transit camp of Westerbork in 1944. She was taken along with her sister Margot and mother Edith to Auschwitz. Ann and Margot were then transferred to Bergen Belsen in October of 1944. Edith Frank died at Auschwitz in January of 1945, and Anne and Margot Frank died of typhus at Bergen Belsen in March of 1945. Witnesses from Bergen Belsen told of the girls' suffering from the cold and from typhus. Anne died only a few weeks before British soldiers arrived at the camp on April 15 where they found a camp full of prisoners suffering from disease and starvation along with many thousands of corpses. Otto Frank, sent to a separate men's camp at Auschwitz survived until he was liberated by Soviet troops.

Death marches

The final act in the history of the death camps came with executions and death marches in which prisoners who had survived up to that point were forced to trek west to what remained of Germany. Accompanying guards shot many. In many cases, nothing is known for certain of the final moments of prisoners who vanished from the face of the earth. Primo Levi, an Italian Jew who survived Auschwitz as a laborer in the Buna forced labor camp told of how his fellow Italian prisoner Alberto suffered this fate. Recalling his friend, Levi writes, "We were inseparable: we were 'the two Italian' and foreigners even mistook our names. For six months we had shared a bunk and every scrap of food. . . ." Levi, ill, remained at the camp and survived, escaping what awaited others. "Almost in their entirely they vanished during the evacuation march: Alberto was among them."

Those who survived the death marches were then packed into ever-more crowded concentration camps in the dwindling area under German control. Here, they died of famine and disease until liberation came with the arrival of allied troops, and even then many were too weakened and depleted to survive. The death marches stand out as evidence of determination to exterminate Jews because by this time it was increasingly obvious that Germany was going to lose the war. The Holocaust ended, therefore, only with complete German surrender.

Regions of genocide: Galicia, Bessarabia, Berlin, Salonica

As in other genocides, there were regional differences in the Holocaust. The drive to destroy Jews stemmed first and foremost from the Nazi hierarchy, but in pursuing a "Final Solution" Germans interacted with local authorities. German power took many forms, ranging from occupation zones such as in the General Government in central Poland to alliances with states such as Hungary that hoped to make gains from an expected German victory. Differences in the proportion of Jews who survived showed the importance of regional conditions. Jews suffered everywhere in occupied Europe, but they did not all face the same likelihood of death.

A much higher proportion of Jews, for example, died in the Netherlands than in France. More than 100,000 or some 75 percent of the 140,000 Jews in the Netherlands died, while some 75,000 or 20 percent of the Jews in France died. Such differences cannot be explained entirely by the response of local police to occupation. Vichy, the collaborationist government created in central and southern France at times deported Jews—especially foreign Jews, but there was no Dutch equivalent to Vichy. Geography and the pattern of distribution of Jews also influenced the chances of survival. The concentration of Jews in Amsterdam made it easier to round up Jews in the Netherlands. In contrast, Jews in France were scattered over a much larger area.

The very concept of a "Final Solution" ignored the variety of Jews in Europe. In the east the death squads and death camps eradicated Jewish communities from cities and from numerous small towns known by the Yiddish term Shtetl that dotted the landscape in rural areas in Poland, but the Jewish population in Galicia, a region held by Austria-Hungary up until the First World War, also included farmers and landowners. Eastern Galicia after the Great War made up southeastern Poland. Germany turned it into part of the General

Government. Killing of Galicia's Jews started earlier than elsewhere in the General Government. Einsatzgruppe C, assisted by Ukrainian militia and in some cases by German soldiers carried out massacres of Jews in July 1941, but there was no immediate counterpart to the sustained killing spree carried out by the Einsatzgruppen in regions such as Lithuania. Instead Galicia's German authorities oscillated between mass shootings, exploiting Jews for forced labor, and setting up ghettos. In 1942, occupation authorities, including Friedrich Katzmann, SS General and Police leader, initiated large-scale deportations of Jews to Belzec. Work ghettos remained, but in 1943 Germans carried out numerous massacres of the dwindling Jewish population. In the final stages of the Holocaust in Galicia, police in 1943 carried out relentless sweeps to seek out and kill Jews in hiding in the district. Katzmann complained of the Jews who tried to flee or hide in underground bunkers.

Within Eastern Europe, the Holocaust took a distinct form in areas controlled by German allies. Romania, Hungary, and Bulgaria cast their support behind Germany (though in Bulgaria's case in more limited fashion) in hopes of gaining favorable territorial adjustments for their efforts, and all three countries displayed varying degrees of ambivalence toward genocide. In contrast, a puppet state in Croatia led by a Fascist movement named the Ustasha demonstrated zeal for killing, but these other German allies generally proved slow to deport their own Jewish populations. Such foot dragging did not prove support for equal treatment of Jews: Hungary and Romania both instituted their own anti-Jewish laws and regulations. However, growing anxiety that they had chosen the wrong side in the war and some level of concern about the actual eradication of their own Jews gave leaders pause about taking part in the "Final Solution."

To stop short of genocide of core Jewish populations did not however prevent genocide for Romania, which carried out ethnic cleansing and extermination in disputed border regions, most notably the area of Bessarabia between the Prut and Dniester Rivers—today the region lies mostly in Moldavia with some sections in Ukraine. Romania gained Bessarabia after the First World War with the collapse of the Russian Empire, but in 1940 the Soviet Union seized the area. Romanian troops reentered Bessarabia in June 1941 as they joined in the German invasion of the USSR. Here, they took part in genocide. The killing started just across the border from Bessarabia as Romanian soldiers, police, and civilians, along with Germans, murdered Jews in a pogrom in the city of Iasi, claiming that the town's Jews were assisting Soviet forces. Posters plastered to walls encouraged residents to join in the pogrom, and soldiers and civilians murdered Jews.

Crossing into Bessarabia, Romanian forces continued to massacre Jews. They forced survivors into temporary ghettos. The Romanian Government also sought to push all remaining Jews out of Bessarabia through a policy called "ground cleansing" by forcing them out of the region entirely to the east. Initially, Romania lacked any such final destination for ethnic cleansing of Bessarabian Jews, but the German award of a strip of territory along the banks of the Dniester, dubbed Transnistria, provided just such a location. Romanian forces drove Jews east as onlookers took part in plunder. Recurrent mocking cries of "Palestine" served as a signal to Jews to get out. Those who survived massacres en route struggled to endure lack of food, disease, and exposure during the harsh winter of 1941-2. This pattern of ethnic cleansing that served genocidal ends recalled the Armenian Genocide more than any other phase of the Holocaust, though where Armenians pushed into the deserts of Syria and Mesopotamia suffered from disease and famine amidst extreme heat, Jews in Transnistria perished from systematic mistreatment amidst severe winter cold. German death squads killed Jews as well.

Even at the very core of German power, the Holocaust remained a more complex process than talk of a single "Final Solution" suggested. As early as August 1941 Minister of Propaganda Joseph Goebbels recorded that Hitler had "promised me that the Jews will be deported from Berlin to the east as soon as possible, once the first transport opportunity arises." In September, Goebbels added, "the first towns to be free of Jew free will be Berlin, Vienna, and Prague. Berlin will be first. . . ."[11] In reality, ridding Berlin of all Jews took longer than anticipated. Transports from Berlin to ghettos in the east began in 1941.—the first left for the Lodz Ghetto on October 18. While some Jews in eastern ghettos resented newcomers, Sierakowiak was complementary, writing "It's really a pleasure to be among them."[12] The actual killing of Jews deported east from Germany proceeded in fits and starts, suggesting that there was as yet no overall decision about their fate in the Fall of 1941. On November 30, Jews arriving in Riga on a train from Berlin were murdered, but other transports were sent to ghettos while some Jews were shot in small groups. In 1942 transports began to take Berlin's Jews to death camps. As late as February 1943, more than 35,000 Jews surprisingly still resided in Berlin; they included Jews deployed for labor. A large action carried out by SS, Gestapo, and police then rounded up those Jews who had previously worked for industry, and deportations to Auschwitz followed, though many Berlin Jews first passed through the transit camp at Theresienstadt. On May 19 Goebbels declared Berlin "free of Jews," and an official declaration of June 19 repeated the claim.

The Holocaust attacked not only European Jews but their distinctive cultures, through the destruction of books, schools, and cultural, civic, and religious institutions. The largest number of victims came from the Ashkenazi Jews, many of whom spoke Yiddish as a language of everyday life in Eastern Europe, but in areas such as southeastern Europe German occupation also targeted Sephardic Jewish communities for destruction. One of the most remarkable and distinctive of all the Jewish communities of Spanish origin was located in the Greek port of Salonica. As recently as the late nineteenth century, Jews speaking Ladino, a dialect of Spanish had constituted the largest single population group in Salonica. A visitor to Salonica at the time would therefore be more likely to hear Ladino than Greek. Their influence dwindled in the twentieth century as Thessaloniki, as the city is now known, became increasingly Greek, but they still made up a large minority when Germany invaded Greece in 1941. In 1942, male Jews in Salonica were sent to forced labor, and beginning in March of 1943 some 48,000 Jews were deported. At Auschwitz, they left an indelible impression on Primo Levi who commented on their solidarity, vigor, and cunning, but most died. Here, the Holocaust brought destruction both of a population and of its culture.

Perpetrators

Though the Holocaust is the single best known case of genocide, its perpetrators are often identified vaguely: commonly used terms such as Nazi or German lack precision. To speak of Nazis as responsible for the Holocaust explains little in that there were millions of Nazi Party members. The Nazi party espoused radical anti-Semitism, and party members worked to advance "solutions" to the Jewish question, but not all perpetrators were literally Nazis.

Indeed, blaming the Holocaust solely on "Nazis" can serve to mask the participation of others in rounding up, deporting, and killing Jews. To describe perpetrators simply as German is no more precise. German expansion drove planning for ridding Europe of Jews and enabled genocide, but perpetrators were not always German. Described simply by nationality or ethnicity, perpetrators came from across much of Europe.

SS and SD

Among perpetrators, some took on core tasks in initiating and carrying out genocide while, at another extreme, some became involved without a great deal of prior knowledge or forethought. Of all institutions, the inner core of perpetrators was most closely linked to the SS and SD. SS, along with security police, furnished personnel for Einsatzgruppen, and the Death's Head units. Led by Theodore Eicke, the Death's Head named for their symbol which they wore on their lapels, staffed concentration camps.

SS General Reinhard Heydrich, until his death in 1942 also led the Security Service or SD as well as the Reich Security Main Office (RSHA). The RSHA linked together normal police branches, or criminal police, with the Gestapo or political police, and the SD. The RSHA oversaw numerous terror functions and took on a key part in organizing the Holocaust. The RSHA, for example, organized the Einsatzgruppen and planned deportations.

The basic truth that SS and SD members were directly involved in all stages of planning and executing the destruction of European Jews neither fully identifies perpetrators nor their motives. As the SS Reichsführer Heinrich Himmler won numerous internal power struggles, personnel under SS command mushroomed to include some quarter of a million by the outset of war, including the German criminal police.

SS staff who were directly involved in carrying out the Holocaust proceeded for different combinations of reasons. While the actions of some support popular images of the SS as a home for the violent and depraved, others organized and carried out extraordinary violence including acts of genocide for ordinary motives. Men eager to advance killing certainly fell into the inner core of SS perpetrators. Christian Wirth, for example, compiled a long career of murder and according to all accounts adapted easily to his role. He worked at the T4 forced euthanasia program and then gained posts as Commandant of Belzec and as Inspector General of the Operation Reinhard camps. He personally shot victims, and whipped Ukrainian guardsmen. Another perpetrator testified that Wirth "was pitiless, and one could easily imagine him capable of shooting a subordinate on the spot."[13] Wirth's nicknames included "Christian the Terrible" and "Stuka" after the German dive bomber.

In other cases, such as that of Franz Stangl, careerist motives blended with ideological goals. Born in Austria Franz Stangl crossed paths with Wirth in the T4 program and worked under Wirth at the Hartheim forced euthanasia killing center. He became Commandant of Sobibor in April 1942 and then of Treblinka in August 1942. Stangl later gave an unusually detailed account of his actions and motives when the journalist Gitta Sereny interviewed him in 1971 after he was extradited from Brazil and convicted to life in prison in West Germany. Stangl depicted his death camp post as yet another job to advance his career. "That was my profession. I enjoyed it. It fulfilled me. And yes, I was ambitious about that, I won't deny it." He sought to distance himself from his victims, dehumanizing them as an indistinguishable mass. "They were cargo. I think it started the day I first saw the Totenlager (extermination area) in Treblinka. I remember Wirth standing there, next to the pits full of blue-black corpses. It had nothing to do with humanity—it could not have. It was a mass—a mass of rotting flesh. . . . I rarely saw them as individuals. It was always a huge mass."[14]

The pursuit of efficiency in killing emerged as a motive in the murderous career of Rudolf Höss, Commandant of Auschwitz. Höss in prison in Poland in 1946 contrasted mass shootings with gassings, which had "a calming effect on me." Employing Zyklon B as the killing agent further advanced the goal of efficient killing. Called as a witness at the Nurember trials, Höss told of the improvements in killing achieved at Auschwitz.

Adolf Eichmann who was captured after the war by Israeli agents came to epitomize bureaucratic elements of the Holocaust. After the Anschluss he led efforts to force Jews to emigrate from Austria. During the Holocaust, he oversaw deportation of Jews from much of Europe. The writer and philosopher Hannah Arendt, a German Jew who escaped Germany and occupied Europe only in 1941, wrote an account of Eichmann's trial, in which she depicted him as a perpetrator who killed mainly to fulfill his bureaucratic tasks and advance in his career. Eichmann, himself claimed that he was following orders-a defense that failed in this case as in others.

Police forces and soldiers

The ranks of perpetrators extended far beyond any inner core of SS and SD personnel: men like Himmler, Heydrich, Wirth, Stangl, and Höss did not carry out the Holocaust alone. It was obvious to the leading architects of death, themselves, that they required resources and assistance, often extending far beyond the SS, SD, and Security Police to achieve their destructive aims. In a memo on the "Solution of the Jewish Question in Galicia" SS and Police Leader Friedrich Katzmann referred to continuing actions by security police, Order Police, Gendarmes, and the Ukrainian police.[15]

Police forces, local and German, took part in rounding up Jews all over Europe. In France, for example, police rounded up Jews. Under German pressure, police collected 22,000 Jews in the region of Paris in July 1942. At least some policemen showed awareness of the tragedy. Annie Kriegel, a 15-year-old, who would later become an historian, recalled a policeman "who was carrying a suitcase in each hand and crying," though other officers, apparently more ready to take to the task at hand broke down doors and searched for Jews.[16] In 1942, French police in the unoccupied zone or Vichy also began to expel Jews, at first targeting those who had entered the country after 1936. In southwestern France in Bordeaux, Maurice Papon, then a secretary general in the Bordeaux Prefecture, signed deportation orders, though he later managed to cast himself as a supporter of resistance and went on to a long and successful postwar career before he was tried and convicted in 1998 of crimes against humanity after a long and drawn-out legal process.

In ghettos of the east, Jewish police also took part in rounding up Jews to be deported. Their actions furnished evidence of what Primo Levi described in a different setting as the "gray zone." We tend to think of perpetrators, victims, and bystanders as distinct, but the boundaries between these positions could and did blur. The ghetto elders and their administrations were in no way responsible for the Holocaust, but Jews who survived for any stretch of time in ghettos or camps soon found distinctions and differences in power and privilege and some, like Dawid Sierakowiak, came to deeply resent the role of Jewish police. He described the roundup at Lodz on September 5, 1942. Accompanied by doctors, nurses, and firemen "policemen entered our building completely unexpectedly. They had lists with the names of the tenants in every apartment."[17]

Where Jewish police took part in roundups in ghettos, other police forces moved from rounding up Jews where they lived to guarding Jews during transit and sometimes to actual murder. German perpetrators included members of police units far removed from the Security Policy. The Order Police, or Orpo, a reserve police force, provided an especially important pool of manpower for helping to carry out the Holocaust. The order or reserve police were civilians who trained for call-up in case of need. Precisely because they were not elite forces, they were available for tasks that required far less military expertise than frontline combat. Order Police rounded up Jews in Poland and elsewhere, including Amsterdam. They guarded ghetto walls at Warsaw and Riga, and on occasion they killed Jews. Even at the height of Operation Reinhard, breakdowns in transport caused interruptions in the killing process, and temporary resumption of mobile killing. In such circumstances, the Order Police were available to shoot Jews.

The ranks of perpetrators extended far beyond any narrow inner circle during the second sweep of Jews in occupied Soviet territories and during operations to round up scattered remaining Jews and Jews in hiding. The Order Police took on important roles in killings through 1942 during the second sweep. German police assisted by even larger numbers of local collaborators and local auxiliaries wiped out temporary ghettos during this period. During the last phases of the Holocaust the Order Police took part in sweeps through the countryside to hunt down Jews in hiding and complete the Final Solution. They also accompanied Jews west on death marches during the last stages of the war.

Along with police, some German soldiers assisted at times with the Holocaust. Their numbers cannot be quantified as a percentage of the German army, but soldiers from the army or Wehrmacht took part in killing Jews during the invasion of Soviet Union in regions including Belarus. Orders to kill partisans and reprisals for partisan attacks provided another route by which the work of the regular military shaded into mass murder of civilians.

Motives

The very diversity of perpetrators suggests that they acted for varied motives. Much of the research into perpetrators' motives has focused on the extent to which ideology motivated them to kill. In a climate where Germans were bombarded with propaganda, anti-Semitism was an obvious possible motive. In practice hatred of Jews, though open and highly radical and vitriolic, also did not form the chief propaganda theme. Still, German propaganda identified Jews with a war against Communism and a war to defend Germany against a threat posed by a Jewish, Communist, Soviet, and sometimes Asiatic enemy. This theme of defending Germany gained increasing importance within German propaganda. It distorted reality, by reversing cause and effect: German forces struggled to defend Germany only because Germany had launched a war of aggression and extermination.

It is difficult to calculate the exact response to wartime propaganda, but at the very least immersion in a highly-anti-Semitic society eased the path to complicity and to outright killing. German personnel on the Eastern Front, and German visitors to ghettos described Jews as filthy, again leaving out German responsibility for increasing deprivation that produced the very conditions that contributed to overcrowding and disease. The more perpetrators adopted such language of Jewish filth, the more easily they could equate murder with a kind of "cleansing."

Along with anti-Semitism, more ordinary motives, also contributed to extraordinary acts of violence against Jews. The seizure of Jews' property and possessions provided economic and material gains for wide circles of Germans, ranging from German settlers in the east to broader circles of Germans living with in the prewar borders. Careerist motives also gave incentives for SS men who aimed to do well in their jobs. Conformity to the group created pressure to fit in by contributing to the work of rounding up, guarding, holding, and even killing Jews. It must be stressed that threats of punishment did not drive the Holocaust forward. Germans did not kill Jews because they would be executed by German authorities if they did not join in murdering Jews. Indeed, the one motive for killing during the Holocaust that seems to vanish on close examination is threat or fear of execution. "Quite simply in the past forty-five years," the historian Christopher Browning wrote in 1992, "no defense attorney or defendant in any of the hundreds of postwar trials has been able to document a single case in which refusal to obey an order to kill unarmed civilians resulted in the allegedly inevitable dire punishment."[18]

Bystanders

Information

Bystanders within Europe, those who lived alongside the Holocaust, outnumbered both perpetrators and victims. Residents of towns and villages closer to the epicenters of killing were certainly more likely on average to be informed about ongoing genocide than bystanders in regions more removed from the sites of massacres and death camps. Proximity whether to concentration camps, train lines traversed by rail cars carrying Jews east, or to actual death camps brought greater knowledge of particular phases of the Holocaust. Guards at concentration camps in Germany and Austria let versions of reality slip out on occasion to civilians in nearby towns. The Operation Reinhard Death Camps were comparatively small and secluded, but Polish peasants witnessed transports, roundups, and hunts for Jews in hiding.

To quantify bystanders' level of knowledge let alone the percentage of bystanders who knew of the Holocaust is impossible, but information was available, for example, even within Nazi Germany. The fact that Jews were deported from German towns and cities was obvious: witnesses to their removal abounded, and there were also abundant witnesses to the transport of Jews on trains. Information about actual killing of Jews reached Germans via several routes. News of massacres carried out in the open filtered back to Germany through comments by soldiers on leave, and those killings were also common knowledge among many in the areas where the shootings took place. Reports of mass murder of Jews in the east were picked up by the English and American press, and, in turn, the BBC German service transmitted news of the killings back to Germany. Individual Germans clearly knew of the mass killing of Jews. The White Rose, a resistance movement founded by students and their friends in Munich, spoke of the horrors in a pamphlet.

Their second pamphlet referred to "the fact that since the conquest of Poland three hundred thousand Jews have been murdered in this country in the most bestial way." Other Germans, including men and women with no obvious expertise or special source of information, spoke of the killing of even larger numbers. Specific knowledge of murder of Jews in gas chambers in particular death camps was harder to come by, but a version of the reality emerged in the form of rumors about killings by gas in wagons or tunnels. As in many other cases, the individual's attitude toward information counted for a great deal: even without any special expertise or high-level sources, those Germans who wished to scrutinize what they did know came to accurate conclusions.

Some significant proportion of Germans could claim to have not known about the Holocaust, but even that lack of detailed specific knowledge about the extermination of Jews did not necessarily equate to total ignorance. Fears of revenge after the German defeat at the battle of Stalingrad in early 1943 drew on a sense that Germans had killed Jews on a massive scale in the east. Even where Nazi propaganda shaped responses to the war's events such as when Germans attributed bombing in some way to international Jews, these myths at their core grew out of the understanding, often half-stated, that Germans had carried out extraordinary violence against Jews.

Gray zone

Most bystanders in the end took little action of any sort with regard to the Holocaust, but ignorance and passivity could blend into forms of complicity. Reports by the SD on the German public indicate that open and intense persecution by no means met with uniform approval among the public. However, the fact that Aryans profited from the seizure of Jews' homes and businesses provided incentive not to think too carefully about Jews' fate.

To be a bystander was not to always remain one: bystanders like others could find themselves in a gray zone. They could also shift into entirely different modes, either directly aiding in deportation or shifting into a stance of resistance and opposition. Jews also learned that bystanders could pose a threat to survival. The librarian Herman Kruk who kept a diary on events in the Vilna Ghetto described the growing danger from those he termed "snatchers." Soon after Vilna fell the snatchers began to seize Jews.

"Groups of Snatchers wander around the streets and courtyards, snatch men wherever they can, and drag them off."[19] Bystanders also aided Germans in killing. German forces seeking to complete the "Final Solution" by hunting down Jews in hiding enlisted the help of Polish peasants, paying for tips on the location of Jews with small gifts of food. Thus, Order Police pursuing Jews in the countryside relied on Poles to locate Jews. Opportunism again provided motive for complicity.

Rescue

At another extreme some apparent bystanders became rescuers. Efforts to rescue Jews could involve careful organization, but some bystanders became rescuers almost on the spur of the moment when they confronted a Jew in need. The accounts of rescues compiled by Yad Vashem, the Israeli memorial to the Shoah or Holocaust, in a listing of Righteous among Nations provide striking example of both heroism and tragedy. Szmuel and Josef Liderman, for example, were brothers who escaped execution twice in September 1942 in the region of Volhynia. They arrived destitute at the house of a farmer named Stanislaw Jasinski in the middle of a forest. Jasinski had known the brothers' father though he had not been a friend. Jasinski let the Liderman brothers hide on his farm and his daughter Emilia helped feed them. Jasinski took in two more Jews who had escaped massacre, but the four Jews had to leave because of rumors that they were hiding at the farm: tragically all except Szmuel were later killed by Ukrainian nationalists.[20]

In Western Europe as well, bystanders displayed a similar wide range of behavior all the way from acts that verged on complicity to acts that shifted toward a stance of resistance. Vichy France had its own anti-Semitic laws and the shock of defeat left the public stunned. Over time however, it took increasing effort to round up and hunt down Jews in France. If this cannot be taken as clear evidence of widespread active support for rescue, the difficulties SS, German police, and their auxiliaries encountered on some occasions in finding Jews suggested that the French public was becoming increasingly less willing to actively help round up Jews. Some, including in the case of the small village of Le Chambon-sur-Lignon, the entire community, ceased to be bystanders. The Pastor André Trocmé encouraged the members of his Protestant congregation to shelter Jews.

Rescuers came from all across occupied Europe. The award of the honor Righteous Among the Nations cannot give a complete listing of all cases of help for Jews, but still shows the efforts of rescuers from across occupied Europe. The largest single number came from Poland, but Poland also had the largest Jewish population. Denmark provided the most effective example of rescue measured in terms of percentage of Jewish survivors, but the position of Jews in Denmark was also very different than in Poland. German occupation was initially less harsh in Denmark than elsewhere, mainly because the occupiers viewed the Danes as Germanic and hoped to win them over for their cause. As Danes generally declined to join the German cause, occupation took a turn toward more severe measures especially after the King of Denmark in 1942 showed little interest in birthday greetings from Hitler. In late September 1943, alerted to imminent plans to deport Danish Jews, Danes rescued some 7,200 Jews, the vast majority of the country's small Jewish population of approximately 8,000. Proximity to neutral Sweden helped in that Danish fisherman could ferry Jews out. Some 500 Jews were deported but most of these were rescued as well with the help of intercession by Danish officials.

Neutrals and Allies

The concept of bystanders has also been applied to citizens of neutral countries and to the allies. The greater the distance, the more questionable it is to speak of merely standing by during the destruction of Europe's Jews, but the very fact that some information about killing became available outside Europe raises scrutiny of the allied response. The escape of four prisoners from Auschwitz in the Spring of 1944 only added to that information. Here again, the availability of information did not ensure that it was widely known or fully grasped or understood.

The allies were not entirely silent about the fate of the Jews. An Inter-Allied Declaration of December 17, 1942 charged Germany with a "bestial policy of cold-blooded extermination" of European Jews. There is no evidence that the allies could have rescued most Jews and only allied victory ended the Holocaust, but debate has raged over the question of whether the allies did their utmost to rescue. The US Assistant Secretary of War, John McCloy, for example, rejected calls by Jewish organizations to bomb rail lines leading into Auschwitz. Such a plan, he stated, "could be executed only by the diversion of considerable air support essential to the success of our forces now engaged in decisive operations."

Letter by Assistant Secretary of War John McCloy September 1944 to Mr. John W. Pehle, Executive Director, War Refugee Board

Dear Mr. Pehle:

I refer to your letter of November 8th, in which you forwarded the report of two eye-witnesses on the notorious German concentration and extermination camps of Auschwitz and Birkenau in Upper Silesia.

"The Operation Staff of the War Department has given careful consideration to your suggestion that the bombing of these camps be undertaken. In consideration of this proposal the following points were brought out:

a. Positive destruction of these camps would necessitate precision bombing, employing heavy or medium bombardment, or attack by low flying or dive bombing aircraft, preferably the latter.

b. The target is beyond the maximum range of medium bombardment, dive bombers and fighter bombers located in United Kingdom, France or Italy.

c. Use of heavy bombardment from United Kingdom bases would necessitate a hazardous round trip flight unescorted of approximately 2,000 miles over enemy territory.

d. At the present critical stage of the war in Europe, our strategic air forces are engaged in the destruction of industrial target systems vital to the dwindling war potential of the enemy, from which they should not be diverted. The positive solution to this problem is the earliest possible victory over Germany, to which end we should exert our entire means.

e. This case does not at all parallel the Amiens mission because of the location of the concentration and extermination camps and the resulting difficulties encountered in attempting to carry out the proposed bombing.

Based on the above, as well as the most uncertain, if not dangerous effect such a bombing would have on the object to be attained, the War Department has felt that it should not, at least for the present, undertake these operations."

Victims and survivors

The Holocaust stands out among many other cases of genocide for the fixed nature of victims' identity in the eyes of perpetrators. Where theories of ethnicity, nationality, race, and even to some degree gender increasingly cast all such forms of human identity as fluid, the assault against Europe's Jews cast all Jews simply as Jews: the individual had no choice in the matter. Even in the Armenian Genocide some Armenian women made their way to a new identity, typically at enormous personal cost and after great suffering, by accepting Islam, but there was no equivalent to this kind of conversion for European Jews. A few Jews pursued survival by passing as Aryans, but to become Aryan, or German was not a decision under the individual's control—indeed even such decision made in the past could be deemed irrelevant. Under the Nuremberg laws a Jew was defined as someone with three Jewish grandparents, but the conversion of any grandparents counted for nothing in determining a grandson's or granddaughter's identity.

An obsession with victims also distinguished the Holocaust among European genocides when it came to expanding and extending the area to be purified through murder. Where genocides often focus on eliminating a group defined as impure from a particular country or from a region identified by perpetrators as their national or racial homeland, ridding Germany of all Jews was not sufficient for the Holocaust's perpetrators. Ethnic war that followed the First World War in eastern Anatolia and Transcaucasia saw violent attacks against groups of civilians spill over the boundaries of fledgling states and collapsing empires, but in no other twentieth-century European genocide did perpetrators strive so consistently to kill an entire group far beyond the borders of the perpetrators' own nation-state. Thus, the declaration that Germany was "Jew free" had no effect on the Holocaust elsewhere in Europe.

Facing deportation

Increasingly isolated and impoverished, Jews lived with growing dread before deportation. A vast series of anti-Semitic measures in all things large and small deprived Jews of the possibility of making a living, stripped away their remaining property, and subjected them to an endless array of humiliations. The requirement to wear a Yellow Star or other similar marker struck many as most offensive and shocking, but discrimination extended to all manner of other activities, ranging from owning a pet to speaking on a public telephone.

Whether in ghettos in Poland, in Jews' houses in Germany, or elsewhere Jews struggled to piece together information about the war: with all restrictions they knew full well that it was going badly, though some still expected an eventual German defeat. As in the case of bystanders, Jews' knowledge of the unfolding Holocaust was patchy and imperfect. Jews far removed from Poland did not by and large know of the operation of the death camps, but they increasingly regarded transport east as a virtual death sentence. Deportations from Germany generated suicides: Martha Liebermann, the widow of the renowned German painter Max Liebermann, was one of thousands of Jews to commit suicide—her husband had died of natural causes in 1935.

KNOWLEDGE OF DEATH CAMPS: WARSAW GHETTO

Jews living in ghettos came to realize the common fate they all shared at different dates. In the Warsaw Ghetto rumors of deportation preceded the actual start of deportations in late July 1942, but the ghetto's Jews did not initially know where they would be sent. Warsaw's Jews also debated the nature of these transports. Precisely because Jews from other areas, including some from as far away as Czechoslovakia and Germany had already been sent to Warsaw, some of Warsaw's Jews reasoned that they too would experience a similar transfer and simply be sent somewhere else. However, glimpses of fragments of a darker future were already providing a more accurate picture. News that 40,000 Jews from Lublin had vanished off the earth raised the obvious question of what could possibly have happened to them, and grave-diggers who had escaped from Chelmno told of gassing. Some of Warsaw's Jews had already predicted mass death awaited them before Germans actually initiated transports from Poland's largest ghetto. Chaim Kaplan wrote in his diary of a friend who declared as early as June, "All of you are already condemned to die, only the date of execution has yet to be set."[21] Adam Czerniakow, the head of the Jewish council, killed himself on July 23 without leaving any note giving the exact reasons why he took poison, but he had learned only the previous day that all Jews would be deported east. German authorities sought to mask their deadly plans with deception. A ruse by which some Jews transported to Treblinka sent letters back just before they were killed calmed and pacified others. Offerings of 3 kilograms of bread and 1 kilogram of marmalade for those who turned up voluntarily for transport at late July gave further incentive to hope for the best. Still, the ghetto's dwindling remnant of Jews increasingly learned the truth about what awaited at Treblinka. Many did not believe the misleading letters: they pressed to find work in hopes that "productive" employment could stave off deportation or tried to go into hiding. Toward the end of his final diary entry on the day of his death Czerniakow remarked, "A sewing machine can save a life."[22] The Jewish labor movement the Bund dispatched an activist who could pass as an Aryan who in turn met an escapee from Treblinka, and others too carried news of the death camp, which was murdering the Jews of Warsaw at breakneck speed. A secondary school teacher named Abraham Lewin recorded the reality in his diary on August 11. At Treblinka, the people "are driven into huge barracks. For five minutes heart-rending screams are heard then silence."[23]

The possibility of escape

Jews, wherever they lived in occupied Europe, faced immense challenges in attempting to escape. A few made it over borders into neutral countries but these by no means welcomed a mass influx: Switzerland refused entrance to more than 20,000 Jews during the Second World War, though the small neutral country on Germany's border admitted others. Escape to Spain became more difficult after the fall of France. Sweden did accept the Danish-Jewish community of some 7,000, rescued suddenly in 1943. Some Jews also managed to get out of Europe via the Balkans. However, for the vast and overwhelming majority of Jews there was no safe haven.

Jews who sought to escape death by hiding within Europe confronted persistent danger. Geography was a critical factor, not just because proximity to swamps or forests might provide someplace to flee to, but also because of the connection between timing of deportations and geography. At the same time, the local views of Jews did matter: in a world where it is easy to assume that the residents of nation-states share a nationality we easily forget just how fragile and tenuous any shared national identity remained in large areas of Central and Eastern Europe, especially in regions where nationalism was new and still contested. It is easy to speak, for example, of Polish-Jews, but the term does not describe how many Poles and Jews thought of themselves. In the new or at best recently recreated state of Poland only a small majority saw themselves as Poles, and Poles and Jews were not the only groups where bonds of solidarity often frayed to the breaking point as the violence carried out by rival Polish and Ukrainian militia forces against each other in the latter years of the Second World War revealed. Poles were victims of Nazi aggression themselves and Poles in many individual cases rescued or helped to rescue Jews, but neither of these important facts can negate another reality that Jews in many cases feared hostility from Poles as well as from other peoples of Eastern Europe.

To survive in hiding depended on good fortune above all but required reserves of endurance and stamina. Rescue in peace-time connotes a sudden escape from danger, but both rescue and survival in the Holocaust were agonizingly slow. Survival might seem much like another form of suffering. Even Jews who found or met local residents willing to rescue them had to spend months and even years living in cramped quarters amidst the constant risk of detection. Raya Weberman, for example, was a young Jewish woman who, along with her father and uncle, found help from a Polish farmer named Adam Butrin. At first they lived in a hole beneath his kitchen, but as German searches continued they moved to the stables and finally to the nearby forest before returning to the pit below the stables.[24] In cities such as Warsaw or Amsterdam Jews might spend months and years in small hiding places, seeking to maintain quiet to avoid suspicion, and dependent on the aid of others to obtain food. Anne Frank along with her sister, mother, and father, lived for more than two years in hiding before being arrested and deported to Auschwitz in September 1944.

HIDDEN JEWS OF BERLIN

Jews hid during the Holocaust even at the heart of Nazi power. Declared free of Jews, Berlin was actually not entirely so. True most Jews had been deported and murdered, but even in the heart of German power there were exceptions. Some were known. Jews in mixed marriages were largely spared until their deportation was ordered in 1945. Others, despite immense obstacles and the ever present danger of falling into the sights of Jew hunters or "catchers" who collected fees for turning in Jews, survived in hiding or sought to vanish from their pasts as u-boats or submarines. Most disturbing was the fact that a few Jews, including a young woman named Stella Kübler or Goldschlag, hunted down fellow Jews as searchers for the Gestapo. Still, others found Berliners or foreign neutrals ready to hide or assist them in other ways. As many as 2,000 Jews survived in Berlin until the war's end. As bombing damaged the city, some told any inquisitive authorities that their personal papers had been destroyed.

Others hid in the open, living as Christians or Aryans. To do so in Poland they first had to escape from ghettos. Everywhere, passing as a non-Jew required gaining and then maintaining a false identity. To pass as a Pole, Jews themselves explained, it helped to possess features that seemed, a subjective judgment, to blend in with those of Poles in general. That was only the start: a Jew who sought to live as a non-Jew had to take care to avoid all manner of expressions and observe small cultural rules and habits to pass convincingly. Vladka Meed (also known as Feigele Peltel) a young Jewish woman who escaped from the ghetto to live in Christian Warsaw, described these pressures in one of the first accounts published after the Second World War. "The so-called 'Aryans,'" she explained, "had to blend with their surroundings, adopt Polish customs, habits and mannerisms, celebrate the Christian festivals, and of course go to church. They had to watch their every movement, lest it betray nervousness or unfamiliarity with the routine and weigh their very word, lest it betray a Jewish accent."[25] Finding a place to live posed another challenge. If Jews who hid in the open sometimes received aid from bystanders, they also faced the constant risk of recognition and blackmail. Memoirs and diaries of Jews in hiding refer to the stress and burden posed by the blackmailers or szmalcowniks.

Resistance

Meed was one of many Jews to move to resistance. The notion that Jews collectively chose not to resist is a myth. If some Jews shifted from their roles as victims to become complicit at some level in transmitting or carrying out German orders, others resisted. Membership in organized armed resistance, such as in the Warsaw Ghetto Uprising of 1943, proved most visible, but resistance took other forms as well in opposition to German wishes and orders. In general, organized armed resistance took place later in the Holocaust. Given German policy of exacting many deaths as punishment for partisan attacks, the prospective resister had to balance his or her determination to fight back against the likely punishment that other Jews would suffer for these acts. The high death rate in ghettos and far higher mortality in camps also worked against any efforts to organize resistance—prospective leaders might be lost to disease or selection at any time. As certainty of death increased, however, the real risks posed by organizing or fighting Germans provided less and less compelling reasons to avoid resistance. Armed resistance was also more commonplace in areas that were slipping away from German control. Jews who escaped murder in the Baltic and Russia had somewhat better chances of getting to forested regions where partisans operated, though some resistance fighters were themselves hostile and a threat to Jews.

In April and May 1943 the Jewish Fighting Organization (ZOB) in Warsaw fought back against German efforts to deport the remnant of the ghetto's Jews after the vast majority had been murdered during Operation Reinhard in 1942. Mordechai Anielewicz, the young commander—he was only 23 or 24, knew there was no chance of actual military victory, though the ghetto fighters fought for many weeks. In his last letter of April 23, he wrote, "Only a few will be able to hold out. The remainder will die sooner or later. Their fate is decided. In almost all the hiding places in which thousands are concealing themselves it is not possible to light a candle for lack of air."

Resistance in death camps typically took place as camps wound down their operations and death became increasingly likely even for the remnant of Jews set to work. Uprisings occurred at Treblinka in August 1943 and at Sobibor in October 1943: in both cases German security tracked down many but not all of those who escaped. On October 7, 1944 prisoners in the Sonderkommando at one of the Crematorium at the Auschwitz Birkenau killing center staged an uprising. At roll call they attacked the SS with axes, picks, and crowbars. The Sonderkommando at another of the Crematorium then attacked their SS guards. Primo Levi, working at the Buna Camp, saw one of the rebels hanged as an example to other prisoners. The SS tortured and killed Jewish women who had smuggled gunpowder that the Sonderkommando used to make small explosives.

Along with these cases of organized resistance late in the war, Jews also sought to resist in other ways. The historian Emmanuel Ringelblum compiled an archive of the Warsaw Ghetto to document the conditions and suffering of ghetto life. He formed a group called Oneg Shabbat that compiled a record of the ghetto along with the unfolding deportations, burying documents and images in three milk cans and metal boxes—metal boxes and two of the milk cans were discovered after the end of the Second World War. Other acts of resistance took place individually: Jews in transports east for example, might be cowed in crammed stockcars filled over capacity with hungry, thirsty civilians in a state of shock and despair, but those Jews who had some sense of what awaited them in camps to the east were sometimes very difficult to control. Guards posted on some transports east spent hours shooting virtually nonstop at Jews trying to break out of rail cars and jump off the moving trains. Deported from Lvov after working in a small labor camp Jacob Gerstenfeld-Maltiel was placed on a train headed for Belzec: as soon as the train was beyond the station, the prisoners began to jump, braving shots by Germans with machine guns on the roof top. With the "rattle of the machine gun" in the air, Gerstenfeld-Maltiel jumped out and made his want into a forest.[26]

Other victims

Nazi Germany carried out violent campaigns against other groups of victims during the Second World War. Within Germany, the Nazi regime persecuted gay men and Jehovah's Witnesses. They targeted Gypsies or Roma and Sinti for persecution across broad areas of Central and Eastern Europe. With the invasion of the east, German forces carried out violent campaigns against Polish elites and an extraordinary campaign of destruction against Soviet prisoners of war. To varying degrees, these campaigns have been identified as genocides, though the term is not uniformly applied in every case. There is also a question of terminology: should other groups of victims be described as victims of the Holocaust or is it more accurate to speak of parallel and sometimes closely related campaigns of destruction? Given differences in goals and in some cases in methods of persecution, the Holocaust most often refers to destruction of European Jews rather than to these other campaigns of violent persecution. However, there were many important connections between parallel Nazi efforts to attack specific groups.

Gypsies

The "Gypsies," a distinct ethnic group that migrated into Europe toward the end of a long sequence of migrations in the late first millennium belonged to several groups, including the Roma and the Sinti. They had endured a long pattern of suspicion and discrimination across much of Europe. Because of their place of origin, somewhere in the north of India, Gypsies could have been classified as closely related to the alleged Aryan racial elite because the actual Aryans of history were thought to have moved south into India during the ancient world, but anthropologists working in the Third Reich claimed that Gypsies had lost their racial purity by intermarrying with Asians en route to Europe.

Nazi persecution of Gypsies built on but vastly expanded on previous discrimination against Gypsies. The state of Bavaria for example, had enacted a law in 1926 for combating "Gypsies, Travelers, and the Work-shy." The Nazi state brought a much harsher crackdown. German authorities interpreted supplemental decrees to the Nuremberg laws to ban marriage between Germans and Gypsies. In 1936 the Nazi regime created a Central Office for Fighting the Gypsy Nuisance. In many cases Gypsies were forced to live in special settlements—they were pushed out of Berlin before the Olympic Games. Gypsies were often classified as "asocial," and more than 2,000 German and Austrian Gypsies described as asocial were imprisoned in concentration camps, including Buchenwald, Dachau, Mauthausen, Ravensbrück, and Sachsenhausen beginning in 1938.

In the Second World War Germany began to expel Gypsies into the General Government zone of occupation in Poland, but as in the case of Jews German authorities disputed where to place Gypsies. Gypsies were deported into ghettos, including Lodz and Warsaw. In 1941, with the invasions of the Balkans and the Soviet Union, Einsatzgruppen as well as other units began to shoot Roma and Sinti. Gypsies were also sent to a "Gypsy Family Camp" at Auschwitz in 1943. Commandant Rudolf Höss expressed a liking for the Gypsies, but oversaw their murder anyway. More than 20,000 were gassed by 1944, and Gypsies counted among those killed to make room for the last large contingent of incoming prisoners, Hungarian Jews.

Of all other groups of victims during the Second World War, Gypsies faced treatment most analogous to that of Jews during the Holocaust. To describe this destruction historians have employed the word Porajmos or devouring. The number of Gypsies killed amounted to some 200,000 or more. There were differences between the Porajmos and the Holocaust. In contrast to the "Jewish Question," Hitler was much less personally interested in a so-called Gypsy Question. In one conversation with Heydrich on October 2, 1941, Hitler talked about Gypsies as pickpockets and "plague," employing language that more closely reflected older forms of prejudice than an obsession with racial purity. But despite these differences, Nazi Germany still carried out a campaign against Gypsies that historians increasingly recognize as genocide.

Poles and Slavs

Driving east, Nazi occupation authorities, Einsatzgruppen, and the German army blurred the lines between combatants and civilians with terror and killing operations. The SS and security forces carried out tens of thousands of murders in Poland, targeting elites in an effort to weaken Polish society. The SS also killed the disabled at clinics and asylums in Poland. Ongoing German occupation was far harsher in Poland than in Western Europe, and the last stages of the war brought further devastation to Poland, including the destruction of much of Warsaw after German forces crushed the uprising of the Polish underground in 1944 and carried out mass shootings of civilians in reprisal. In all, the toll of those deliberately murdered counted in the hundreds of thousands and a total of more than 3 million non-Jewish Poles died during the war—the postwar Communist government gave out a figure of close to 6 million total wartime deaths of the residents of Poland.

Goals for Poland, as elaborated by Himmler called for eventually doing away altogether with Polish nationality. The SS Reichsführer did not expect to proceed only by killing. Rather he wished to undermine Polish nationality by breaking down the population into an "ethnic mush," taking out any components with Germanic roots, and withholding all but the very most rudimentary education from the remainder.

Invading the Soviet Union in 1941, German forces subjected still more groups to terror and in some cases to mass killing. Even before the start of Operation Barbarossa, German commanders conceived of their campaign in the Soviet Union as a war of extermination. In May 1941 General Erich Hoepner who would later be executed for participation in a plot against Hitler in 1944 stated, "... Every military action must be guided in planning and execution by an iron will to exterminate the enemy mercilessly and totally. In particular, no adherents of the present Russian-Bolshevik system are to be spared."[27] Along with massacring Jews, and executing commissars and partisans, German forces carried out mass killing of captured Soviet soldiers.

Germany carried out a systematic campaign of destruction of Soviet prisoners of war or POWS. Soviet prisoners of war were shot and hung, subjected to death marches, and provided with food at a starvation level. Daily rations in 1941 could amount to as little as 20 grams of millet and 100 grams of bread or even 100 grams of millet without bread: death was the expected outcome of such a diet kept up for any significant amount of time. As of late 1941 large proportions of all Soviet prisoners of war subjected to such mistreatment were dying in what amounted to death marches. The contrast with the First World War was striking. Slightly more than 5 percent of all Russians taken prisoner by German forces during the First World War died in captivity, but of some 5.7 million Soviet soldiers taken prisoners just under 1 million were still alive in 1945.[28] The scale of killing and the predictable outcome made the policy genocidal in all but one respect: the Genocide Convention did not clearly list the victims among the groups whose destruction amounted to genocide. However, the German mass killing of Soviet prisoners of war had a clearly genocidal quality.

Civilians in Soviet cities under German control also suffered from lack of food and hunger. Plans for the new east called for taking away Soviet food supplies. With food in short supply, occupation authorities in areas such as Ukraine and Belorussia let urban populations starve. Indeed some of the same areas previously devastated by famine in the 1930s suffered still more deaths from starvation under German occupation.

The conquest of much of the Soviet Union encouraged German plans for moving peoples on a still grander scale. A plan prepared for Himmler in 1941 by Professor Konrad Meyer foresaw expelling some 31 million people, including 16 to 20 million Poles, along with millions of Ukrainians and White Russians to the east. A revised version of this General Plan East in 1942 envisioned creating a chain of German settlements, though Himmler continued to insist on Germanization of the General Government and eventually pushing German settlements all the way to the Urals. However, completing programs that mixed ethnic cleansing with an effort to do away with many Slavic peoples awaited a final German victory that never came.

Without undertaking a program of extermination of Poles or of other Slavic peoples identical to the "Final Solution" of European Jews, Germany unleashed massive killing of Polish elites, as well as repeated killing of civilians and of Soviet prisoners of war. German plans for the future of both Poland and of the East stretching far into the Soviet Union called for ethnic cleansing on an enormous scale as well as the breakdown of unwanted national and ethnic groups. Despite references to a "Holocaust" or genocide of Poles, there is not a historical consensus that German persecution of Poles was genocide. Plans to deport Poles raised concerns among German occupation and military authorities about the possibility of labor shortages. However, even if mass killings and terror in Poland are defined as war crimes and crimes against humanity other than genocide, the Holocaust still fit into a broader project of forcibly redrawing the ethnic and racial map of occupied areas of Eastern Europe in the interests of creating an Aryan racial empire.

Communists, gay men, Jehovah's Witnesses

Within Germany itself, the Nazi regime persecuted several groups. The security and terror forces crushed political opposition, targeting Communists in particular. As the T4 program demonstrated, mass killing of civilians actually began in an effort to purify the Aryan race by eliminating those deemed to have undesirable characteristics. Nazi Germany also expanded upon and intensified punishment of German gay men or homosexuals, claiming that they weakened German masculinity and the racial community. Some 100,000 German men were punished on this basis between 1933 and 1944. From 1936 onward convicted men upon release from prison were increasingly sent to concentration camps where they were forced to wear the pink triangle. The 10,000–15,000 German men placed in concentration camps as homosexuals were subjected to harsh treatment.

Where claims of a threat to race or racial purity underlay persecution of many other groups, the Nazi regime singled out the small community of some 25,000–35,000 German Jehovah's Witnesses for their objections to oath taking and rejection of military service. In contrast to Jews and Gypsies, Jehovah's Witnesses received the option of escaping persecution by renouncing beliefs held objectionable by the state. Some 10,000 were imprisoned at some time, and more than 2,000 were sent to concentration camps.

The Holocaust and genocide

Often overlooked at the time, the Holocaust became not only the most infamous example of genocide in European history, but the best known of all cases of genocide. The massive outpouring of research confirms that the Holocaust, much like the Armenian Genocide, stemmed from no single cause or simple sequence of events. Deep-seated hatred of Jews provided the indispensable ideological basis for extermination, and more pervasive anti-Semitism helped to explain the passivity of many bystanders, but the Nazi regime seriously considered varied solutions to the "Jewish Problem." Jews under any such solution faced suffering and likely death, but there was not a single plan for genocide created far in advance of the Holocaust. The Nazi regime instituted an extraordinary sweeping series of exclusionary policies and it piloted extermination with the forced euthanasia of disabled Germans, but war still brought a further stage in radicalization.

As in the Armenian Genocide, the Holocaust also included multiple forms of genocide. The most obvious, evident both in the killings by the Einsatzgruppen and in the operation of the death camps was "killing members of the group." Other phases of the Holocaust also brought genocide through "deliberately inflicting on the group conditions of life calculated to bring about its physical destruction in whole or in part." Romania's deportations of Jews into Transnistria led to genocide by this method, and the ghettos as well, moved toward such an outcome, though the prospect of genocide through incarceration in ghettos was cut short by the more rapid killing of most ghetto residents in death camps. In contrast to the case of the Armenian Genocide, however, the Holocaust did not include any significant attempt in the case of Jews at "forcibly transferring children of the group to another group." Some Jewish children survived after being passed as Christians in orphanages or other institutions, but the racial core of Nazi ideology held that Jews were inherently contaminated and could not be remade into Germans.

Study questions

- What were the chief causes of the Holocaust, including but also extending beyond Hitler's own views and goals?

- What were the chief phases and methods of killing during the Holocaust?
- How was the Holocaust both related to but also distinct from other twentieth-century European genocides?
- What was the "gray zone" and how did boundaries between perpetrators, bystanders, and victims sometimes shift?
- What problems lie in stressing themes of survival or triumph of the "human spirit" as major themes in the history of the Holocaust?
- What were the chief obstacles to survival for Jews during the Holocaust?
- When did information about the Holocaust become known to Jews, to Germans, and to people living outside occupied Europe?

Further reading

Browning, Christopher R., *Ordinary Men: Reserve Police Battalion 101 and the Final Solution in Poland* (New York: Harper Perennial, 1993).

Dwork, Deborah and Robert Jan van Pelt, *Holocaust: A History* (New York: W. W. Norton, 2003).

Friedlander, Henry, *The Origins of the Nazi Genocide: From Euthanasia to the Final Solution* (Chapel Hill: University of North Carolina Press, 1997).

Friedlander, Saul, *The Years of Extermination: Nazi Germany and the Jews, 1939–1945* (New York: Harper Perennial, 2008).

Levi, Primo, *Survival in Auschwitz: The Nazi Assault on Humanity* (New York: Collier, 1961).

Longerich, Peter, *Holocaust: The Nazi Persecution and Murder of the Jews* (Oxford: Oxford University Press, 2010).

5

Ethnic cleansing and acts of genocide in the former Yugoslavia

In her memoir of the violent breakup of Yugoslavia, Jasmina Dervisevic-Cesic describes growing up in the late 1980s and early 1990s in the eastern Bosnian town of Visegrad. Situated at the meeting point of the Drina and Rzav Rivers, Visegrad was a town with a mixed population that included both Serbs and Bosnian Muslims, a group sometimes termed Bosniaks. Growing up Dervisevic-Cesic recalled a closely integrated community where Serbs and Bosnian Muslims lived and worked together, and her friends included both Serbs and Bosnian Muslims.

Ethnic fault lines soon opened up as Yugoslavia broke apart. On a visit to Belgrade, she saw "Chetniks everywhere," men with beards who wore insignia of the Second World War when the Chetniks had comprised a Serbian nationalist movement. Back in Visegrad demonstrations by Serbian nationalists began to shake her sense of security even near her home. With the outbreak of war in Croatia in 1991 the community began to break apart. Many Serbs left Visegrad, and Jasmina, who had just married, left the town after it was shelled and sought refuge in Bosnia's capital Sarajevo.

From Sarajevo, she learned that the Muslims of Visegrad were being expelled, and worse news followed: her father and her younger brother Samir, also known as Charlie, had not made it out with the rest of the family. Her father would be held in a camp, but Samir was killed in Visegrad. Dervisevic-Cesic recounts how her brother

Almir, Samir's twin, saw Samir taken by a man named Lukic who seized Charlie and two other boys, who were playing on the street and forced them into a car. Almir learned of Charlie's fate from the only one of the boys to survive. "Lukic and his companions took all three boys to a bridge. They threw Charlie from the bridge and shot at him on the way down, as if for target practice."[1] They killed another boy, a refugee from the town of Foca who had been taken in by Jasmina's family. They let the third boy live: obviously terrified he told them which neighbors had previously owned guns.

Milan Lukic became notorious for unleashing a reign of terror in Visegrad. In October 26, 1998, the International Criminal Tribunal for the former Yugoslavia (ICTY) at the Hague, a court established by the UN Security Council to prosecute those responsible for crimes in the wars for Yugoslavia, indicted Lukic. The indictment charged that Lukic had formed a Bosnian Serb paramilitary and spread terror. He was also charged with specific crimes, including forcing some 70 Bosnian Muslims into a house on June 14, and then, along with his associates setting it ablaze and shooting at those who tried to escape. Another charge in the indictment referred to an almost identical case of arson and murder on June 27. Lukic escaped, but in 2005 was found and arrested in Argentina and subsequently extradited. In 2009 he was found guilty of numerous crimes. The Trial Chamber convicted him of murders, as violations of crimes against humanity and crimes against the laws of war, and with one dissent found him guilty as well of "Extermination, a crime against humanity."

Milan Lukic was not charged or convicted of genocide but the indictments and convictions in his case serve to compare ethnic cleansing and genocide. Contemporaries during the wars for the former Yugoslavia referred to "ethnic cleansing," and a UN Commission of Experts described a policy of ethnic cleansing. However, the term ethnic cleansing did not appear in the judgment for Lukic because ethnic cleansing, unlike genocide, is not defined under international law. The case against Lukic presented evidence of specific crimes, such as murder. The convictions also extended beyond such acts of violence against individuals to crimes against humanity, crimes against the laws of war, and extermination or the "act of killing on a large scale."

Mass violence in the former Yugoslavia gave rise to popular usage of the term ethnic cleansing and to debate over the relationship between ethnic cleansing and genocide. Ethnic cleansing soon came to refer to campaigns of violence and intimidation designed to force a particular group to leave a place or territory. The killings carried out by Milan Lukic took place within a broader series of acts of violence that attacked Bosnian Muslims while leaving Serbs in place. Thus, the Dervisevic family and other Bosnian Muslims were terrorized into fleeing Visegrad and other areas in eastern Bosnia.

One issue with ethnic cleansing concerns the very suitability of the term. Because of the extreme violence often employed in ethnic cleansing, the term has sometimes been condemned as a euphemism for genocide. Indeed, ethnic cleansing was apparently initially employed by supporters of such cleansing operations. Cleaning, after all, can be presented as a virtuous activity. Such fears of mistaking ethnic cleansing for something benign, however, are overstated because the term ethnic cleansing soon became synonymous with violence and massive human rights abuses: it is so closely connected with the killings, rapes, and forced migration carried out in regions like Bosnia that ethnic cleansing can no longer be used to cover up killings or other violent acts.

UN COMMISSION OF EXPERTS ON ETHNIC CLEANSING

In its first interim report (S/25274), the Commission stated: "55. The expression 'ethnic cleansing' is relatively new. Considered in the context of the conflicts in the former Yugoslavia, 'ethnic cleansing' means rendering an area ethnically homogenous by using force or intimidation to remove persons of given groups from the area. 'Ethnic cleansing' is contrary to international law.

56. Based on the many reports describing the policy and practices conducted in the former Yugoslavia, 'ethnic cleansing' has been carried out by means of murder, torture, arbitrary arrest and detention, extra-judicial executions, rape and sexual assaults, confinement of civilian population in ghetto areas, forcible removal, displacement and deportation of civilian population, deliberate military attacks or threats of attacks on civilians and civilian areas, and wanton destruction of property.

Those practices constitute crimes against humanity and can be assimilated to specific war crimes. Furthermore, such acts could also fall within the meaning of the Genocide Convention.

57. The Commission is mindful of these considerations in the examination of reported allegations."

Upon examination of reported information, specific studies, and investigations, the Commission confirms its earlier view that "ethnic cleansing" is a purposeful policy designed by one ethnic or religious group to remove by violent and terror-inspiring means the civilian population of another ethnic or religious group from certain geographic areas. To a large extent, it is carried out in the name of misguided nationalism, historic grievances, and a powerful driving sense of revenge. This purpose appears to be the occupation of territory to the exclusion of the purged group or groups.

A second issue raised in connection with ethnic cleansing focuses on the question of whether ethnic cleansing is simply genocide. Ethnic cleansing is closely related to genocide and it may overlap with genocide, but it is also at times distinct from genocide. Both ethnic cleansing and genocide employ violence to pursue a goal of creating purity by removing unwanted groups. In genocide destruction of the group provides the method, but ethnic cleansing can employ other methods of forced migration. Ethnic cleansing and genocide can overlap in two respects. The first comes when the methods used to remove a group amount to destruction—this was the case in the Armenian Genocide when forced relocation was also a campaign of destruction. The second, and more complex area of overlap, comes through what the UN Genocide Convention refers to as acts of genocide. The Genocide Convention refers both to "genocide" and to "acts." Such acts committed with "intent to destroy in whole or in part, a national, ethnical, racial, or religious group as such" include "killing members of the group" but also a series of other acts. A massacre no matter how terrible might not fit the definition of an act of genocide, but a massacre carried out with intent to destroy a group could be seen as a genocidal massacre, though this then raises the complex issue of determining criteria for distinguishing between massacres and massacres that are also acts of genocide. Visegrad, for instance, was not referred to by the ICTY as the site for acts of genocide, but the Tribunal brought up acts of genocide in proceedings in other massacres, most notably the massacre of Bosnian Muslim men and boys at Srebrenica.

Toward ethnic cleansing

Ethnic and national tension in Yugoslavia

Jasmina Dervisevic-Cesic, like many other witnesses to the wars in the former Yugoslavia, recalled bewilderment as well as fear as her country began to break apart. Growing up in Visegrad, she had not paid much notice to ethnic or religious divisions. "Although some of us were Muslims and some were Serbs, we all thought of ourselves as Yugoslavians." She "didn't look at friends . . . any differently because they were Serbs."[2] Visegrad was not unusual: in many other communities Yugoslavs of different ethnic and religious backgrounds lived alongside each other, attended the same schools, and worked together. As late as 1990, a public opinion survey revealed that most respondents rated ethnic relations in the workplace and neighborhoods as either good or satisfactory.

Yugoslavia, or the country of the south Slavs, was founded after the First World War on the assumption of such unity. The country had experienced previous periods of tension between different groups of south Slavs. Conflict between Croats and Serbs shaped politics in Yugoslavia, or the Kingdom of the Serbs, Croats, and Slovenes as it was officially known until 1929, and ethnic and religious conflict intensified during the Second World War. Numerous political movements fought a kind of war for Yugoslavia within the broader war. The Ustasha, the Fascist movement whose exiled leadership had been brought back by the axis powers, engaged in widespread killing and expulsion of Serbs, as well as murder of Jews. Chetniks, Serbian monarchists and nationalists, fought the Ustasha and engaged in their own massacres of Croats as well as Bosnian Muslims who the Chetniks saw as Ustasha allies. Neither Ustasha nor Chetniks, however, won the war for Yugoslavia. Instead the Partisans, the Communist resistance, led by Marshall Tito won the bitter war for Yugoslavia and forged a postwar country that in principle united southern Slavs.

Yugoslavia was actually a complex assemblage of Slavs and other groups. Serbs, Croats, Bosnian Muslims (or Bosniaks), Slovenes, and also Macedonians (though Macedonia was itself a mix of varied groups) were indeed Slavs who could communicate with each other. The Serbo-Croatian spoken, for example, in Bosnia by Serbs, Croats, and Bosnian Muslims was a single language. Thus Bosnian Muslims like Jasmina Dervisevic-Cesic and her Serb class mates took the same lessons in the same language. There was a difference of alphabet: Croats employed a Roman alphabet and Serbs used Cyrillic. In contrast to language, religion was a main dividing line that in turn shaped ethnic identity: Slovenes and Croats were Catholic, Serbs were Orthodox, and Bosnian Muslims were obviously Muslim. In addition there were non-Slavic groups in Yugoslavia, including a significant Hungarian minority in the north of Serbia in an area called Vojvodina, as well as Jews, Roma or Gypsies, and Albanians. The Albanian population was concentrated in particular in the province of Kosovo, though there were also large numbers of Albanians in Macedonia.

Ethnic and religious tensions increased in Yugoslavia after the death of Marshall Tito in 1980. The country did not seek to replace him with a single figure but instead turned to a rotating Presidency, which gave the office in turn to the different members of a collective head of state that represented different republics and autonomous provinces. The individual republics began to drift apart as nationalist movements gained strength and support among Serbs, Croats, and others.

Rising Serb nationalism in the 1980s focused first and foremost on Kosovo rather than the sites where war would first break out in the 1990s. For Serb nationalists, Kosovo was both a site of national greatness and a place where the Serb nation faced a growing threat. Serb nationalists traced the importance of Kosovo back to the middle ages: in 1389 a Serb prince had suffered defeat at Kosovo Polje or Kosovo field at the hands of an Ottoman army. Many details of the battle were uncertain, but in memory it became a key symbol of Serb national sacrifice and persistence. Serb monasteries in Kosovo further added to the association between Kosovo and Serbian identity. A key site for Serb identity in this nationalist reading of history, Kosovo was actually predominantly Albanian. Serbia only gained the region in the First Balkan War of 1912–13, taking it from the Ottoman Empire. Serbia regained Kosovo after the First World War, but the Albanian majority only grew over time. Marshall Tito responded to the strong Albanian presence in Kosovo by making the region autonomous, but with Tito gone Serb nationalists and intellectuals drew attention to what they described as an Albanian threat to Serbs in Kosovo. Members of the Serbian Academy of Arts and Sciences drafted a *Memorandum* that saw a growing threat to Serbs' very survival in Kosovo. Officially denounced but leaked to the press, the Memorandum referred to "open and total war" against Serbs.

The nationalist ferment over Kosovo produced startling shifts in Yugoslav politics, none more so than the emergence of Slobodan Milosevic as a Serb nationalist. Milosevic was a longtime member of the League of Communists, which was officially committed to brotherhood and unity among the peoples in Yugoslavia. However, on a trip to Kosovo in 1987, Milosevic identified himself with the Serb cause. As Serbs clashed with Albanians, he declared, "No one should dare to beat you!" Milosevic pursued an increasingly nationalist course in politics and managed by 1989 to rescind Kosovo's autonomy.

Serb authorities engaged in extensive and far-ranging human rights abuses in Kosovo, ranging from dismissal of Kosovar Albanians from state employment to arrests and beatings. In 1992, President Bush issued a Christmas warning in a December 24 telegram to Milosevic, "In the event of a conflict caused by Serbian action, the US will be prepared to employ military force against Serbians in Kosovo and against Serbia proper."

As Kosovo generated a surge in nationalism, another fissure widened in the late years of Yugoslavia between Serb and Croat nationalists. In Croatia, Franjo Tudjman, a former general in the Yugoslav army, gained increasing prominence as a nationalist politician. Tudjman, who also wrote history, gained notoriety for downplaying the number of victims killed during the Second World War in camps in the Independent State of Croatia or NDH, a puppet state run by the Croatian Fascist movement the Ustasha. Tudjman even served prison sentences, but in 1989 he helped found a new political party, the HDZ.

Serb and Croat nationalists alike dwelt on themes of national greatness and victimization. Both created narratives of history that stretched back to the middle ages, but both also emphasized recent oppression. Where Serb nationalists referred to killings of Serbs by the Ustasha, Croatian nationalists described Partisan massacres of Croats. Television and newspapers in Belgrade featured stories on killings carried out by Croats, while the equivalent media in Zagreb depicted Croats as victims of massacres. These themes of victimization gained a public airing through the media in the last years of Yugoslavia.

The nationalists in Serbia, Croatia, and elsewhere did not win the support of all, but they made political gains. With some 42 percent of the vote, the HDZ outpaced all other parties and won a majority of seats in the Croatian elections in 1990, and in Serbia, the Socialists with Milosevic at the head won 48 percent of the vote in December of 1990. Milosevic himself was reelected President of Serbia with a large majority of 65 percent. Some of the citizens of Yugoslavia still identified themselves first and foremost in national terms as Yugoslavs, but they increasingly represented a beleaguered minority. In Bosnia-Herzegovina, for example, 5.5 percent of citizens identified themselves as Yugoslavs in the census conducted in 1991 as Yugoslavia approached its end.

The breakup of Yugoslavia

From 1990 to 1991 Yugoslavia broke apart into multiple fledgling states and varied self-declared Republics. In December of 1990 almost 90 percent of voters backed independence for the northern Republic of Slovenia, and in May 1991 a similar referendum in Croatia produced similar results. Slovenia and Croatia both declared independence in 1991. Voters in Macedonia similarly overwhelmingly backed independence in September 1991, and in March 1992 almost all of the voters in a referendum boycotted by Bosnian Serbs backed independence for Bosnia-Herzegovina.

The swift moves toward independence demonstrated widespread support for an end to Yugoslavia but also deep divisions and cleavages over the future national boundaries. A host of other votes held in the final years of Yugoslavia declared that varied regions wished to go their own way. In Kosovo the majority of voters backed independence in 1991. Serbs, for their part, made clear that they were not willing to live in an independent state of Croatia or

Bosnia-Herzegovina. Serbs predominated in a swathe of Croatia known as the Krajina, an old term for border or frontier. A Serb government of Krajina declared its secession from Croatia. Across the old Yugoslav border in Bosnia-Herzegovina, Serbs asserted their independence from Bosnia-Herzegovina declaring the founding of a Serb Republic.

The international response reinforced the trend toward independence. Germany took the lead in recognizing the independent states of Slovenia and Croatia in 1991. Some observers criticized that decision as contributing to the violent breakup of Yugoslavia, but there was little evidence of widespread popular support for the continued existence of Yugoslavia, and the former Yugoslav republics that opted for independence generally gained international recognition.

In contrast, ethnic enclaves within former Republics failed to gain international legitimacy. Kosovo formed a partial exception to that rule: it had a long history of autonomy, and an overwhelming Albanian majority that had already created parallel institutions separate from those of Serbia. Although foreign states did not immediately recognize Kosovo as independent, the United States indicated that Serb power was not unlimited there.

War

The breakup of Yugoslavia brought a series of wars. Slovenia's declaration of independence in 1991 met with attacks by a comparatively small contingent of the Yugoslav military. Dozens died before the European Union brokered a cease-fire. Even as Yugoslav military forces withdrew from Slovenia they became increasingly involved in fighting in Croatia. A comparatively homogenous former Yugoslav Republic like Slovenia could make the transition to peace, but in Croatia the Yugoslav military (the JNA) sided with Serb militias that wished to separate from any independent Croatia. With control over heavy weapons, the JNA provided invaluable aid to Serbs in the Krajina and in Slavonia, a region in eastern Croatia. In Slavonia, the Yugoslav military shelled the Danube port of Vukovar, a mixed city of Serbs and Croats as well as ethnic Hungarians and after months of siege took Vukovar in November. On Croatia's Adriatic coast, the JNA shelled the port of Dubrovnik. The bombardment of Dubrovnik, a UNESCO world heritage site that only had a small Serb population, quickly gained widespread attention and notoriety.

In 1992 war spread to Bosnia-Herzegovina. Many forces took part: troops of the self-declared Bosnian Serb Republic, remnants of the JNA, and a myriad of Serb paramilitaries and militias as well as police. Croatians in the west in the region of Herzegovina created their own republic of Herzeg-Bosnia with a military, the HVO or Croatian Defense Council, and Bosnian Muslims formed their own military forces. Serb forces, backed with heavy weapons, generally prevailed during the early stages of the wars for Bosnia. They took power in most of eastern Bosnia in towns like Visegrad as well as in much, though not all, of the north. Croatian forces meanwhile took over the west. Sarajevo, the capital remained under the control of the Bosnian government, but fell under prolonged attacks by Bosnian Serbs who took hold over Pale, a ski resort just above Sarajevo. From this high ground that had served as a site for skiing events during the 1984 Winter Olympics, Bosnian Serbs laid siege to the capital below. Sarajevo's residents endured intermittent shelling and sniper fire. To leave the city could mean risking death.

From the start, the wars for the former Yugoslavia uprooted and displaced large numbers of civilians. The fighting in the Krajina in 1991 caused both Serbs and Croats to flee, depending on which militias gained the upper hand, but the phenomenon first gained greater attention with the Serb victories in Eastern Slavonia. Croats poured en masse out of towns, including Vukovar. A diplomat, describing Croat mass evacuation of a town south of Vukovar, observed that this "could be the start of something much bigger. We could see an attempt at large-scale population transfers."[3] War in the collapsing state of Yugoslavia, redrew not only boundaries defined by military power but also shifted the ethnic and religious balance.

Ethnic cleansing

Ethnic cleansing begins

War itself and the fear of injury and death propelled civilians to gather their belongings and leave cities, towns, and villages under attack, but ethnic cleansing was not simply an effect of war. In campaigns of ethnic cleansing, the forces that entered into mixed communities and regions made driving out unwanted populations a prime goal of violence. As in mass killing, perpetrators specifically aimed to attack noncombatants. In contested regions of Bosnia-Herzegovina, paramilitaries and others targeted groups of victims based on their ethnic identity and resorted to murder, intimidation, and varied forms of terror to redraw the ethnic map.

Ethnic cleansing began almost as soon as war started in Bosnia-Herzegovina. From the start and for much of the war Serb forces had the upper hand, and carried out the largest number of expulsions. In one of the earliest cases, the paramilitary organized by Arkan took over the town of Bijeljina. Zeljko Raznatovic, to use Arkan's real name, was a bank robber, who escaped prison, returned to Yugoslavia, and formed a paramilitary known as the Serbian Volunteer Guard or Tigers. Arkan recruited his troops from supporters of a soccer or football team. On April 1, a unit moved into the town of Bijeljina. There they harassed, intimidated, and murdered Bosnian Muslims or Bosniaks.

EYEWITNESS TO ETHNIC CLEANSING

In April 1992 Arkan, the leader of the paramilitary known as the Tigers, invited the American photojournalist Ron Haviv to follow the Tigers into the eastern Bosnian town of Bijeljina. Haviv attributed the invitation to Arkan's ego, pride in "liberating" Bijeljina, and belief that he could control his image. At Bijeljina Haviv witnessed one of the early examples of ethnic cleansing. He also managed to take photographs documenting the violence.

"They had taken a middle-aged man and a woman out of one of the houses. And the woman was screaming. And the soldiers were screaming. And they were screaming at me not to take photographs. And some shots rang out and the man fell to the ground. A few minutes later, they brought out another woman and then they shot her as well. And, and then things sort of calmed down for a bit, and then they brought out two more people, and they said 'Look, look, he's from Kosovo. He's a fundamentalist.' And he put his arms up and basically looked at me as if I was probably the only person that could save him, which, probably in his mind I was, but unfortunately there wasn't really anything I could do.

They brought him to the headquarters and as I was standing there I heard a great crash and I looked up and out of a second floor window, this man came flying out and landed at my feet.

And amazingly, he survived the fall and they came over and they doused him with some water.

They said something like, 'This is to purify Muslim extremists,' as they doused him in the water.

And they started kicking him and beating him and then dragged him back into the home. I had to make sure there was a document, that there had to be evidence of this crime, of what was happening.

And that, I think, gave me the courage to try—to take those photographs.

I was shaking, for sure, when I was doing it because I realized how precarious everything was, but I really thought it was unbelievably important to be able to have the world see what happened." (United States Holocaust Memorial Museum)

Another early ethnic cleansing operation targeted the Bosnian Muslims of the eastern Bosnian town of Zvornik. Arkan was also present during this attack. In Zvornik, like Visegrad, relations between Bosnian Muslims and Serbs had previously been good but deteriorated markedly by 1991. Many Serb families received some kind of advance warning and left before Zvornik was attacked from April 8 to April 10. Paramilitary forces thereupon occupied Zvornik, instituted a curfew, and began ethnic cleansing.

Methods of ethnic cleansing

Ethnic cleansing subjected targeted populations to multiple forms of terror. Killings like the murder of Samir Dervisevic in Visegrad or the shootings in Bijeljina not only devastated survivors, but also created a wider climate of fear. The deaths terrorized the population targeted for removal. The dead included men, women, and children, but the violence did vary to some extent by gender: those murdered were most often men. The shootings, especially during the early assaults by paramilitary forces at times had an indiscriminate quality. However, the killing process at times also aimed to break down local communities by eliminating leaders: the dead included judges, physicians, and business and civic leaders. In some cases, such as at the town of Kozarac in northern Bosnia, Serbs selected names of Bosnians from a list.

After initial seizing power, Serb forces swept Bosnian men into such camps. Schools, soccer stadiums, and industrial sites functioned as holding places for the unfortunate prisoners. At the Luka Camp, for example, at Brcko in northern Bosnia, Serb forces held hundreds and possibly even thousands of prisoners, the vast majority of whom were Bosnian Muslim men. Prisoners were killed, especially in the early days of the camp from May until early July 1992, and subjected to beatings and torture. The Keraterm camp was located at a former ceramics factory near the town of Prijedor. Prisoners at Keraterm who were not killed received meager rations, and like those in other camps suffered from ill nutrition and extreme loss of weight. Omarska, a former iron ore mine near the town of Kozarac, acquired international notoriety after reporters, including Roy Gutman and Ed Vulliamy, broke the story of the camp.

OMARSKA

The camp of Omarska at a village near Prijedor held thousands of prisoners, mostly Bosnian Muslim men. The reporter Roy Gutman traveled to Banja Luka in northern Bosnia-Herzegovina and learned of and collected information on Omarska from refugees and survivors. Gutman described how Serbian guards executed Muslim and Croat prisoners. "They would take them to a nearby lake. You'd hear a volley of rifles, and they'd never come back," one said.[4] The Omarska camp held thousands of prisoners, including hundreds in a pit previously used for mining. Plans for killing extended beyond the executions described by survivors. The UN Commissioner for refugees quoted a guard from Omarska discussing plans for murder: "We won't waste our bullets on them. They have no roof. There is sun and rain, cold nights, and beatings two times a day. We give them no food and no water. They will starve like animals." In August of 1992 British reporters Ed Vulliamy, Penny Marshall, and Ian Williams actually gained access to the camp when Bosnian Serb President Radovan Karadzic surprisingly granted sudden access. Vulliamy described emaciated prisoners at the facility which Serbs dubbed an "investigation centre." It was hard to get the prisoners to speak openly. One told him, "I don't want to tell any lies, but I cannot tell the truth." Watching the prisoners at a brief meal, Vulliamy wrote "The men are at various stages of human decay and affliction; the bones of their elbows and wrists protrude like pieces of jagged stone from the pencil-thin stalks to which their arms have been reduced. Their skin is putrefied, the complexions of their faces have been corroded."[5] Trials later carried out by the International Criminal Tribunal for the Former Yugoslavia (ICTY) confirmed the initial reports of the horrors of Omarksa. In the first such case five Bosnian Serbs were convicted in 2001, found to have taken part in or known about killings, torture, and rape. Mass graves containing hundreds of bodies were also later discovered in the vicinity.

Along with murders, sexual assault and rape spread further shock and suffering among those targeted for ethnic cleansing. Victims included women and men, and all sides engaged in such assaults, but in particular Bosnian Serbs repeatedly carried out sexual assaults against Bosnian Muslim women. Serb forces often seized women and placed them under detention as virtual sex slaves. In the southern Bosnian town of Foca, Bosnian Muslim women and girls were held in one such camp and repeatedly beaten and raped. Visegrad was another of the towns where women were thrown into a kind of rape camp. The UN High Commission compiled extensive evidence of rape and sexual assault from locations in Bosnia as well as Croatia, but victims have also charged that the persecution of war crimes and crimes against humanity committed in the former Yugoslavia has not adequately addressed charges of sexual assault. Thus survivors of the attack on Visegrad decried the fact that the ICTY did not indict Milan Lukic and his cousin for these crimes.

Constant acts of intimidation and harassment further reinforced the climate of fear. Patrols enforced curfews against targeted population. Theft mixed with politically motivated violence. The armed men who made up paramilitary and militia took what they wished with impunity. Those who remained from populations under attack lost their jobs, and people sold their belongings at cut-rate prices to try to survive.

After the initial shock of military assault, murder, and rape, ethnic cleansing also developed a bureaucratic side. In larger towns such as Banja Luka, administrative authorities encouraged and arranged for the departure of civilians who gave up their property and left their former homes on buses. In similar fashion, Serbs in Zvornik set up an agency for exchange of houses, in which Bosnian Muslims were to trade their dwellings with Serbs said to be leaving other regions. Such measures created the illusion of voluntary departure and of legality, but all of the violent methods of ethnic cleansing, and the fear created by the reports of terror disposed members of targeted communities to get out while they still could. Departing Bosnian Muslims in communities such as Zvornik also had to relinquish and sign up their property before leaving.

RICHARD HOLBROOKE ON BANJA LUKA AUGUST 14, 1992

American Diplomat Richard Holbrooke who would later be instrumental in the negotiations at Dayton Ohio that brought an end to the war on Bosnia described the pressure employed to get Bosnian Muslims to leave Banja Luka:

"An extraordinary day! It begins with loud noise and shooting outside our hotel rooms. We go outside to find armed Serbs conducting a 'mild' form of ethnic cleansing right in front of journalists with television cameras. . . . At close to gunpoint, Muslims are signing papers giving up their personal property, either to neighbors or in exchange for the right to leave Bosnia. Then they are herded into buses headed for the border, although they have no guarantee they will actually be able to leave the country. Some leave quietly, others crying."

"After this terrible scene, which leaves us shaken and subdued, we pile into white UNHCR vehicles. A few miles north of Banja Luka, we begin to see terrible signs of war—houses destroyed all along the route. As we progress toward the front lines, the destruction increases. We encounter the occasional house left completely undestroyed in a row of ruined ones— its occupant a Serb, not a Muslim. Such destruction is clearly not the result of fighting, but of a systematic and methodical pogrom in which Serbs fingered their Muslim neighbors."[6]

A campaign of cultural destruction accompanied and reinforced ethnic cleansing. Along with attacking unwanted ethnic and religious groups, perpetrators also knocked down and blew up the cultural and religious symbols of their victims. Ruins of mosques and in some cases of churches dotted the landscape. A survey completed in 1996 recorded the destruction of mosques as well as Islamic shrines, towers, schools, and libraries. In areas that had been held by Bosnian Serb forces many such sites were heavily or completely destroyed. Most, except for a minority of more lightly damaged buildings in Sarajevo, bore the marks of deliberate sabotage. Some were razed to the ground. Catholic sites, as well, in areas that came under Bosnia Serb control during the wars for Bosnia also suffered extensive damage.[7] In areas that came under Bosnia Croat control Orthodox religious sites were similarly blown up, and Serbs and Kosovar Albanians damaged each other's cultural and religious symbols in parts of Kosovo as well.

Initial outcomes of ethnic cleansing

Early waves of ethnic cleansing ravaged Bosnian Muslim and in some cases Croat communities in mixed areas of Bosnia-Herzegovina. The first strikes aimed at communities in northern Bosnia, including

Prijedor and Banja Luka. Serb forces also targeted communities like Bijeljina on the far northeastern edge of Bosnia in order to create a corridor to connect northern Bosnia with areas of eastern Bosnia. In Bosnia's east, ethnic cleansing struck towns, including Zvornik and Visegrad as well as towns to the south such as Foca.

THE RESULTS OF ETHNIC CLEANSING

Reporter Maggie O'Kane described the results of ethnic cleansing along a corridor linking Serbia with western Bosnia:

In the last two weeks, a new bus route has been opened up along the corridor. It is bringing Serbs home to the towns and villages that have been "cleansed" of the Muslims. Along the Belgrade corridor, the early "cleansing" was done in April. Here, only the shells of the Muslim houses remain. In the roofs are the ragged round holes where the tank shells punched in.

The tanks are still there in the villages, but resting, like the soldier in red swimming trunks taking the sun at the river with the Kalashnikovs leaning on the bridge.

Further through the corridor in the villages more recently cleansed, busy green Serbian army trucks shuttle up and down the roads, green worker ants emptying the houses before they are torched.

The Serbs on the bus are silent. As we pass through the charred wastelands they watch from the windows. Mouths slightly open. Shocked. You wonder about the efficiency of it all. It's an 11-hour journey and thousands and thousands of houses have been burned. . . .

Banja Luka, in the north of this new Serbian republic, is a city waiting to be cleansed. The men at the front make no secret of their plans. "We have cleaned Foca and Visegrad of Muslims and now we will clean Gorazde," predicts a Serbian commander at Foca.

The Muslims and Croats know what's coming. Here in Banja Luka, an apparently sophisticated town with its parks and street cafes, the curfew begins at 10 pm. During what local people call "the police hour," the machine gun fire starts in town. Rat-a-tat-tat, rat-a-tat-tat, somewhere out in the darkness.

In the morning there's another Muslim shop with smashed windows, the facade of another Muslim house riddled with bullets.

One woman, who until a month ago had worked for 26 years at the same import-export firm, said: "I came back from lunch on Friday and they handed me a little note saying I didn't work here anymore. All the Muslims were sacked together that Friday. We need papers to move around our own town."[8]

With their early gains Bosnia Serb forces took over some 70 percent of Bosnia-Herzegovina. Estimates of the numbers killed and driven out varied widely. Many of the victims of ethnic cleansing were classified as Internally Displaced Persons or IDPs rather than as refugees because they had not crossed officially recognized international boundaries. The UNHCR set the number of people displaced by November 12, 1992 at 740,000 within Bosnia and at 725,000 in other parts of the former Yugoslavia. By November of 1995 the CIA set the numbers even higher, estimating that up to 1.2 million had become refugees and that some 1.5 million were internally displaced.

The cleansing operations created several enclaves—communities surrounded by territory under hostile control. In eastern Bosnia, Muslims remained in a few such enclaves, including Srebrenica. In 1993 the United Nations established Srebrenica, a town in eastern Bosnia, along with Gorazde and Zepa, Tuzla, Bihac, and Sarajevo as "safe areas." This designation did not prevent attacks by Serb forces. The United Nations authorized a UN Protection Force or UNPROFOR, first created to ensure demilitarization in selected areas of Croatia, to protect the safe areas including Srebrenica and Zepa.

For years, the insecurity of safe areas was evident to the world as fire rained down on Sarajevo from the Serb forces above the city. Thousands were killed. Within the city, the remaining residents struggled with a lack of electricity and running water and shortages of food: people obtained water from wells. To try to get out by air meant risking sniper fire at the airport.

Expansion of ethnic cleansing

Bosnian Serb forces carried out the most extensive ethnic cleansing campaigns throughout most of the war for Bosnia-Herzegovina, but all sides took up the practice of employing terror to drive out unwanted populations. Bosnian Muslims and Croats were only nominal allies in the war with Bosnian Serbs. The targeting of victims depended in large part on which group held power in a particular region of Bosnia-Herzegovina. In the west, Bosnian Croats created their own state of Herzeg-Bosnia and then proceeded to conduct ethnic cleansing operations against Muslims in contested regions. Mostar, the Bosnian Croats' chosen capital, was a mixed city on the Neretva River with a significant Muslim population. To make Mostar Croat, the Croatian Defense Council (HVO) and Bosnian Croat paramilitaries attacked the city's Bosnian Muslims, pushing them east across the Neretva River and then shelling them. Bosnian Croat forces also attacked Bosnian Muslims in the Lasva River Valley of Central Bosnia. In one of the single worst incidents of violence, more than 100 Bosnian Muslims were killed at the village of Ahmici on April 16, 1993. Tensions between Ahmici's Croats and Bosnian Muslims increased in 1992 until Bosnian Croatian forces attacked and drove out the village's Muslims.

Bosnian Muslims, for their part, struck against Bosnia Croats. Bosnian forces formed in part from refugees driven out of other regions by Bosnian Serbs seized towns in Central Bosnia in 1993. The Croat-Bosniak struggle for Central Bosnia reached a peak in October and November of 1993 with victory by Bosnian Muslims propelling flight by thousands of Bosnian Croats. Bosnian Serbs generally held the upper hand during the war's early years, but at times they too counted among victims of ethnic cleansing. Thus, Croats pushed Serbs out of communities along the Neretva River.

After the early waves of ethnic cleansing, the ethnic borders of Bosnia-Herzegovina and Croatia stabilized. Ethnic cleansing continued at a sporadic pace, but there was little change in the balance of power in disputed regions of Bosnia and Croatia until 1995 when there was a new surge in ethnic cleansing. Croatian forces went on the offensive against Serbs in disputed areas of Croatia, retaking Western Slavonia in May and Krajina in August. The kind of military backing that Serbs of Krajina had received from well-armed Serb forces in

1992 was utterly absent in 1995. Instead, a rearmed Croatian military pushed out Serbs—some 150,000 left the Krajina for Serbia.

In eastern Bosnia, Serb forces meanwhile completed their ethnic cleansing operations by attacking safe havens in the summer of 1995. Bosnian Serbs entered Srebrenica despite the presence of a small detachment of Dutch peacekeepers. The small force of some 600 lacked either the weapons or air support necessary to fulfill their ostensible mission of protecting the 40,000 Bosnian Muslims who had crowded into the safe area, though a 2002 report by the Netherlands Institute for War Documentation also criticized both the UN and the Dutch Government and military for the shortcomings of the missions. Expelling women and children, Bosnian Serb forces killed some 7,000–8,000 Bosnian Muslim men and boys at Srebrenica (Figure 5.1). Taking Zepa, a town with an even smaller

FIGURE 5.1 *Srebrenica Genocide Memorial.*

Photo by Michael Bueker (http://commons.wikimedia.org/wiki/File:Srebrenica_massacre_memorial_wall_of_names_2009_4.jpg). Reproduced under the Creative Commons copyright.

contingent of peacekeepers—79 Ukrainian troops—Bosnian Serbs expelled those Bosnian Muslims who did not flee.

From this apparent pinnacle of power, the Bosnian Serbs soon suffered sharp reversal. After the shelling of a Sarajevo market on August 28, 1995 killed 37 people, NATO intervened by bombing Bosnian Serb positions. Bosnian Croats and Bosnian Muslims joined in an offensive, taking much of Western Bosnia and precipitating flight by tens of thousands. Military setbacks brought Serbs to join negotiations. The Dayton Peace Accords reached at Dayton Ohio in November solidified new borders with regions under Serb control reduced from 70 to 49 percent of Bosnia-Herzegovina.

Kosovo

The last major pulses of ethnic cleansing in the conflicts in the former Yugoslavia took place in Kosovo. In the 1990s Slobodan Milosevic had capitalized on the growing tensions between the large Kosovar Albanian majority (some 90%) and Serbs. Repression of Kosovar Albanians continued as an armed movement called the Kosovo Liberation Army or KLA formed by 1996 and soon began to carry out attacks. By 1998 Serb forces and the KLA were involved in an armed conflict. In October 1998, following NATO warnings of intervention, Serbia withdrew some forces, but violence soon escalated again. In January 1999, 45 bodies were found at the village of Racak. Renewed NATO military threats led to talks in France at Rambouillet. The KLA, after facing much pressure finally agreed to the Rambouillet Accords. Serbia, in contrast, rejected the Accords and as Serbia gathered forces and attacked Albanians, NATO began airstrikes.

Serbian forces in Kosovo countered with a wave of ethnic cleansing. Murders and threats propelled Albanians into massive flight from the chief city Pristina and towns throughout the region. Refugees crossed into Montenegro and piled up on Kosovo's borders with Macedonia. From the western borders of Kosovo many pressed into Albania, a desperately poor country ill prepared to handle the influx. Thousands camped out in the open near the Albanian town of Kukes. Others fled within Kosovo itself and became IDPs. In this peak phase of ethnic cleansing some 863,000 refugees left Kosovo and nearly 600,000 were internally displaced.

On June 10, after more than two months of NATO bombing, Serbia announced a pull-out from Kosovo. The sharp military turn-about reversed the flow of refugees. Kosovar Albanians reentered Kosovo and many Serbs in turn fled. Many feared revenge, but intimidation, beatings, and even murders spurred their flight in a new pulse of ethnic cleansing. Driven out of much of Kosovo, Serbs remained chiefly in the area of the town of Mitrovica.

Ethnic cleansing, genocide, and acts of genocide

Camps

The very fact that the crime of genocide was well established by the 1990s raised almost immediate comparisons between the campaigns of ethnic cleansing in the former Yugoslavia and genocide. The sight of emaciated prisoners and the evidence of torture and killings at camps such as Omarska recalled images of survivors of concentration camps. The journalists who broke the story perceived the parallels, though they did not always refer to Omarska or other camps as concentration camps.

Subsequent accounts sometimes, though not always, applied the term concentration camp to the sites that held prisoners during the wars for the former Yugoslavia. Human Rights Watch alternately referred to Omarska as a collecting center, a detention camp, and a concentration camp. The ICTY customarily described these simply as camps. The larger camps served to detain, collect, and concentrate thousands from targeted populations, and they were sites for extensive torture and murder. In these respects, the parallels to concentration camps were striking. Mark Danner was one of several journalists to make the comparison in writing about Omarska, "In Omarska as in Auschwitz the masters created these walking corpses from healthy men by employing simple methods: withhold all but the barest nourishment, forcing the prisoners' bodies to waste away; impose upon them a ceaseless terror by subjecting them to unremitting physical cruelty; immerse them in degradation and death and decay, destroying all hope and obliterating the will to live."[9]

THE *TENTH CIRCLE OF HELL*

In his book the *Tenth Circle of Hell*, Rezak Hukanovic, a journalist who survived Omarska, describes torture and killings. Hukanovic writes about himself as Djemo. He details mass killings.

"Most of the time other prisoners loaded the corpses onto the van; usually they too ended up as corpses on the same van, to eliminate the possibility of leaving living witnesses."

Hukanovic was himself badly beaten—the following excerpt only describes the beginning of the assault he endured.

"Žiga kept hitting Djemo the whole time on the back and head with a club that unfurled itself every time he swung it to reveal a metal ball on the end. Djemo curled up, trying to protect his head by pulling it in toward his shoulders and covering it with his right hand. Žiga just kept cursing as he hit, his eyes inflamed by more and more hatred. The first drops of blood appeared on the tiles under Djemo's head, becoming denser and denser until they formed a thick, dark red puddle. . . . At some point a man in fatigues appeared at the door. It was Šaponja, a member of the famous Bosnamontaža soccer club from Prijedor; Djemo had once known him quite well. He came up to Djemo and said, 'Well, well, my old pal Djemo. While I was fighting in Pakrac and Lipik, you were pouring down the cold ones in Prijedor.' He kicked Djemo right in the face with his boot."[10]

The functions and goals of the camps overlapped with but did not in all respects duplicate those of concentration camps, and in particular the death camps, of the Second World War. Camps in former Yugoslavia advanced ethnic cleansing by intimidating, terrorizing, and removing groups, most often but not always Bosnian Muslims, to achieve ethnic purity. However, the camps of the wars for Yugoslavia were not set up like the smaller number of killing centers of the Second World War with the specific purpose of destroying groups at the highest possible speed. Guards at Omarska and other camps in the former Yugoslavia beat and shot prisoners, but there was no exact equivalent to the efficient killing carried out at Nazi death camps that annihilated entire Jewish communities. At the same time, camps like Omarska functioned as an effective instrument for erasing unwanted groups from particular areas through terror and murder, and in this respect their purpose overlapped with that of concentration camps.

Acts of genocide

Ethnic cleansing and genocide shared related goals of purifying areas through violence and at times shared the same methods when ethnic cleansing incorporated acts of genocide. The ICTY in its prosecution of individuals identified larger massacres carried out in Bosnia as acts of genocide, most notably the killings in 1995 at Srebrenica and Zepa.

In a war full of atrocities, Srebrenica stood out for the organization and scale of murder. Entering and taking Srebrenica Serb forces systematically separated women, children, and the elderly apart from men and boys. After sending other Bosnian Muslims away on buses, the Bosnian Serbs who had taken the town then began to kill the remaining 7,000 to 8,000 Bosnian Muslim men and boys. They killed in groups, forcing 1,000 to 1,500 into a warehouse and then shooting them and lobbing in grenades. The Bosnian Serb forces gathered some 1,000 more Bosniak men and boys in a school before taking them outside to kill them. Some 1,500 to 2,000 were shot next to a dam, and others were shot at a military farm.

SREBRENICA BY A SURVIVOR FROM THE KRSTIC TRIAL

Testimony from April 7, 2000 of a witness from the trial of Bosnian Serb General Radislav Krstic included charges of genocide:

"And then when we got to where this gunfire was coming from, the buses stopped, and no sooner did they stop and the doors opened. Serb troops all around the buses, 'Get off now. Fuck your mothers and Alija's and everybody's. Get off. Alija doesn't want you.' A group got off the bus, up to half of the bus, and then they stopped. 'Enough,' they said, 'for the moment.' And I was in that second half of the bus. I watched as the column goes down a path, and I watched to where the dead ones are. I got there and I heard Serb troops cursing, making noise. Bursts of fire simply mowed them down. They all fell to the ground. Serb soldiers came back to fetch us, that half of the bus, and drove us off the bus, as we were stepping down from the bus. So the column headed for the shooting area. As I stepped down, a Serb soldier tells me, 'You, give over the marks.' I said I didn't have them because I didn't, and he kicked me in the stomach. I fell to the ground, on my knees. Another Serb soldier behind my back said, 'Don't commit genocide. Get your rifle and kill as the soldiers do.' They forced me, and I stood up and I followed the column along. Along that path, a dead body here and there I could see. And the one who kicked me, the same one asked, 'Does anyone want to say that he is a Serb so that we let him be?' and two said they would, just to stay alive, but nothing came out of it. Another one in the column, one of ours, asked, 'Give us water to drink, and kill us after that,' but nothing doing again. When I got to where those killed were, they were all in a row, they looked like lines which had been lodged, and there were many, many of them. And then I saw that those who had supposedly left to Sarajevo, paid for the buses, had been killed. They were giving money and then their lives. When we passed between those rows, towards the end of those rows, between them, they said, 'Turn your backs and line up with them.' We turned our backs and lined up. Then he orders not 'Fire,' he orders 'Lie down,' but at that moment bursts of fire cut us all down. And I fell, and they also fell, cropped down by the bursts of fire. When the gunfire stopped, then a Serb soldier asked, 'Is there anyone alive?' and two made out that they were alive. One said, 'I am,' and another one said, 'I am. Come kill me.' I kept silent. If need be, I'd let them know that

I'm alive later on and let them kill me then. And so column after column, they drove up there. I was lying down. They drove up some six columns more, and below me, lining them up, and bursts of fire just cropping them down. . . ."

The ICTY identified Srebrenica as a case of genocide. The key issue, as the Presiding Judge explained, in bringing this charge "was whether genocide was committed against in the Prosecutor's words, 'a part of the Bosnian Muslim people as a national, ethnical, or religious group.'" Bosnian Serb forces, the Trial Chamber found, first planned to carry out ethnic cleansing, and proceeded to transfer women and children, along with the elderly. However, they then moved to kill all men: "The result was inevitable: the destruction of the Bosnian Muslim population in Srebrenica." The Appeals Chamber in turn reviewed the issue of whether the killings met the language of the Genocide Convention that referred to destruction of the group "in whole or in part." At this point, the Genocide Convention itself provided little direct guidance—the Appeals Chamber determined whether the part of the group targeted for destruction was "substantial." If the 7,000–8,000 dead by themselves did not make up a substantial part of all Bosnian Muslims they did account for a very substantial portion of the targeted population group in eastern Bosnia. Killing this group constituted a larger attempt to destroy the Bosnian Muslim population of Srebrenica.

Applying a similar understanding of genocide, other acts of destruction in Bosnia could also be termed genocide. At times, the ICTY described Prijedor as a site of genocide. In the case against Milan Kovacevic of the Prijedor Crisis Staff, which took control over the town, the ICTY charged in the indictment that the plan to expel Bosnian Muslims and Croats included killing, causing serious bodily and mental harm and "deliberately inflicting on the Bosnian Muslims and Croats conditions of life calculated to bring about the physical destruction of a part of the Bosnian Muslim and Croat populations." However, Kovacevic died before the conclusion of his trial. A subsequent trial found Milomir Stakic, a physician and official on the Bosnian Serb Crisis Staff at Prijedor guilty of numerous crimes, including extermination, but not of genocide. The Trial Chamber found a "comprehensive pattern of atrocities against Muslims in Prijedor," but did not find the necessary special intent for genocide.

Killings in other towns, including Brcko and Visegrad, have sometimes been described as genocide, though these sites of destruction are not cited as acts of genocide nearly so often as Srebrenica. An indictment of Goran Jelisic, a Bosnian Serb commander in Brcko, included a charge of genocide, also stating that he had termed himself a "Serb Adolf." Witnesses spoke of Jelisic's goals for killing: one testified that Jelisic spoke of having to execute 20 to 30 people to drink his morning's coffee. Jelisic himself pled guilty to numerous charges, including crimes against humanity and violations of the laws of war, but in this case the Trial Chamber did not find evidence to establish "beyond all reasonable doubt . . . a plan to destroy the Muslim group in Brcko. . . ." An Appeals Chamber found errors in this standard, stating that "the existence of a plan or policy is not a legal ingredient of the crime of genocide, although it may be evidentially of assistance" but did not call for further legal proceedings. As for Visegrad, some accounts of the killings and massacres in the town on the Drina refer to genocide. The ICTY charged Milan Lukic with extermination, including the burning alive of civilians trapped in houses, but not with genocide.

Gendercide and genocide in Bosnia

Killing and assaults in Bosnia and elsewhere during the wars for the former Yugoslavia frequently targeted victims by gender. The Genocide Convention does not directly list gender as a class among the groups whose destruction amounts to genocide, though it lists "imposing measures intended to prevent births within the group" as act of genocide. Building on analysis of genocide, scholars such as Mary Anne Warren and Adam Jones have outlined the concept of gendercide. Though gendercide is not part of international law, genocide and related crimes have often involved selection of victims by gender.

The violence in Bosnia, as well as elsewhere in Yugoslavia, demonstrated that gendercide or massive violence and destruction aimed at particular gender brought devastation for women and men. Both men and women suffered sexual assault, but women were the chief victims of abuse and assault in so-called rape camps set up by varied forces. Sexual assaults in such camps were crimes against individuals but also advanced ethnic cleansing campaigns against the ethnic group under attack.

Massacres throughout the wars for Yugoslavia and Bosnia also repeatedly involved killing by gender. As in the case of sexual assault, both men and women counted among those slaughtered. At the same time, the massacres repeatedly targeted men and boys. This reflected the fiction that all men were inherently military combatants, and as in the case of rape also served as an attack on the group itself, advancing the ethnic cleansing and destruction of communities.

Perpetrators

Perpetrators of ethnic cleansing and related crimes in the conflicts in the former Yugoslavia came from the military and from civilian life and included both leaders with official posts as well as members of unofficial paramilitaries and militias. Many perpetrators came from the breakaway regions that declared themselves states, including the Republic Serpska and Herzeg-Bosnia, but others were residents of and in some cases leaders of internationally recognized states.

The ICTY pursued investigations of perpetrators at the highest ranks of government, most notably in the case of Slobodan Milosevic, the President of Serbia from 1989 to 1997 and then of what remained of Yugoslavia from 1997 to 2000. Charges of war crimes and crimes against humanity brought by the ICTY against Milosevic focused on the terror campaign carried out against Kosovar Albanians living in Kosovo—in this case forces of the Serbia had taken part directly in attacks against civilians in 1999. The court also charged Milosevic with crimes against humanity in Croatia during the war that broke out in 1991. In 2001, a further indictment focused on Milosevic's ties to Bosnian Serbs, charging him with genocide along with war crimes and crimes against humanity.

A key issue centered on Milosevic's relationship with Bosnian Serb forces that carried out massacres, most notably at Srebrenica. The Republic Serpska was highly dependent on Serbia itself, but the two did not always march in lockstep as the Dayton Accords revealed when the Bosnian Serb leadership was shut out of the negotiating process. According to the Tribunal, Milosevic nonetheless acted as a "dominant political figure." The case reached no conclusion because Milosevic died in March 2006 before the trial was completed. The slow pace of the trial, which endured for five years attracted widespread criticism.

In the case of Kosovo, Serbian authorities were closely involved in carrying out ethnic cleansing. The question of whether Serbian authorities had already drawn up a particular plan for ethnic cleansing has been debated. Here, as in other cases of related violence, proving the existence of such a specific plan has proven difficult. However, the combined assault of the Serbian military and paramilitary forces propelled the flight of Kosovar Albanians. The organization of transport out of some towns and cities by bus or train indicated a high level of coordination, and refugees told of being forced out of their homes by military personnel, police, or militia.

CHARGES AGAINST SLOBODAN MILOSEVIC—FROM THE INDICTMENT AT THE ICTY

In very brief, summary form, the allegations are as follows. The indictment is concerned with events which took place in Bosnia and Herzegovina between 1992 and 1995. The Prosecution case is that this accused, together with others, participated in a joint criminal enterprise, the purpose of which was the "forcible and permanent removal of the majority of non-Serbs, principally Bosnian Muslims and Bosnian Croats, from large areas of the Republic of Bosnia and Herzegovina." It is alleged that this criminal enterprise was carried out by means of the commission of numerous crimes during a series of offensives against the non-Serb population. . . .

These offensives are alleged to have been carried out by "Serb forces" in attacks on towns and villages in over 40 municipalities in Bosnia and Herzegovina which were taken over by such forces. It is further alleged that during these attacks thousands of Bosnian Muslims and Bosnian Serbs were killed (including the thousands executed after the fall of Srebrenica). Thousands more were imprisoned in over 50 detention facilities such as camps, barracks, police stations and schools: while there, they were subjected to inhuman living conditions and forced labour; many were murdered and others subjected to torture, beatings and sexual assault. Of those not imprisoned, thousands were forcibly transferred and deported from their homes: the total expelled or imprisoned is alleged to have been over a quarter million people. . . .

It is alleged that as the dominant political figure in Serbia, SFRY, and FRY, the accused exercised effective control or influence over the other participants in the joint criminal enterprise and himself participated in it; and that he did so *inter alia*, by controlling, directing, or supporting the units of the JNA, VJ, Bosnian Serb Army (VRS), MUP, and Serb paramilitaries who carried its objectives out; by assisting the RS leadership in the take-overs of municipalities and participating in the planning of the same; and by manipulating and controlling the Serb state-run media in order to spread false reports, which were intended to create an atmosphere of fear and hatred.

Unlike Milosevic, Franjo Tudjman, the President of Croatia during the breakup and wars for the former Yugoslavia was never indicted. In March 1995 Tudjman warned that he was ready to attack Krajina. He then said he would not, but Croatia retook Krajina anyway in August. At the time of his death in 1999 Tudjman had not been charged with responsibility for ethnic cleansing of Serbs from the Krajina. However, investigators for the Tribunal found that "In a widespread and systematic manner, Croatian troops committed murder and other inhumane acts upon and against Croatian Serbs." The scrutiny of perpetrators focused on other leaders of the Croatian campaign of 1995 in Krajina, including General Gotovina, a former member of the French Foreign Legion who had joined the Croatian military. In 2011 the ICTY found Gotovina guilty of multiple charges of crimes against humanity and war crimes, but in November 2012 an appeals chamber acquitted him. A key issue concerned the question of whether artillery shells had been directed against civilians.

Perpetrators of serious crimes included both civilian and military leaders from the breakaway Bosnian Serb region. Biljana Plavsic, the onetime President of the Republic Serpska, was sentenced to eleven years for supporting and contributing to the campaign to drive out Bosnian Muslims and Croats. The ICTY in 2006 convicted Momćilo Krajišnik, another important Bosnian Serb political figure, of crimes against humanity while acquitting him of genocide. In particular, the Tribunal pointed to Krajisnik's actions within the Bosnian Serb Assembly "when he called for 'implementing what we have agreed upon, the ethnic division on the ground.'" Former officers from the Bosnian Serb military were also convicted. The ICTY convicted Vidoje Blagojević and Dragan Jokić for crimes against humanity and war crimes for their role at Srebrenica, though the Appeals Chamber voided Blagojević's initial conviction for complicity in genocide. The Bratunac Brigade under Blagojević's command provided "practical assistance" to the attacks which resulted in more than 7,000 deaths at Srebrenica. In particular, men from the Brigade separated out Muslim men and boys.

At the top of the Bosnian Serb military and civil apparatus, former military commander Ratko Mladic and former President Radovan Karadzic faced multiple charges but remained at large for years. Karadzic, a psychiatrist, was arrested only in 2008, while Mladic escaped arrest until 2011. Mladic's indictment charged the former Bosnian Serb general with participating in genocide and complicity for genocide as well as extermination, murder, and deportation.

Even before all trials were concluded, the sentences handed down by the ICTY documented the key work of civilian and military leaders in driving out unwanted groups, but the work of ethnic cleansing also required repeated individual violent acts. Many of the perpetrators who carried out ethnic cleansing on the ground belonged to paramilitary or militia forces. For all the notoriety that surrounded Arkan's Tigers, multiple such groups carried out ethnic cleansing in different locales across the former Yugoslavia. The attack on Zvornik provided an example of the variety of units involved. Troops of the former JNA carried out the assault on

Zvornik, but numerous different forces then entered the city where they attacked and intimidated Bosnian Muslims.

IRREGULAR SERB FORCES AT ZVORNIK

A report by Ludwig Boltzmann Institute for Human Rights detailed the multiple forces that carried out ethnic cleansing in Zvornik in 1992. Because so many different types of units were involved in the attack, it was often difficult to clearly identity and distinguish between them.

- Yugoslav National Army (JNA): the JNA was nor formally involved but witnesses said that "former JNA troops . . . participated in the course of the attack."
- Territorial Defense (TO)—these units were recruited from local Serb populations in the area: "Being from the area themselves, its members are said to have been under special orders to act as informants for the military; later, they reportedly identified many wealthy and prominent Muslims who were subsequently robbed and arrested."
- Arkanovci (Serb Volunteer Guard)—forces of Arkan: "Reportedly, it was the Arkanovci in particular who, accompanied by local Serbs, were systematically involved in house searches, killings, rapes, and lootings."
- Seseljevci—Vojislav Seselj was a Bosnian Serb politician and sometime rival of Milosevic's: "According to witness accounts they were frequently drunk; they repeatedly recruited criminals and 'weekend fighters.' They are said to have been particularly active as regards acts of violence against civilians."
- Beli Orlovo (White Eagles)—said to be associated with Seselj as well as other leaders.
- Draganovci—named for their commander and involved in occupation rather than in attack.
- Other formations, including Zute Ose (Yellow Wasps).[11]

To a large degree the paramilitaries and militias that carried out ethnic cleansing functioned much like criminal gangs, but this was more than a campaign carried out by a small number of violent interlopers. Milan Lukic, for example, was well known in the town of Visegrad—he was born and lived in the region before spending time abroad and in Serbia and then returning during the wars for the former Yugoslavia. One witness at his trial testified that she knew him, "because he was a schoolmate of my husband in elementary school..." If some militia members came from outside the immediate area, others traveled from nearby towns: in the case of Zvornik, for example, members of the White Eagles came from towns in adjacent areas of Serbia. The Serb Volunteer Guard apparently went through hard training, but for others ethnic cleansing appeared to be something of a weekend hobby. Rezak Hukanovic described much the same mix of perpetrators at Omarska. "The guard," he stated, "were all young men from surrounding villages.... They were Serb volunteers; there were no regular troops among them." Weekends, however, brought newcomers: "regular troops from Banja Luka came to the camp." These specialized in brutal beatings.[12]

Even as militias and paramilitary bands entered war zones to carry out ethnic cleansing, local residents also acted as perpetrators. In the former Yugoslavia neighbors turned on one another. One of the very first cases brought to trial at the ICTY brought the conviction of Duško Tadić in 1997 for crimes against humanity and violations of the laws of war, for acts including various assaults, as well as "forced transfer" and taking part in the attack on the town of Prijedor. Tadić was not some outsider, who had undergone any kind of intensive paramilitary training, but a local café owner, well known to many who witnessed and experienced ethnic cleansing. One of the witnesses who had lived in the town of Prijedor explained that she had known Duško Tadić, as well as his wife, since 1983 and that he had once worked at the same company as her husband. As Tadić's case suggested, ethnic cleansing emerged both from the top down and from the grass roots. Popular participation in ethnic cleansing repeatedly shocked survivors. At Kulen Vakuf toward the west, a Bosnian witness to a Serbian attack on a nearby village told of seeing "my former colleagues, people I used to work with" helping to load looted goods onto a truck.[13] Fahrudin Alihodzic, a Bosnian forced out of Sanski Most—another northern town—recalled, "I grew up with Serbs, shared good and ill with them.

That's the first great disillusion to me, that those friends were the people who arrested me." At a camp at Manjaca, "unbelievably, my former friends were actually beating us. . . ." One of the guards was his best friend.[14]

TESTIMONY FROM CASE IT-97–25-T, THE PROSECUTOR VERSUS MILORAD KRNOJELAC

Krnojelac commanded the KP Dom detention camp at Foca and in 2002 was found guilty on counts of crimes against humanity and war crimes.

At the trial a witness named Amir Berberkic testified about attacks on villages near Foca and stated that he personally knew many men in the Serb force.

Q. "You said the Chetniks arrested you. Did you know them? Could you say who arrested you, neighbours or soldiers from other areas?

A. All the soldiers that entered the weekend cottage were my neighbours, most of them. I knew them. Only one of them was not from Bosnia. Judging by his accent, by the way he spoke, I came to the conclusion that he was from Serbia. I knew all the rest from before, and I had even treated some of them, as a doctor, while they were in hospital."

After being taken to a hospital where he had previously worked and therefore trusted the staff, Dr. Berberkic was taken to the KP Dom. He knew the two soldiers from the special police who escorted him there, and he knew the investigator who interrogated him. "I knew him from before, and we even cooperated on business. We even cooperated on certain cases before the war." The investigator, according to Berberkic, accused him of belonging to a group of doctors "who wanted to organise themselves to poison Serbian children and patients in hospitals . . ." On the other hand, Dr. Berberkic also met detainees in the camp who were Serb neighbors who did not want to fight.

As in any example of genocide or related violence, in the former Yugoslavia ethnic cleansing, it remains difficult to identify the motives of perpetrators. Many of the same interpretations that emerged in study of the Holocaust applied as well to the destruction in the former Yugoslavia. Focusing on groups such as Arkan's points to the importance of indoctrination. Originally formed from supporters of the Red Star Belgrade soccer team, the recruits went through extensive training and were subject to harsh discipline.[15] They also memorized songs in which they vowed to fight for Serbia. However, discipline only extended so far: Arkan's men repeatedly stole, and so too did many of those involved in ethnic cleansing.

Dispossessing targeted groups served as an opportunity to take anything and everything that armed men could seize. Indeed, ethnic cleansing has been described as an essentially criminal activity carried out by comparatively small numbers of groups acting much like gangs in the pursuit of personal power and profit. Many units that engaged in ethnic cleansing were not highly professional. The opportunity for personal gain gave inducement for taking part in driving targeted populations out of their homes and towns.

Neither training nor avarice, however, was likely to lead to the extraordinary violence and rupture of normal everyday social norms without some other ingredient. Ideology, as well, propelled ethnic cleansing. Combatants increasingly adopted both old nationalist symbols and referred to their victims as historical enemies: as Chetniks, Ustasha, or Turks. The testimony at the trials at the ICTY was full of references to ethnic and religious slurs employed by perpetrators. Mixing and combining claims of past and present victimization, perpetrators sought to justify destruction and removal of peoples who had grown up in the same country.

Bystanders

Ethnic cleansing in Bosnia, Croatia, and Kosovo proved both shocking and bewildering. The use of insignia and names from the past identifying combatants with Chetniks or Ustasha and the claims that Muslims were Turks made little sense to many who well remembered years of comparatively peaceful ethnic and religious relations. The minority who chose to define themselves as Yugoslavs in the country's last census in some sense found themselves living without a country that corresponded to their own past understanding of the nation.

The violence in the former Yugoslavia exemplified the idea of a gray zone in that bystanders could easily move to aid perpetrators or could easily find themselves victims. Some bystanders became complicit in ethnic cleansing by extending help or providing vital information to the armed bands intent on driving out or destroying unwanted groups. Perpetrators cooperated with and drew on the knowledge of local residents. At Zvornik, for example local Serbs reportedly created lists of Muslims for Arkan's men to rob. Perpetrators also tipped off their own ethnic community in many cases. The sudden departure of members of a community of a particular ethnic and religious group provided a clue of imminent attack. Where isolated houses still stood in areas decimated by arson, the pattern suggested not just chance, but also a practice of marking homes to be spared by advancing paramilitary units.

At the same time, other bystanders chose to aid those affected by or endangered by ethnic cleansing. Svetlana Broz, a cardiologist and granddaughter of Tito, later compiled an account of such efforts by ordinary people to befriend and aid others across the ethnic lines that increasingly divided the former Yugoslavia.[16] Bystanders also extended help to others from their own group. There is no equivalent to the Righteous among the Nations, the title awarded by Yad Vashem for non-Jews who put themselves into danger to rescue Jews, but US Secretary of State Hilary Clinton in 2011 honored Mina Jahic, a Bosnian Muslim, who in 1994 took Ferid Spahic, a wounded Bosnian Muslim man, into her house—Jahic's own son was murdered in 1995 at Srebrenica.

Victims

Ethnic cleansing in the former Yugoslavia inflicted a heavy toll on victims. The total number of deaths proved difficult to calculate. A total of 200,000 dead in Bosnia alone was often cited during the conflict, but the OTP or Office of the Prosecutor of the ICTY later arrived at lower estimates, finding 104,000 killed from conflict in Bosnia-Herzegovina between 1992 and 1995, though these figures did not distinguish between deaths in combat and noncombat deaths. Men with military status, for example, could count among victims of war or among victims of executions or abuse and ill-treatment at camps.

For victims of ethnic cleansing, return proved difficult. The military campaigns of 1995 and the Dayton Accord created new de-facto and official ethnic and religious boundaries. By 2004, more than a million, according to the UNHCR, had returned to Bosnia, but of that number many did not return to their former towns which now lay in areas dominated by other ethnic groups. Despite efforts by international agencies to support reintegration, many remained displaced years after the end of war—some 113,000 in Bosnia-Herzegovina in 2010. Some displaced persons filed claims for their old homes, but still feared returning or did not wish to do so. Control over property pitted the interests of new settlers with those of the displaced, but even with restitution, or the restoration of property, original owners or residents did not necessarily return.

Campaigns of ethnic cleansing waged in the name of Serb nationalism, not only failed to create a greater Serbia, but left many Serbs displaced. In the case of Serbs who were forced from or fled Croatia, 125,000, according to the UNHCR, registered as returning, but many did not actually go back. The Serb flight out of Kosovo added to the number of the displaced: as of 2012 there were still some 210,000 people classified as IDPS living in Serbia.

Genocide and ethnic cleansing in the former Yugoslavia

The violence that erupted with the breakup of Yugoslavia both helped to give rise to the term ethnic cleansing and became the most well-known case of ethnic cleansing. The origins of the term as a phrase coined by perpetrators attracted criticism that ethnic cleansing was simply a euphemism for genocide.[17] Ethnic cleansing, however, quickly lost any positive connotation: observers of the wars in the former Yugoslavia and later accounts uniformly understood it as violent and highly destructive.

Another objection to the idea of ethnic cleansing focuses on the difficulty identifying an exact boundary between ethnic cleansing and genocide, but that can also be seen as a problem of defining genocide. The former Yugoslavia was not the first example of destruction of unwanted populations in twentieth-century Europe that also overlapped with genocide. The concept of ethnic cleansing emphasizes the particular means or methods employed to achieve purity through force. The Armenian Genocide was both ethnic cleansing and genocide, but in the case of Yugoslavia the relationship between genocide and ethnic cleansing was more complex. This chapter has documented perpetrators employed in acts of genocide, but their overall goal often lay first and foremost in driving out groups of victims through those acts.

Study questions

- Given the strong evidence that many of the residents of Yugoslavia had good relations with Yugoslavs of differing ethnic and religious identities what factors led to the breakup of Yugoslavia after the death of Marshall Tito?
- What were the chief methods of ethnic cleansing?
- How did ethnic cleansing target Yugoslavs by gender?
- What were the chief outcomes of ethnic cleansing?
- What were the chief groups of perpetrators?
- What factors motivated continuing ethnic cleansing?
- What was the relationship between ethnic cleansing and genocide in the former Yugoslavia?

Suggestions for further reading

Holbrooke, Richard, *To End a War* (New York: Random House, 1998).

Judah, Tim, *The Serbs: History, Myth and the Destruction of Yugoslavia* (New Haven: Yale University Press, 1997).

Maas, Peter, *Love thy Neighbor: A Story of War* (New York: Vintage, 1997).

Rohde, David, *Endgame: The Betrayal and Fall of Srebrenica* (New York: Farrar, Strauss & Giroux, 1997).

Silber, Laura and Alan Little, *Yugoslavia: Death of a Nation* (New York: Penguin Books, 1997).

Conclusion

As one of the core areas in the field of genocide studies the history of twentieth-century European genocide offers key insights not only into the patterns of genocide in Europe but also into the broader history of genocide. The study of European genocides has revealed patterns in the causes of genocide, the actual processes and acts of genocide, and the behavior of perpetrators, victims, and bystanders, and many of these patterns are now fundamental to the entire field of research into genocide. In addition, European genocides shared important common features with other major twentieth-century genocides, including the Cambodian Genocide and the Rwandan Genocide. The aftermath of genocide and efforts to come to terms with the past of European genocides had important consequences for the development of international law. Finally, as the setting for the acts that first made genocide widely known, Europe's tragic history of genocides offers important lessons for efforts to detect and prevent possible future genocides.

Patterns in european genocide

Prior intent and radicalization

Multiple paths converged to lead to European genocides. Extremist nationalist and racist ideologies and prior cycles of violence contributed to genocide and related violence. Groups targeted for extermination, ethnic cleansing, and mass killing endured prior attacks that in some cases already caused many deaths well before the actual onset of genocide. In the Ottoman Empire, nationalists in the CUP already viewed Armenians with suspicion before the First World War, though the revolutions against Sultan Abdul Hamid II also created the potential for solidarity between the Empire's varied ethnic and religious groups. In the case of Germany, Hitler espoused hatred of Jews throughout his entire political career. Both Armenians and Jews had also suffered prior attacks before the outbreak of genocide. In the Ottoman Empire, Armenians died in large numbers in the massacres of the Abdul Hamid era in the 1890s and again at Adana in 1909. Jews, had previously associated Eastern Europe more than Germany with the danger of attack, but rising discrimination in the Nazi era before the Second World War culminated with the violence of Kristallnacht in 1938. There were no equivalent outbreaks of massive violence in the last years of Yugoslavia, but Serb intellectuals accused Kosovar Albanians of threatening Serbs in Kosovo. Serb-Croat tensions meanwhile increased as Serb politicians and media raised animosity against Croats just as Croatian politicians and media intensified fear and mistrust of Serbs.

Even where a long pattern of prior threats indicated the potential for violent action, a process of radicalization led to actual genocide. War was an obvious common thread: the Armenian Genocide, the Holocaust, and the ethnic cleansing and acts of genocide in the former Yugoslavia all took place during war. The famine terror in the USSR was different in that it did not take place during a war between states, but Stalin and Soviet security forces sought to pacify suspect populations, and the NKVD carried out sudden deportations of entire ethnic groups during the Second World War.

In almost all cases perpetrators of genocide and ethnic cleansing claimed to be victimized themselves, and war intensified their charges of victimization and betrayal. The leaders of CUP, already disposed to extreme suspicion of Armenians, were quick to accuse Armenians of treason and of undermining the war effort in 1914 and 1915. The early events of the war, including Turkish defeat at the battle of Sarikamis, the British landing at Gallipoli, and the uprising at Van all fit into a narrative which depicted Turkey as victimized both by external and internal enemies, in particular by Armenians. In the case of Nazi Germany, Hitler had long claimed that Jews betrayed Germany and asserted that they would face destruction in the event that they again, as he put it, led to world war. Jews had no effect whatsoever on the broadening war in 1941, but the onset of a world war still brought German planning to a new stage in expanding the Holocaust. In Yugoslavia many of the claims popularized by politicians and the media in the late 1980s and early 1990s depicted a picture of ethnic and religious animosity often at odds with the normal realities of daily life. However, the onset of war reinforced propaganda that depicted those nearby of a different ethnic or religious background as dangerous enemies.

With radicalization, the range of options narrowed in societies that moved toward genocide. The possibility of an inclusive Ottoman identity vanished for the CUP leadership. Nazi Germany's leaders and varied experts who served the Nazi state considered multiple possible "solutions" for dealing with Jews, including emigration and resettlement, before opting for the "Final Solution" of mass extermination of European Jews. In the former Yugoslavia, the Yugoslavs—those who identified with the idea of solidarity and a common identity that united southern Slavs—became a marginalized minority.

Perpetrators, victims, and bystanders

European genocides of the twentieth century also demonstrated common patterns in the experiences of perpetrators, victims, and bystanders. In most cases an inner core of perpetrators took on key roles in initiating and organizing genocide, but broader circles of perpetrators also carried out genocide. In the Armenian Genocide the leadership of CUP and of the Special Organization and in Nazi Germany the leadership of the SS and SD drove forward genocide. Mass killing in the Soviet Union, whether identified as genocide or as closely related to genocide, drew heavily on central initiative from the highest levels of the Soviet state and terror apparatus. In the case of the former Yugoslavia, the incomplete trial of Slobodan Milosevic prevented a legal ruling on key questions of responsibility for ethnic cleansing, but other trials outlined the planning and organization of crimes against humanity and acts of genocide.

To describe genocide as a crime organized and executed by a narrow inner core of perpetrators, however, leaves out the role of broader circles of perpetrators. Survivors of the Armenian Genocide told of attacks carried out by diverse groups, including Kurds, along the deportation routes. In the Holocaust, police assisted in rounding up Jews and reserve police took part both in collecting victims and at times in shooting them. Units of the Wehrmacht or German Army also became involved in carrying out killings even if it is not possible to determine the percentages of such "ordinary" perpetrators. In the late twentieth century, paramilitaries carrying out ethnic cleansing in Bosnia brought in outsiders, though these had grown up in the same country as their victims, but many of those who survived ethnic cleansing also stated that the perpetrators included former neighbors and colleagues.

In no case were the victims in a position to by themselves halt genocide. Perpetrators pulverized the local leadership of targeted groups, disarming victims, and attacking communities without significant military resources of their own. In the Armenian Genocide, the special organization, Kurds, and armed bands assailed Armenians, mainly women, children, and the elderly, as they tried to make their way across mountain ranges into deserts. In the opening phases of the Holocaust, Einsatzgruppen swept through communities in the eastern Soviet Union, rounded up, and shot Jews. In ethnic cleansing in Yugoslavia irregulars, aided and assisted in many instances by the forces of client states that sought to divide up Bosnia, shot down residents of mixed towns and carried out massacres.

The inability of victims to by themselves halt genocide did not preclude the possibility of any resistance. The CUP vastly exaggerated any threat presented by Armenians to justify a wholesale campaign of deportation and slaughter, but Armenians close to the Ottoman-Russian border staged an uprising at Van. In the Holocaust, Jews did not represent any military threat to Germany, but still resisted both on an individual level, and with acts of armed defiance, especially at the point when it became clear that Germany aimed at nothing less than the annihilation of all Jews.

Acts of resistance by victimized groups did not make genocide an equivalent to war. Indeed, perpetrators repeatedly broke laws and customs of war even before the creation of the Genocide Convention. Civilians suffered grievous injuries from the wars of Europe's twentieth century, but in genocides perpetrators saw combatants and civilians as one and the same. This often began with treating all men as armed combatants, regardless of their age or military status, and ended with treating entire populations of targeted groups as enemy combatants. In genocide there was no battlefield in a conventional sense: instead perpetrators killed behind the front lines in areas where they already had full control.

Debate persists over the level of knowledge possessed by bystanders to genocide and related violence, but there is abundant evidence that significant numbers of bystanders either knew directly of the genocides of twentieth-century Europe or had sufficient information to be able to reach that conclusion. In Anatolia in 1915, the expulsions of Armenians were visible to onlookers in numerous towns and villages, and the evidence of slaughter was also clear to see in dead bodies in lakes, rivers, and along roads. In the case of the Holocaust, some killing was more secluded in the death camps, but many Germans as well as local residents witnessed the slaughter of mobile killing, and even the news of gassing leaked out through rumors. Deportations of Jews were also visible to many onlookers. In Yugoslavia in the 1990s, the killings carried out by paramilitaries and soldiers were also visible, and camps like Omarska and the many sites where rape was carried out soon became notorious in the surrounding areas.

Bystanders' attitude toward information was as important as the actual availability of information in shaping their responses to genocide. Different factors reduced the chances that bystanders would seek out or endeavor to comprehend the signs of genocide in their midst. Passivity in the face of expulsion and genocide reflected lack of solidarity that in some cases preexisted before the onset of war. Nazi Germany actively promoted the breakdown of solidarity by excluding Jews from the racial community and then by promoting the Aryan ideal through a barrage of propaganda. In parts of occupied Europe, the lack of apparent interest in the fate of Jews also reflected the fragility of relatively new nation-states and the breakdown of social solidarity during war and occupation. In all cases of genocide and related violence, preoccupation with the effects of war understandably caused many to think first of their own immediate families when they were not focused on war itself. Along with all these reasons, however, opportunism and the chance to gain economic benefits also contributed to passivity. In Anatolia, bystanders found they could snap up goods cheaply as Armenian were deported, and the seizure of Jews' homes, businesses, and goods, also brought gains to others through the process of Aryanization. Ethnic cleansing in Yugoslavia provided the chance to take over others' land and apartments, though newly created ethnic enclaves often suffered from very poor economic conditions.

Many bystanders were in the end mainly onlookers, but bystanders, like others in genocide, could also come to occupy a gray zone. Some, moved to assist perpetrators as did Kurds or others who attacked columns of Armenians, peasants who tipped off Germans looking for Jews, or the residents of Bosnian towns slated for ethnic cleansing who helped invading paramilitary forces to find and pick out victims. On the other hand, members of some of the very same groups moved in some cases to rescue. Thus, Kurds offered a comparatively safe haven for Armenians who could make it to the region of Dersim, some peasants in occupied Europe made the decision to allow Jews to hide in their houses or farms, and ordinary people in wartime Yugoslavia also on occasion aided those who faced ethnic cleansing.

Cycles of violence

In twentieth-century Europe, genocide frequently took place within longer cycles of violence—these cycles are most obvious when history looks beyond genocide and covers both genocide and related forms of violence such as ethnic cleansing. Genocides repeatedly occurred within longer cycles of violence in which episodes of related violence, including ethnic cleansing, took place before and after genocide.

The Armenian Genocide was both a devastating campaign against Ottoman Armenians and the peak of violence within a much longer cycle that began before the First World War and persisted for years after the war. Early forms of ethnic cleansing immediately preceded and followed the genocide. The violent breakup of the Ottoman Empire in Europe culminating in the First Balkan War sent Muslim refugees into the remaining core of the empire. Precipitated by waves of killings and arson attacks carried out both by irregulars and also by soldiers, this wave of ethnic cleansing radicalized Turkish nationalists in the Committee of Unity and Progress and fed a search for scapegoats. Within the First World War, the Armenian Genocide was part of a broader sequence of deportation of Greeks, and destruction of Assyrians carried out as part of the attack against population groups accused of disloyalty. The aftermath of war and genocide, in turn encouraged further violent ethnic and religious warfare in the Transcaucasus that lasted until 1920 and the final victories of the Turkish nationalists in Turkey and of the Bolsheviks in the Russian Civil War, though between 1918 and 1920 it was often difficult to distinguish between victims and perpetrators in ethnic warfare in the Transcaucasus. In the west, war followed the end of the First World War with the Greek-Turkish war that produced renewed ethnic cleansing along with population exchange.

The Holocaust, as well, was part of a longer cycle of violence, though in a less direct fashion than the Armenian Genocide. Jews represented no political or military threat to Germany, and were in no position to threaten the German war effort, despite such acts of resistance as the Warsaw Ghetto uprising. The German war of extermination, however, gave rise to a longer cycle of destruction, violence, and ethnic cleansing. Germans had reason to fear that they would pay a terrible price for the war of extermination waged by their armies in the east, but it was not specifically the Holocaust, but the German assault on the Soviet Union that led to the end of the German east. Germany's war in the east ended, not only with total German defeat, but also with the flight, ethnic cleansing, and expulsion of Germans from the short-lived Nazi empire and from regions in Eastern and Central Europe where Germans had lived long before the Third Reich. Germans fled in large numbers from across Eastern Europe before advancing Soviet forces. With German defeat, militias began to expel ethnic Germans from countries including Czechoslovakia and Poland before the Potsdam Accords of 1945 arranged for "population transfer" out of Czechoslovakia, Hungary, and Poland.

Ethnic cleansing and acts of genocide in the former Yugoslavia also fit into longer cycles of violence. The breakdown of Yugoslavia took place amidst a revival of very selective memories of the Second World War in which nationalists publicized accounts of terror from the Second World War. Once war started in the former Yugoslavia, all sides engaged in acts of vengeance. Serb forces typically gained the upper hand and carried out the bulk of ethnic cleansing in the early phases of the war, but in 1995 Serbs suffered ethnic cleansing when Serb forces were driven from the Krajina and from parts of Bosnia. After Serb forces drove Croats from the Krajina in 1991, Croat forces overran the Krajina in 1995, propelling mass flight of Serbs. In a similar pattern, Serb forces engaged in massive ethnic cleansing in Kosovo in 1999 before the tables turned there as well and Serbs poured out of much of Kosovo.

Charting these cycles of violence reveals two major points about genocide. First, victimization is closely linked to aggression. Secondly, the cycles show that the categories of perpetrators and victims can be fluid or at least can change over time. Victims typically had no chance to escape being killed in camps, massacres, and death marches. However, power relationships changed abruptly with the start and end of wars, so that ethnic or national groups that had once benefitted from the aggression of perpetrators themselves became victims of ethnic cleansing, and populations that had once suffered ethnic cleansing and even on occasion genocide, in some instances engaged in ethnic cleansing themselves.

Aftermaths of genocide

Knowledge of genocide

Twentieth-century European genocide left legacies of destruction that survivors, bystanders, and perpetrators as well as later generations struggled to confront. It was psychologically tempting to isolate the stories of survival and rescue to attempt to find an uplifting message of perseverance and courage. The theme of the triumph of the human spirit recurs in artistic representations of genocide. However, memoirs and diaries often ended with misery and devastation: Dawid Sierakowiak died, so too did Anne Frank and there were millions others who suffered the same end. Entire communities were devastated, and many never recovered. The Armenian communities of Central and Eastern Anatolia of towns and cities like Harput, Erzurum, and Diyarbakir and many others were gone for good. Former centers of Jewish culture and life stretching from the Baltic to the Balkans, from Vilnius to Salonica, suffered irreparable blows and many disappeared for good.

It can be hard to imagine but acts of genocide were often overlooked within years. The level of interest in discussing the past varied enormously. In the case of the Armenian Genocide, the deportations and massacres sparked significant attention during the First World War, and the memory of starving Armenians survived into early postwar years. There was still a nation-wide appeal in the United States in 1921 to provide aid for "starving Armenians" as well as other Christians in need in the Near East. Nonfiction and literature of the interwar years contained references to both Armenian massacres and to starving Armenians. However, the memories of the genocide dissipated among a broader public. The statement attributed to Hitler, "Who, after all, speaks to-day of the annihilation of the Armenians?" may not have been a major factor in a path toward the Holocaust, though the language suggested awareness of the low costs incurred from mass killing. However, the statement also revealed a larger truth: fading knowledge of genocide after genocide.

As in the case of the Armenian Genocide the level of interest and knowledge of the Holocaust varied enormously after the genocide itself. Despite the evidence of massive killings of Jews during the war, the extermination of European Jews only became widely known toward the war's end. Even then, shocked observers often saw the fate of Europe's Jews as part of the broader pattern of killing and suffering. Thus, accounts of liberation of concentration camps were more likely to stress shared suffering than to note the special effort to exterminate Jews.

The allies and the press, nonetheless, began to outline the dimensions of the campaign to exterminate European Jews. By May 2, 1945 the *New York Times* told of a campaign that "ended with the physical extermination of more than 3,000,000 men, women, and children of the Jewish faith." The Allied Military Government stated on June 8, 1945 that Nazis had exterminated at least 80 percent of Germany's Jews (this was an underestimate) and targeted every European Jew for murder by the end of 1946. And the International Military Tribunal received evidence of the murder of some 6 million European Jews. Major William Walsh presented the affidavit of Wilhelm Höttl, an SS Major, who said Eichmann had told him that 4 million had been killed in camps and 2 million in other ways.

The Holocaust was never entirely forgotten, but it was not a major topic of public discussion in the immediate postwar era. Primo Levi's account of Auschwitz, for example, gained some readers but did not achieve major success during its initial publication in 1947. Some of the unsold copies were later damaged in a flood. Republished in 1958, it subsequently remained in print, but Levi still only gradually won international recognition. Published in translation in the United States in 1959, it gained positive reviews without attracting much broader interest or sales. A German translation in

1961 initially did better, but it was years before Levi and his work gained international acclaim.

The situation was somewhat different in Israel, which instituted an official Holocaust and Ghetto Revolt Day in 1951. The linking of commemoration with the Ghetto Uprising with the Holocaust reflected Israeli ambivalence toward the Holocaust. The Israeli declaration of Independence of 1948 placed the Holocaust in a history of Jewish struggle that culminated with the founding of Israel: "The catastrophe which recently befell the Jewish people—the massacre of millions of Jews in Europe—was another clear demonstration of the urgency of solving the problem of its homelessness. . . ." However, in the early years of Israel, the fate of defenseless victims did not conform to the image of the rugged Israeli fighter.

From modest early postwar interest, efforts to represent and understand the Holocaust increased in the 1950s and 1960s. The publication of Anne Frank's *Diary* and the production of a play based on the *Diary* brought a key shift. Recovered by her father Otto after the war, the *Diary* was initially rejected by several Dutch publishers, and the first print run was only 1,500. It was published in German in 1950 and went on to sell 700,000 copies in paperback between 1955 and 1960. In the United States, the play based on the book won the Pulitzer Prize in 1956, and the play was also widely performed in the Federal Republic of Germany.

In the 1960s, a series of trials, most notably the trial of Adolf Eichmann held in 1961 in Israel, further increased interest in the Holocaust. Eichmann had escaped to Argentina and lived there under an assumed name, remarrying his wife before Israel mounted an operation with intelligence and security agents to capture him in 1960. Israel's prime minister David Ben-Gurion expressly saw the trial as an opportunity to tell Israelis who had grown up after the war about the past: "It is necessary that our young people remember what happened to the Jewish people . . ." He also wrote, "We want the nations of the world to know." The trial also yielded more problematic possible lessons such as debate over the role of Jewish councils, which Hannah Arendt noted in her influential book on the Eichmann trial, *Eichmann in Jerusalem: A Report on the Banality of Evil*. In the Federal Republic of Germany or West Germany, a series of trials of perpetrators, included a trial of perpetrators from Auschwitz carried out in Frankfurt between 1963 and 1965. The trial attracted much attention from the press and public, though a narrow legal framework for the charges focused more on individual criminal acts than on a broader campaign of extermination.

Even in the early 1970s, the Holocaust in public memory was not the Holocaust as it later came to be seen as a central and pivotal modern historical event. The term Holocaust was occasionally attached to the extermination of Jews as far back as during the war itself, sometimes referred to as "Hitler's holocaust" but the widespread discussion of "the Holocaust" only began to become more common in the 1970s. A key turning point surprisingly came with the Holocaust miniseries, broadcast in the United States in 1978 and in Germany in 1979. The miniseries received mixed reviews, but still presented the destruction of the Holocaust to a mass audience. In the 1980s and 1990s virtually all forms of discussion and representation of the Holocaust, ranging from books, to museum exhibits, to films, increased in number. This was the period of the film *Schindler's List* and of a long string of movies and documentaries.

KATHARINA VON KELLENBACH ON WATCHING THE HOLOCAUST MINISERIES

Kellenbach, a Professor of Religious Studies, was born in West Germany and like so many others watched the Holocaust miniseries in 1979 "In January of that year, the television miniseries *Holocaust* was broadcast to unprecedented numbers of viewers and extraordinary media attention . . . I was eighteen years old and determined to watch this series despite the Bavarian regional channel's refusal to broadcast it and my mother's attempts to prevent me from doing so. The series personalized the Holocaust by focusing on one Jewish family's experience and refocused what had been most Germans' prevailing political approach to the Third Reich. . . ." Kellenbach recalled how she had learned in the 1970s that her "uncle, Alfred Ebner, was accused of killing 20,000 Jews and that his trial had been discontinued because of the defendant's health." However, he regularly attended family events. "What was I to make of the fact that my relatives did not censure him? Wouldn't my family treat him as a murderer if he had killed one person? The fact that he sat among us unperturbed implied that the murder of tens of thousands never happened. I wondered how and where he did it, and who his victims were. But my attempts to make sense of this information were brushed off. 'Of course, he didn't do these things, these are all lies. Leave this old man his deserved peace, he has suffered enough.' In her family he was 'accepted as a victim of war and of postwar harassment.' However, von Kellenbach later carried out research into her uncle's wartime record." "In my own case, while some relatives don't talk to me anymore, others have begun to admit their knowledge: that they knew about Ebner's activities from letters he had sent during the war; that his wife, Margaret, joined him in Pinsk to work as a secretary in the civil administration, leaving her newborn son in the care of a grandmother in Germany; that they received gifts they vaguely were aware had come from Jewish victims. To face one's own closeness to horrific crimes is a painful process that requires great honesty and courage."

In the case of Yugoslavia in the 1990s, there was a much more rapid shift toward public attention. Many observers found the reports from the collapsing Yugoslavia confusing or bewildering, but reporters on the scene noted similarities between the slaughter and past episodes of European destruction such as the Holocaust. By the 1990s, the crimes of the Second World War provided a template for describing and debating the new tragedies. The lack of intervention to attempt to curb ethnic cleansing prompted charges that Europeans risked allowing another outbreak of genocide to develop despite the devastating lessons of the Second World War. Even more so than the Holocaust itself, the lack of response to the Holocaust provided a warning. The events, most observers stated were not identical, but the amount of information was incomparably greater than during the Holocaust.

LOUIS GENTILE ON BOSNIA AND "SCHINDLER'S LIST," JANUARY 10, 1994

In a lengthy letter to the editor to the *New York Times*, the Canadian diplomat Louis Gentile then on leave to the UN High Commissioner for Refugees made the case that events reminiscent to those described in "Schindler's List" were taking place again:

"I wonder how many of your readers have seen Steven Spielberg's 'Schindler's List' and how many hear of Banja Luka, Bosnia, in the heart of Europe . . . severe persecution has become a way of life. Minorities have been systematically stripped of all civil rights. . . . The terror continues, terror attacks by armed men at night, rape and murder. . . . To those who have said to themselves after seeing 'Schindler's List,' never again, it is happening again. The so-called leaders of the Western World have known what is happening here for the last year and a half. They receive play by play reports. They talk of prosecuting war criminals, but do nothing to stop the crimes. May God forgive them. May God forgive us all."

Coming to terms with the past

In debating how to understand Europe's history of genocide, Europeans as well as others have struggled to come to terms with past violence. Remembering, forgetting, and, in some cases, denying genocide have shaped national consciousness and identity. In the case of the Armenian Genocide commemorating genocide and winning acknowledgment of the reality of genocide became a focus of Armenian nationalism. Armenia ceased to be independent in 1920, but pressure for commemorating genocide emerged within the Soviet Republic of Armenia in the 1960s. On the fiftieth anniversary of the Armenian Genocide thousands gathered in Lenin Square in the Yerevan, the capital of the Armenian Soviet Socialist Republic. In 1967 the Armenian Genocide monument was completed on a hill atop Yerevan. The 1960s also saw many Armenian diaspora groups build genocide memorials. Armenian activists, intellectualists, artists, and musicians have continued to publicize and demand recognition of the genocide.

As Armenians called for recognition of genocide, Turkey and Turkish nationalists stepped up their assertions denying that genocide had occurred. For decades the Republic of Turkey denied genocide and pressured other countries to refrain from officially recognizing genocide. Turkey, for example, annually pressed successive Presidential administrations in the United States, both Democratic and Republican, to counter any congressional measures to recognize the genocide. The presence of a vast NATO airbase at Incirlik near Adana and Turkey's strategic position provided Turkey with leverage. Turkey's Foreign Ministry has also maintained a website that stressed Armenian killings of Turks, including assassinations of Turkish diplomats and that also provided samples of literature rejecting the genocide.

SPEECH OF TURKISH DEPUTY PRIME MINISTER AND MINISTER OF FOREIGN AFFAIRS GÜL 2005

This speech of Turkish Foreign Minister Gül provides an example of the Turkish government's rejection of the very idea of an Armenian Genocide:

"For a long time, Turkey has faced an extremely well organised campaign regarding genocide allegations which has not refrained from using any available opportunity. This organised campaign is based on prejudices, slander, lies, exaggerations and fabrications concerning our nation and our country which began to be disseminated nearly one century ago.".... "The efforts to depict the events of 1915 as genocide by distorting all these historical realities are also devoid of any legal basis." .... "The circles claiming genocide, despite their 90 year long tremendous efforts, could not find a single document suggesting the intent of the Ottomans to destroy Armenians. What they call documents proved to be fake.".... "Armenian allegations were not on the agenda for half a century after the foundation of the Republic. It seems that these allegations were accelerated after 1965 and turned into a campaign. Views and speculation about the motives behind it are various.

Some Armenian groups chose terrorism as a vehicle for promoting their so-called genocide allegations in world opinion.". . . . "The joint declaration of 8th March 2005 by our distinguished Prime Minister and the distinguished Chairman of the main opposition party has been an important turning point in indicating our perseverance of struggle in fighting against the Armenian allegations. Turkey has shown the whole wide world that she will commence a common struggle both with its political parties in power and opposition."

For both Armenians and Turks the issue of genocide became central to national identity. For Armenians who had suffered genocide, denying genocide constituted a second attack on their identity. For Turks, acknowledging genocide could be seen as a stain on the very founding of the Turkish Republic—the new Turkish state created in 1923 anchored national identity in a country from which most Armenians had been swept away. In principle, it might be possible for Turks to describe the Armenian Genocide as a destructive campaign carried out by discredited perpetrators who lost power (and in the case of Enver and Talat their lives), before the founding of the Turkish Republic, but the relationship between the Turkish Government of the First World War and the later Turkish Republic founded by Mustafa Kemal or Kemal Ataturk, remains complex. Entitling his book *A Shameful Act*, the Turkish historian Taner Akcam, who has held posts in Germany and the United States, quoted from Kemal Ataturk to make the case that if Kemal could refer to the killings of Armenians as a shameful act, other Turks should also be able to make their way to acknowledge the past.[1] However, Kemal's attitude toward the destruction of the Ottoman Armenians remains debated.

Amidst continued denial, some Turks have sought to come to terms with the past and with the mass killings of Armenians.

The notion of full-scale and monolithic Turkish rejection of the reality of the destruction of the Ottoman Armenians is not accurate. The use of the term "genocide" remains fraught, but a growing number of Turkish academics are coming to recognize the scale of the killings of Armenians. On a personal level, some Turks have also started to wonder if they might have Armenian ancestry, most often through a woman brought into a Turkish family during or immediately after the genocide. Fethiye Cetin, for example, a prominent human rights lawyer in Turkey, learned that her grandmother Seher had actually been born with the name Heranus as an Armenian in a Christian family. She wrote a book, *My Grandmother*, describing her grandmother's ordeal and survival in a new family.

FETHIYE CETIN MY GRANDMOTHER

Cetin tells how she revealed her grandmother's true past at her funeral:

"We, the women, stand waiting in the most isolated corner of the courtyard. As we stood there, embracing and weeping with the newcomers, a man from among the male throng came over in a flurry and asked:

'What are the names of Aunt Seher's mother and father?'

There was no immediate answer to this question from the group of women. We each gazed at the others. Our silence went on for a noticeably long time. Then finally, the silence was broken by one of the women, my aunt Zehra:

'Her father's name is Huseyin, her mother's Esma.'

As soon as she uttered these names, my aunt turned her eyes to me as if asking for affirmation, or so it seemed to me.

Just as the man turned away, relieved finally to have extracted an answer from this strangely reticent crowd of women, the following words tore themselves from my heart and broke out of my mouth:

'But that's not true! . . . Her mother's name is not Esma, it is Isquhi. And her father is not Huseyin, but Hovannes!'"

Still, recognition of genocide places Turks outside of the mainstream of political opinion and carries real risks. The clash between recognition of the past and denial took most violent form with the 2007 assassination of Hrant Dink, a Turkish Armenian journalist. A 17-year-old was found guilty, but many thought that he had acted with the support of others. A 2012 decision by a court holding that his killer had acted alone led to a protest in Istanbul.

The process of coming to terms with the past in the aftermath of the Holocaust was difficult even without a serious debate over denial. Holocaust denial has persisted but it remains largely restricted to a subculture—there is no counterpart, for example, to the official Turkish efforts to reject the label of genocide. Indeed, there are few if any other historical events so widely recognized. The Federal Republic of Germany recognized the reality of the Holocaust. In 1953 a reparations agreement arrived at between the Federal Republic and Israel the previous year went into effect. In the German Democratic Republic or East Germany, the Communist leadership took the position that it was inherently an anti-Fascist state that had inherited the anti-Fascism of opposition to the Nazi regime.

CHANCELLOR KONRAD ADENAUER ADDRESS TO BUNDESTAG SEPTEMBER 1951

Adenauer, first Chancellor of the Federal Republic of Germany, minimized public participation in the Holocaust but still spoke of the crimes carried out against Jews.

"Recently the world has on various occasions occupied itself with the attitude adopted by the Federal Republic toward the Jews. . . . The Federal Government and with it the vast majority of the German people is conscious of the immeasurable suffering that was brought upon the Jews in Germany and in the occupied territories during the period of National Socialism. The great majority of the German people abhorred the crimes committed against the Jews and had no part in them. . . . But unspeakable crimes have been committed in the name of the German people, which impose upon them the obligation to make moral and material amends both as regards the individual damage which Jews have suffered and as regards Jewish property for which there are no longer individual claimants. . . ."

The approach taken by the Federal Republic of Germany illustrated both real steps and sharp limits in coming to terms with the past. Denial was out of the question, but Adenauer asserted, without any evidence that most Germans had opposed crimes against Jews. This left entirely unresolved both the questions of what Germans had actually known about the Holocaust and of the participation of perpetrators beyond the leadership.

Without denying the Holocaust, West German memories of the Second World War often focused on German victimization. There was abundant reason for Germans to remember the bombing that had severely damaged much of the country including cities such as Dresden, the expulsion and flight of millions of Germans from Eastern and Central Europe, the violence and rape that many Germans suffered in the early period of occupation, especially in areas entered by the Soviets, and prisoners who in some cases languished in Soviet camps for years after the war. This strong sense of victimization in the early postwar era also resurfaced decades later in the Federal Republic with books and documentaries on subjects such as the bombings and expulsions.

Beginning in the 1960s a generational shift led to an increase in questioning about the role of ordinary Germans both in the Nazi dictatorship and more specifically in the Holocaust. Interest in the history of daily life turned up more details about life and death in the Third Reich at the local level. In place of Adenauer's effort to separate Germans in general from the crimes of the Third Reich, Germans increasingly came to terms with the idea that Hitler and the SS had not carried out the Holocaust without broader participation. This was a very gradual and incomplete shift in opinion. From the

1980s onward, discussion of the role of the military in the war of extermination on the Eastern Front and in crimes of the Holocaust caused recurrent controversies.

Other European countries faced much the same changes in coming to terms with the Holocaust. Where Germans shortly after the war tended to blame the Nazi leadership for genocide, blame in other countries fell to the Germans. But though Nazi Germany clearly initiated the Holocaust, apportioning blame only to Germans had the effect of shielding the actions of the local population from greater scrutiny. The fact that Germany had victimized so many other peoples did not prevent the possibility of passivity or actual complicity in genocide. In France for example, collaboration in general with the Germans was assigned to a small group. That picture collapsed in the 1960s, especially after the release of the 1969 Marcel Ophuls documentary, "The Sorrow and the Pity." A broader public discussion of French complicity in the Holocaust took still longer to emerge, and in 1995 President Jacques Chirac acknowledged a French role in the Holocaust. In even stronger terms, Poland after the Second World War took the country's status as a victim during the Second World War to reject any complicity in the Holocaust. In fact, German occupation was especially harsh in Poland, but after the end of the Cold War research on pogroms and on relations between Poles and Jews during the Holocaust cast doubt on the idea that Poles had always stood apart from the Holocaust. The publication in 2001 of the book *Neighbors* by Jan Gross that detailed Polish participation in a pogrom at the town of Jedwabne in 1941prompted controversy in Poland.

The process of coming to terms with the past for other possible cases of genocide during the Second World War and the period leading up to the war revealed a common pattern in which genocide or related crimes were both ignored by much of the wider world but also emerged as major focal points for research and in some cases for debates about national identity. The literature on the Roma and Sinti, or as they are more commonly known Gypsies, told of the devouring or the Porajmos. Genocide emerged as a major theme in Ukrainian identity. In the late Soviet era and even more so after the breakup of the Soviet Union, Ukrainians both abroad and in Ukraine popularized the use of the term Holodomor or famine murder as a kind of equivalent for genocide by deliberate starvation. The Holodomor has been commemorated through a remembrance day and the construction of monuments. In republics of southern Russia, Chechens and Ingush recalled their deportation into Central Asia by Stalin, and Chechen rebels fought a long war for independence after the breakup of the Soviet Union, which Russia suppressed only after years of fighting.

The process of coming to terms with the past across much of Eastern and Central Europe was both fragmented and competitive. Remembering the past became caught up in the politics of both the Cold War and of the period after the Cold War. The identification of Fascism, Nazism, and the extreme political right with genocide prompted a backlash by opponents of Communism, who did not typically deny the Holocaust, but stressed crimes carried out under the Soviet Union and other Communist regimes.

For more recent acts of genocide in the former Yugoslavia, any process of coming to terms with the past is just beginning. Here again, separate and often competing narratives of victimization have emerged among peoples left traumatized by war, ethnic cleansing, and massacres. In Serbia, for example much of the population saw Serbia as the victim of war. Still, Serbs began to confront the violence of the breakup of Yugoslavia—the release of a video of Srebrenica in 2005 that showed Serb paramilitary police carrying out torture and murders prompted shock and the arrest and trial of several of the men who appeared in the video. In 2010 the Serbian Parliament narrowly passed a resolution that condemned the massacre at Srebrenica. In July 2010 Serbian President Boris Tadić attended a ceremony in Srebrenica commemorating the fifteenth anniversary of the massacre, and though he did not receive a warm welcome from some at the event placed a wreath "to the innocent victims from Serb President Boris Tadić."

Europe genocide and the world

Europe during the twentieth century was a key site for genocide but not the only major site for genocide. Indeed, genocide was a global phenomenon. As in the case of Europe, the level of acceptance of the term genocide for examples of mass killing elsewhere varies. Of all the many examples of mass killing outside of Europe during the twentieth century, the Cambodian Genocide and the Rwandan Genocide count among the core examples of genocide. These genocides, as well as others, shared common elements with Europe's twentieth-century genocides, and a history of prior contact with Europe actually shaped conditions for genocide.

Imperialism, decolonization, and genocide

Some of the roots of European genocide have been traced to European imperialism, but the decline of European imperial power had decidedly mixed effects. The twentieth century saw a drastic decline in European overseas power marked by rapid decolonization after the Second World War. European decolonization in Asia and Africa gave rise to local self-determination and the possibility of democratization. However, decolonization not only sometimes failed to bring democracy, but also helped, in some instances, to give rise to genocide and to related violence.

The connection between imperialism, decolonization, and subsequent ethnic violence was most obvious in the case of Rwanda. This small country, bordered on the west by the Congo, was placed under imperial rule by Germany and then transferred to Belgium in 1919 when the Treaty of Versailles removed all colonies from Germany. Colonial rule consolidated ethnic distinctions between Rwanda's Hutu majority (some 85–90% of the population) and Tutsi minority (some 10–15% of the population)—there was also a smaller Twa minority.

In principle Tutsis were described as pastoralists who raised herds of cattle and held greater power than Hutu farmers, but theories of racial origins introduced by Europeans obscured any actual differences between the two groups. A Hamitic hypothesis, named after Ham the son of Noah, identified the Tutsis as descendants of invaders from the north and justified a colonial policy of privileging the Tutsi minority over the Hutu majority. Belgium made these identities official and in 1933 required the population to carry identity cards marking individuals as Hutus or Tutsis. With the approach of independence, however, Belgium shifted course, to seek closer ties with the Hutu majority.

Sharply divided by the experience of colonial rule, Hutus and Tutsis engaged in multiple waves of violence after independence. Attacks on Tutsis in 1962 prompted the flight of refugees. In 1963

Tutsi exiles attacked from the neighboring country of Burundi, which shared a similar ethnic makeup to Rwanda, but these attacks led to further massacres of Tutsis in Rwanda. There was further violence in 1967 and in 1972–3. Violence spiked again in the early 1990s with a new campaign led by the Rwandan Patriotic Front or RPF, a movement led by Tutsi exiles living in Uganda. Under pressure, the Rwandan Government reached a peace accord in 1993, but in 1994 genocide started shortly after a plane carrying the Presidents of Rwanda and neighboring Burundi was shot down in Kigali on April 6, 1994, an act usually attributed to Hutu extremists.

Former European imperial powers counted among the many countries, including the United States, that failed to prevent or halt genocide. At the very start of the killing wave, Rwandan soldiers murdered ten Belgian soldiers who had been sent to Rwanda as peacekeepers. The killings led Belgium, the former colonial power, to withdraw all of its peacekeepers. Other countries followed, leaving a small peacekeeping contingent under the command of Canadian General Romeo Dallaire that lacked the mission or the force to curb the escalating killing.

France, though never the colonial power in Rwanda, was also involved in the country. As part of a broader policy of maintaining close connections with French-speaking African countries, France had helped to sustain the Habyarimana regime. Even after Habyarimana's death, France maintained ties with the succeeding Rwandan Government. Only during the late stages of genocide did France intervene in western Rwanda in Operation Turquoise. This controversial mission was described as creating a safe haven, but France also faced charges that the intervention was ineffective and offered protection to Hutu militias.

The Rwandan genocide took place at a rapid pace. Hutu militias called Interahamwe searched for and killed Tutsis, taking advantage of the official system of identity. Demanding identity cards provided a ready way to find and murder Tutsis at roadblocks. To seek to evade death some Tutsis discarded their cards, but then had to gain temporary papers from local magistrates. The killing was typically very direct: the perpetrators used machetes to murder their victims. Survivors also told of seeing their friends, relatives, and neighbors killed with stones. Hate radio broadcast by Radio Television des Mille Collines urged the killers on to the task with messages such as: "Ah, they must be exterminated. Let us sing! The Tutsi have been killed. God is always just." By July some 800,000 Rwandans had been killed—mostly Tutsis but also some moderate Hutus. The genocide ended abruptly when the RPF gained control of Rwanda, and many Interahamwe as well as other Hutus fled the country.

Decolonization led to extreme violence in other instances, though, seldom to examples so clearly identified as genocide. In South Asia, partition and independence led to a massive flow of population. On August 15, 1947 Britain withdrew from India through a plan that created two new states separated by religion: Pakistan—a largely Muslim state, and India—a state with a large Hindu majority. Independence soon gave rise to religious violence concentrated in particular regions such as the Punjab. Propelled in many cases by attacks, millions of Hindus fled Pakistan and millions of Muslims fled regions of India, though many Muslims remained in the new India. In all some 500,000 to 1 million died.

More indirectly, decolonization also created potential for ethnic and religious violence when the transition to independence left diverse ethnic or religious groups competing for power within the boundaries of a former colonial state. The country of Sudan, for example, saw repeated outbreaks of extreme violence during conflict between the north and southern regions. Ethnicity and religion divided the predominantly Muslim north from a largely Christian or animist south and contributed to multiple phases of civil war that ended with the independence of South Sudan in 2011, though further rounds of ethnic violence broke out almost immediately within the new state. In the Darfur region of western Sudan, warfare that broke out in 2003 pitted the government of Sudan and militias called Janjaweed against populations that shared Islam, but that were identified more as African than as Arab. Many scholars and prominent observers identified the destruction of villages, massacres, and ensuing mass flight from Darfur as escalating to the level of genocide.

The Cambodian Genocide

Along with Rwanda, the example almost uniformly seen as genocide struck the Southeast Asian country of Cambodia. Bordered on the east by Vietnam and the west by Thailand, Cambodia endured a long and complex struggle for power that led to genocide carried out by the Khmer Rouge or Cambodian Communists between 1975 and 1979. Both Cambodia and Vietnam, along with the country of Laos, had been part of French Indochina. In 1945, shortly before the end of the Second World War, Cambodia's King declared the country's independence, and in 1953 France relinquished control of the country to Cambodians. The Khmer Rouge itself emerged from young Cambodians who traveled and lived in France and Europe in the early 1950s and then returned to organize a revolutionary communist movement. By the 1970s they fought against a civilian government led by Prime Minister Lon Nol in a country severely damaged by the Vietnam War. The United States launched bombing raids on the country to attack Viet Cong (guerillas supported by North Vietnam) supply routes, even though Cambodia was not a party to the Vietnam War. The millions of tons of munitions dropped on the country caused deaths, disrupted agriculture, terrified the peasant population, and led to further instability. In 1975, Khmer Rouge forces overthrew the government of Cambodia.

Entering the capital of Phnom Penh the Khmer Rouge ordered the residents to evacuate on the pretext that the city faced attack from the United States and the CIA or that urban areas lacked food. The Khmer Rouge forced hundreds of thousands of residents of Phnom Penh and the country's other urban areas out of their homes. This marked a sweeping attack on urban areas and the elites associated with them that extended to all Cambodians held to be influenced by foreign views. In this climate to even possess and wear eye glasses was dangerous. In the country side the former urban residents became "new people." Hard labor and ideological indoctrination were supposed to rid the new people of foreign contamination and bring them to the presumed purity of the Khmer peasants who were designated "base people."

The perpetrators of genocide in Cambodia both drew on and reacted against the influence of Europe and of the West more broadly. The irony, of course, was that many of the chief Khmer Rouge leaders themselves had lived abroad before they undertook a campaign to eliminate their country of foreign influences. In their attacks on minorities and obsession with purity, they drew on strains of nationalism and racism that had emerged in large part in Europe. However, in their attacks on urban residents and Cambodians who displayed any trace of foreign education, they attacked and killed those most like themselves.

The Khmer Rouge embarked on a campaign of slaughter to purify the population. Revolutionary cadres called Angkar carried out killings. They murdered most of their victims in the countryside in the open air in what became known as killing fields. Later investigations turned up some 19,000 grave pits. The Khmer Rouge also killed thousands at the Tuol Sleng detention center housed in a former school. Murdering Cambodians accused of lacking purity the Khmer Rouge also targeted ethnic minorities, including Chinese, Vietnamese, and the Cham Muslim minority. In all the killings and the deaths from famine and starvation mounted to some 1.8 million people before a failed Khmer Rouge attack on Vietnam prompted a Vietnamese invasion and the fall of the Khmer Rouge in 1979.

Genocide in the world and genocide in Europe

Genocide in Rwanda and Cambodia shared several key features with European genocides. The ideological pursuit of national and racial purity so central to the genocide in twentieth-century Europe also helped to propel genocide in Rwanda. Newspapers and radio broadcasts in Rwanda called for separation and purification. The Khmer Rouge similarly aimed to purify society through violence and spoke of eliminating sources of contamination. The Khmer Rouge did in principle try to remake some of the new people into base people, but others, much like Jews in Nazi Germany, were presented as a kind of essential biological threat.

1976 KHMER ROUGE REPORT ON MICROBES

A 1976 Khmer Rouge report sometimes attributed to Pol Pot spoke about threats to the Khmer Rouge in biological terms:

There is a sickness inside the party. . . . We cannot locate it precisely. The sickness must emerge to be examined. Because the heat of the people's revolution and the heat of democratic revolution were insufficient at the level of class struggle among all layers of the national democratic revolution, we search for the microbes within the party, without success. They are buried. As our socialist revolution advances, however, seeping into every corner of the Party, the army and among the people, we can locate the ugly microbes.

In Cambodia the focus on class enemies was also reminiscent of the Soviet Union and of purges in other Communist states such as China. The Soviet Union had persecuted so-called bourgeois experts as well as Kulaks for their insufficient dedication to Communism. Like the Soviet Union, the Khmer Rouge employed concepts of class and ethnicity in targeting victims. Building up a preferred class in opposition to those the Khmer Rouge termed the "oppressor class" was reminiscent of the kind of social engineering carried out by Communist regimes, though the Cambodian focus on the peasantry drew much more closely on the Chinese than on the Soviet model. Mao in China had launched a cultural revolution that swept many accused of insufficient revolutionary loyalty out of urban communities. As in Cambodia, traits associated with Western-style education brought the risk of being forced into a process of reeducation through hard labor.

As the case of terror in the Soviet Union demonstrated, the classifying of purges in Communist states may not literally fit the UN definition of genocide, which does not mention a political group among the list of possible victims. However, efforts to destroy class enemies could also acquire a strong ethnic, national, or racial dimension. Thus, class and racial purification overlapped in Cambodia. The Cambodian Genocide stood out from other genocides in one respect: in Cambodia, genocide was directed not just at ethnic minorities, but at the Khmer themselves. Nazi Germany killed many Germans in pursuit of racial purity, but the Khmer Rouge leaders proved even more intent on mass killing of their own people.

Major genocides within and outside of Europe also shared some of the same methods, though the role of death camps for killings was not nearly as central as in the Holocaust. The Cambodian

Genocide, for example, employed killing at discrete physical sites such as Tuol Sleng—photographs taken of those about to be killed document the moments before death. However, while death camps and in particular Auschwitz became central symbols of genocide after the Holocaust, genocides elsewhere more often relied on massacres. Neither the killing fields in Cambodia nor the murders carried out at roadblocks or at scattered sites around the country, including churches, where Tutsis tried in vain to find refuge closely resembled the death camps of the Holocaust or the Gulag of the Soviet Union.

Most killing in Rwanda took place through more or less the same method of swift massacres, but the Cambodian Genocide, like most European genocides, also included multiple acts of genocide. The Angkar carried out repeated massacres and shootings, but Khmer Rouge policies also ensured mass death among even those who were not immediately murdered. The Khmer Rouge made targeted populations undertake forced labor with meager rations. In this way, they subjected persecuted populations to "conditions of life calculated to bring about its physical destruction in whole or in part."

The genocides of twentieth Europe stand at the center of what has often been described as a "century of genocide." Even though the Holocaust was not the first genocide, the comparative analysis of genocide began with research into the Holocaust and then branched out into other examples both within and beyond Europe. The industrialization of killing in the Holocaust drew attention to the connection between modernity and genocide, and the tragic reality that genocide recurred repeatedly after the Holocaust suggested that genocide was a feature of modernity. Even as researchers followed the path of genocides as far back as the ancient world with examples such as the destruction of Carthage by Rome in the Punic Wars, the field of genocide studies also identified modern elements of genocide, including the power of racist and nationalist ideologies, the effort to classify and categorize populations according to abstract criteria, and the role of powerful modern states and bureaucracies.

The modern element to the Cambodian and Rwandan genocide did not lie in particular in the means of killing. In Rwanda, Interahamwe used comparatively simple means to kill at a rate equivalent to that of the Holocaust, although for a much shorter period of time. On the other hand, Rwandan killers employed a scheme of population classification introduced under imperial rule to select and identity victims. Such methods of categorizing victims were reminiscent of the Holocaust where Nazi Germany forced Jews to mark themselves as separate though varied means including passports, officially accepted names, and the mark of the yellow star.

Cambodian perpetrators embraced modern ideologies even as they also distanced themselves from some of the very foreign ideas that had shaped the emergence of the Khmer Rouge. The Khmer Rouge introduced new schemes to classify the population but also consistently targeted symbols of modernity. Urban residents counted among the first wave of victims of persecution and the genocide also targeted professionals with any of the kind of credentials of modern society. Thus, the Cambodian Genocide, through drawing on modern ideologies, in some ways sought to attack modern society.

Law and prevention

Genocide and international law

The responses to twentieth-century European genocides were instrumental both in creating the concept of genocide and in placing genocide in international law. Raphael Lemkin was already interested in past massacres and in what he termed acts of barbarity and acts of vandalism before the Second World War. In 1933 he wrote of the dangers of "acts of extermination directed against the ethnic, religious, or social collectives." But he invented the concept of genocide during the Second World War. Contrasting genocide with the long-term trend toward creating laws of war, Lemkin wrote in 1944, "In the present war, however, genocide is widely practiced by the German occupant."

The experience of the war and recognition of the abuse and killing of civilians contributed to the passage of the UN Convention on the Punishment and Prevention of the Crime of Genocide in 1948. In 1945 the indictment of the International Military Tribunal at Nuremberg, formed to prosecute German leaders, charged the defendants with "deliberate and systematic genocide, viz., the extermination of racial and national groups," in particular "Jews, Poles, and Gypsies, and others." Some of the subsequent military tribunals focused on cases related to genocide, but dismay with absence of genocide from the verdict of the International Military Tribunal motivated Lemkin to lobby the United Nations to make genocide a crime under international law. Lemkin's quest to advance a law of genocide was also personal: he learned that 49 of his relatives had died in the Holocaust, though he also referred to other cases of destruction and abuse of human rights to make his case to delegates of the United Nations.

In the late twentieth century, international responses to ethnic cleansing in the former Yugoslavia gave impetus to renewed efforts to investigate and persecute acts of genocide, along with other related crimes against human rights, under international law. The international tribunals created to investigate war crimes and crimes against humanity carried out by Nazi Germany and by Japan concluded their work without establishing any successors to prosecute related crimes, including genocide, elsewhere. However, in the early 1990s the violence in Bosnia gave rise to calls for legal action against possible genocide. Following preliminary investigation by a Commission of Experts, the UN Security Council established in 1993 a Tribunal for Yugoslavia (ICTY)—shortly afterwards in 1994 it also created an International Criminal Tribunal for Rwanda (ICTR).

Both the ICTR and ICTY further developed international law for the crime of genocide. The ICTR established precedent finding that rape was an act of genocide as a method to destroy a group. The Tribunal determined that rape caused "serious bodily or mental harm to members of the group" and also imposed "measures intended to prevent births within the group."

The ICTY established precedents for the scope of its work investigating and prosecuting charges of war crimes, crimes against humanity, genocide, and major "breaches" of the 1949 Geneva Conventions. The ICTY attracted criticism at times for what some saw as its caution and the slow pace of proceedings, most notably in the case of Slobodan Milosevic who died before the conclusion of his trial. On the other hand, the ICTY tried numerous cases and sought to take a balanced approach. Through 2011, the ICTY indicted 161 individuals and heard testimony from more than 4,000 witnesses, creating a detailed historical and legal record. The International Criminal Tribunal for Yugoslavia or ICTY tried many cases related to ethnic cleansing, without actually placing charges of ethnic cleansing at the center of the court's work, in large part because ethnic cleansing was not a recognized crime under international law. In contrast, several trials yielded detailed analysis of the procedures for convicting individuals of the crime of genocide, and the ICTY also broke major ground in international law by clearly establishing that rape is a form of torture.

Lessons from Europe—preventing genocide

Of all cases of genocide, none was more central than the Holocaust in giving rise to the statement "never again" or to the determination that genocide should never recur. But as the history of Europe itself, not to mention that of Rwanda and Cambodia indicated, genocide has in fact recurred. The effort to glean useful insights from the history of genocide has led to efforts to identity warning signs to detect possible future cases of genocide at an early stage. This is no easy task because selecting key warning signs depends in large part on which cases of genocide are seen as most likely to predict future threats.

One major approach to detecting possible early signs of potential genocide begins with the best-known case: the Holocaust. If the Holocaust is taken as a norm or template for genocide, we should look for early signs of racial discrimination, classification, and categorization of populations, and state-directed terror in highly organized and powerful dictatorships. The example of the Soviet Union reinforces that advice, even for those authors who see Soviet terror and response to famine as closely related to genocide rather than as genocide.

Other cases of genocide from twentieth-century Europe while sharing many common features with the Holocaust, however, offer some different lessons for detecting possible warning signs of genocide. In the Armenia Genocide and in the former Yugoslavia, genocide and acts of genocide emerged from ethnic and religious conflicts. In contrast, German Jews had for the most part seen themselves very much as members of the same nation as Germans, which made the onset of radical anti-Semitism all the more shocking. Both the Armenian and Yugoslav cases also reveal the potential for genocide and acts of genocide to take place in weakening or fragmenting states: the Ottoman Empire had just lost much of its territory on the eve of the First World War and ethnic cleansing immediately followed the actual breakup of Yugoslavia. Based on these examples, efforts to detect early warning signs of possible genocide should look for outbreaks of ethnic and or religious violence in divided or even in collapsing states.

Along with combining lessons from different cases of genocide to watch for very different warning signs for genocide, efforts to prevent genocide need to also take into account the varied acts of genocide and the very close relationship between genocide and related ethnic cleansing and mass killing. We can only hope that there will never be another case of killing in death camps, but even if efforts at genocide prevention focus on signs of massacres, multiple examples from the history of Europe also show the need to watch for policies that intentionally create conditions that will predictably lead to the destruction of populations in whole or in part. In addition, though targeting of victims by gender is only implied in the Genocide Convention, the prevention of genocide must also watch for policies that attack particular genders. Finally, efforts to detect potential genocide must also be alert to warning signs of closely related forms of violence. It will be of no consolation if experts after the fact conclude that a particular campaign of destruction was due to mass killing or to ethnic cleansing rather than to genocide.

Along with the providing insights into how to detect potential early warning signs of genocide, the history of twentieth-century European genocide also offers instructive lessons about the challenge of responding to genocide. The record is not by and large encouraging. Again and again, perpetrators killed without facing much intervention or active resistance beyond the efforts of victims themselves who invariably lacked the means to stop genocide on their own. In a world organized around states in which nation-states act first and foremost in their own national interests, attempting to stop the slaughter of other peoples will always prove difficult.

The tragic series of European genocides does offer some ideas for how to respond to genocide. Along with taking news of genocide seriously and looking out for signs of genocide, punishing perpetrators can create awareness of the costs of engaging in genocide. In halting fashion, international law has slowly built up legal precedents for investigating and punishing the crime of genocide. In principle the prosecution of perpetrators by international tribunals may cause some potential perpetrators to think twice before embarking on policies of destruction. Even in the Second World War, some German allies held back from deporting their own Jewish populations and tried to extricate themselves from their alliance with Germany as the war turned in favor of the allies.

Publicity and the threat of punishment can provide incentives to refrain from genocide, but the history of the twentieth century also indicates that some perpetrators will continue to kill until they are stopped. In the case of the Holocaust only total defeat of Germany ended the killing, and even though the allies did not intervene to stop the Holocaust their victory had that effect. Bosnia provides an instructive example of both the failure and potential for intervention. The disaster at Srebrenica demonstrated the failings of peacekeeping operations that lack sufficient force or that operate within narrow mandates. On the other hand, NATO intervention in 1995 did have a decisive effect because it both demonstrated broad will on the part of NATO allies and because the military means were sufficient to persuade key parties to the conflict to negotiate.

The history of twentieth-century European genocide gives cause to monitor conditions likely to lead to genocide and to act to prevent potential future genocides. It is easy to say never again without doing anything to seek information about potential genocide let alone to seek to stop genocide, and the recurrence of genocide and ethnic cleansing also makes clear that preventing genocide is no easy task. On the other hand, the insights that can be gained from reviewing these tragedies in Europe's tumultuous twentieth century offer possible approaches for monitoring the approach of genocide, raising the costs of engaging in mass killing, and creating pressure to stop genocides.

Study questions

- What common patterns is it possible to find in the causes of twentieth-century European genocides?
- What common patterns do twentieth-century European genocides reveal in the actions of perpetrators, victims, and bystanders?
- How did twentieth-century European genocides fit within longer cycles of violence that began before and continued beyond genocides?
- How did public knowledge of genocide increase after twentieth-century European genocides?

- How did European come to terms with the past reality of genocide?
- How were other cases of twentieth-century genocides outside of Europe related to European genocides?
- How did twentieth-century European genocides shape the development of international law?
- What lessons does the history of twentieth-century European genocides offer for seeking to prevent future genocides?

NOTES

Introduction

1 Mark Mazower, *Dark Continent: Europe's Twentieth Century* (New York: Alfred A. Knopf, 1998).

Chapter 1

1 Bartolomé de las Caass, *A Short Account of the Destruction of the Indies*, ed. and trans. by Nigel Griffin (London: Penguin, 1992), 11.
2 Henry Morton Stanley, *Through the Dark Continent*, vol. 2 (London, 1878), 51.
3 Adam Hochschild, *King Leopold's Ghost: A Story of Greed, Terror, and Heroism in Colonial Africa* (Boston: Houghton Mifflin, 1998), 202.
4 Jürgen Zimmerer, Joachim Zeller and Edward Neather, *The Genocide in German Southwest Africa: The Colonial War (1904–1908) and its Aftermath* (Merlin Press, 2008), 134.
5 Hull, *Absolute Destruction*, 86–7.
6 Anthony Trollope, *Australia and New Zealand*, vol. 1 (London: Chapman and Hall, 1873), 499.
7 Patrick Brantlinger, *Dark Vanishings: Discourse on the Extinction of Primitive Races, 1800–1930* (Ithaca: Cornell University Press, 2003).
8 Dominik J. Shaller and Jürgen Zimmerer, "Settlers, Imperialism, Genocide: Seeing the Global without Ignoring the Local— Introduction," *Journal of Genocide Research* 10 (2008): 192–4.
9 R. J. Crampton, *Bulgaria*, The Oxford History of Modern Europe (Oxford: Oxford University Press, 2007), 82.
10 Houston Stewart Chamberlain, *Foundations of the Nineteenth Century*.
11 Ian Kershaw, *Hitler: 1889–1936 Hubris* (New York: W.W. Norton, 1999).

12 Adolf Hitler and Clemens Vollnhals, *Hitler: Reden, Schriften, Anordnungen: Februar 1925 bis Januar 1933* (München: K.G. Saur, 1992), vol. II/1, 612.

13 Chris Bellamy, *Absolute War: Soviet Russia in the Second World War* (New York: Knopf, 2007), 9.

14 Benjamin Madley, "From Africa to Auschwitz: How German Southwest Africa Incubated Ideas and Methods Adopted and Developed by the Nazis in Eastern Europe," *European History Quarterly* 35 (2005): 429–64.

15 Hitler, *Reden Schriften Anordnungen* Band IV Teil 1, 407.

Chapter 2

1 Grigoris Palakéan, Peter Balakian, and Aris G. Sevag, *Armenian Golgotha: A Memoir of the Armenian Genocide, 1915–1918* (New York: Vintage Books, 2010), 45, 57, 127, 136, 139.

2 Leon Trotsky, George Weissman, and Duncan Williams, *The Balkan Wars, 1912–13: The War Correspondence of Leon Trotsky* (New York: Monad Press, 1980), 255.

3 Taner Akçam, *The Young Turks' Crime against Humanity: The Armenian Genocide and Ethnic Cleansing in the Ottoman Empire* (Princeton: Princeton University Press, 2012), xvi, 48, 130–4.

4 Clarence D. Ussher and Grace Higley Knapp, *An American Physician in Turkey: A Narrative of Adventures in Peace and in War* (Boston and New York: Houghton Mifflin Company, 1917), 239.

5 Henry Morgenthau, *Ambassador Morgenthau's Story* (Garden City, NY: Doubleday, 1918), 345.

6 Taner Akçam, *A Shameful Act: The Armenian Genocide and the Question of Turkish Responsibility* (New York: Metropolitan Books, 2006), 155.

7 Ussher, *An American Physician in Turkey*, 218.

8 Henry H. Riggs, *Days of Tragedy in Harput: Personal Experiences in Harpoot, 1915–1917* (Ann Arbor: Gomidas Institute, 1997), 47–9.

9 Arnold Toynbee and James Bryce Bryce, *The Treatment of Armenians in the Ottoman Empire, 1915–16: Documents Presented to Viscount Grey of Fallodon, Secretary of State for Foreign Affairs, by Viscount Bryce* (London: H.M.S.O, 1916), 573.

10 James L. Barton, *Turkish Atrocities: Statements of American Missionaries on the Destruction of Christian Communities in Ottoman Turkey, 1915–1917* (Ann Arbor, MI: Gomidas Institute, 1998), 23.

11 Leslie A. Davis and Susan Blair, *The Slaughterhouse Province: An American Diplomat's Report on the Armenian Genocide, 1915–1917* (New Rochelle, NY: A.D. Caratzas, Orpheus Pub. 1989), 60.
12 Davis, *Slaughterhouse Province*, 80.
13 Wolfgang Gust, *Der Völkermord an den Armeniern 1915/16: Dokumente aus dem Politischen Archiv des deutschen Auswärtigen Amts* (Springe: Zu Klampen, 2005). Or see the site www.armenocide.de
14 *Armenian Genocide Documentation*, vol. 2, 205.
15 Davis, *Slaughterhouse Province*, 52.
16 Riggs, *Days of Tragedy in Harput*, 140.
17 Morgenthau, *Ambassador Morgenthau's Story*, 337, 352.
18 Balakian, *Armenian Golgotha*, 79, 81.
19 Vahakn N. Dadrian and Taner Akçam, *Judgement at Istanbul: The Armenian Genocide Trials* (New York: Berghahn Books, 2011), 299–300.
20 Balakian, *Armenian Golgotha*, 139.
21 Balakian, *Armenian Golgotha*, 145.
22 www.armenocide.net/armenocide/armgende.nsf/$$AllDocs/1915–07–17-DE-002
23 Akçam, *Young Turks' Crime against Humanity*, 304–8.
24 Mary Caroline Holmes, *Between the Lines in Asia Minor* (New York: Fleming H. Revell Co., 1923), 29.
25 Davis, *Slaughterhouse Province*, 54.
26 Barton, *Turkish Atrocities*, 210.
27 Gust, *Der Völkermord an den Armeniern 1915/16*; and www.armenocide.net/armenocide/armgende.nsf/$$AllDocs/1915–08–05-DE-002*Armenian Genocide Documentation*, vol. 2, 205.
28 Armin T. Wegner, "Letter to Hitler," *Journal of Genocide Research* 2 (2000), 139–44.
29 Henry Morgenthau, *I was Sent to Athens* (NY: Doubleday, Doran & Co., 1929), 16.
30 David Gaunt, *Massacres, Resistance, Protectors: Muslim-Christian Relations in Eastern Anatolia During World War I* (Piscataway, NJ: Gorgias Press, 2006), 121.
31 Balakian, *Burning Tigris*, 342–4; and Balakian, *Black Dog of Fate*, 254–8.
32 Akçam, *The Young Turks' Crime against Humanity*, 311–20.

Chapter 3

1 Robert Gellately, *Lenin, Hitler and Stalin: The Age of Social Catastrophe* (New York: Alfred A. Knopf, 2007), 52.

2 Aleksander Solzhenitsyn, *The Gulag Archipelago: An Experiment in Literary Investigation,* vol. 1 (New York: Harper & Row, 1976), 37.

3 Miron Dolot, *Execution by Hunger: The Hidden* Holocaust (New York: W. W. Norton, 1987), 140.

4 Dolot, *Execution by Hunger,* 180.

5 Timothy Snyder, *Bloodlands: Europe between Hitler and Stalin* (New York: Basic Books, 2010), 72, 81.

6 Solzhenitsyn, *The Gulag Archipelago,* 442.

7 Snyder, *Bloodlands,* 104.

8 Terry Martin, "The Origins of Soviet Ethnic Cleansing," *Journal of Modern History* 70 (1998): 848–9; and Amir Weiner, *Making Sense of War: The Second World War and the Fate of the Bolshevik Revolution* (Princeton: Princeton University Press, 2002), 26, 143.

9 Snyder, *Bloodlands,* 104; and J. Arch Getty and Oleg V. Naumov, *The Road to Terror: Stalin and the Self-Destruction of the Bolsheviks, 1932–1939* (New Haven: Yale University Press, 1999), 492.

10 Martin, "Origins of Soviet Ethnic Cleansing," 813–14, 851.

11 Jeffrey Burds, "The Soviet War against 'Fifth Columnists': The Case of Chechnya, 1942–4," *Journal of Contemporary History* 42 (2007): 267–314.

12 Snyder, *Bloodlands,* 109.

13 Brian Glyn Williams, "Hidden Ethnocide in the Soviet Muslim Borderlands: The Ethnic Cleansing of the Crimean Tatars," *Journal of Genocide Research* 4 (2002), 362–3.

14 Aleksandr Nekrich, *The Punished Peoples: The Deportation and Fate of Soviet Minorities at the End of the Second World War* (New York: W. W, Norton, 1981), 110–11.

15 Michaela Pohl, "'It Cannot be that Our Graves will be Here' Chechen and Ingush Deportees in Kazakstan, 1944–1957," <www.chechnyaadvocacy.org/history/Graves%20-%20MPohl.pdf>

16 Williams, "Hidden Ethnocide," 365–6.

17 R. J. Rummel, *Death by Government* (New Brunswick, NJ: Transaction Publishers, 1994).

18 Benjamin Valentino, *Final Solutions: Mass Killing and Genocide in the 20th Century* (Ithaca: Cornell University Press, 2004), 10–13.

19 Paul Preston, *The Spanish Holocaust: Inquisition and Extermination in Twentieth-Century Spain* (London: HarperPress, 2011).

Chapter 4

1 Dawid Sierakowiak, Alan Adelson, and Kamil Turowski, *The Diary of Dawid Sierakowiak: Five Notebooks from the Łódź Ghetto* (New York: Oxford University Press, 1996), 63.

2   Sierakowiak, *Diary of Dawid Sierakowiak*, 143.
3   Sierakowiak, *Diary of Dawid Sierakowiak*, 173.
4   Chaim Aron Kaplan and Abraham Isaac Katsh, *Scroll of Agony; the Warsaw Diary of Chaim A. Kaplan* (New York: Macmillan, 1965), 297.
5   Gerald Fleming, *Hitler and the Final Solution* (Berkeley and Los Angeles: University of California Press, 1984), 51.
6   Michael Burleigh and Wolfang Wippermann, *The Racial State Germany 1933–1945* (Cambridge: University of Cambridge Press, 1991), 152.
7   Christian Gerlach, "The Wannsee Conference, the Fate of German Jews, and Hitler's Decision in Principle to Exterminate All European Jews," *The Journal of Modern History*, vol. 70, no. 4 (December 1998), 785, 790.
8   Jan T. Gross, *Neighbors: The Destruction of the Jewish Community in Jedwabne, Poland* (New York: Penguin Books, 2002), 71, 73.
9   Martin Gilbert, *The Holocaust: A History of the Jews of Europe during the Second World War* (New York: Henry Holt and Company, 1985), 203.
10 Martin Seckendorf, *Die Okkupationspolitik des deutschen Faschismus in Jugoslawien, Griechenland, Albanien, Italien und Ungarn (1941–1945)* (Berlin: Hüthig, 1992), 168, 173, 176–9.
11 Beate Meyer, Hermann Simon, and Chana C. Schütz, *Jews in Nazi Berlin: From Kristallnacht to Liberation* (Chicago: University of Chicago Press, 2009), 173.
12 Sierakowiak, *Diary of Dawid Sierakowiak*, 142.
13 Henry Friedlander, *The Origins of Nazi Genocide: From Euthanasia to Final Solution* (Chapel Hill: University of North Carolina Press, 1995), 203.
14 Gitta Sereny, *Into that Darkness: An Examination of Conscience* (New York: McGraw Hill, 1974).
15 Nationalsozialistische deutsche Arbeiter-Partei, and Katzmann, *Lösung der Judenfrage in Galizien*.
16 Susan Zuccotti, *The Holocaust, France, and the Jews* (New York: Basic Books, 1993), 98, 104.
17 Sierakowiak, *Diary of Dawid Sierakowiak*, 218.
18 Christopher Browning, *Ordinary Men: Reserve Police Battalion 101 and the Final Solution in Poland* (New York: HarperCollins, 1993), 170.
19 Herman Kruk and Benjamin Harshav, *The Last Days of the Jerusalem of Lithuania: Chronicles from the Vilna Ghetto and the Camps, 1939–1941* (New Haven: YIVO Institute for Jewish Research, 2002), 61.

20 The Righteous Among the Nations, Yad Vashem, <www1.yadvashem. org/yv/en/righteous/stories/jasinski.asp>

21 Kaplan, *Scroll of Agony*, 347.

22 Adam Czerniaków, Raul Hilberg, Stanislaw Staron, and Joseph Kermish, *The Warsaw Diary of Adam Czerniakow: Prelude to Doom* (Chicago: Ivan R. Dee, 1999), 385.

23 Abraham Lewin and Antony Polonsky, *A Cup of Tears: A Diary of the Warsaw Ghetto* (Oxford: Basil Blackwell in association with the Institute for Polish-Jewish Studies, Oxford, 1988), 320.

24 Gilbert, *The Holocaust*, 670.

25 Feigele Peltel Miedzyrzecki, *On Both Sides of the Wall: Memoirs from the Warsaw Ghetto* (New York: Holocaust Library, 1979), 194.

26 Jacob Gerstenfeld-Maltiel, *My Private War: One Man's Struggle to Survive the Soviets and the Nazis* (London: Vallentine Mitchell, 1993), 154.

27 Michael Burleigh, *The Third Reich: A New History* (New York: Hill and Wang, 2000), 521.

28 Burleigh, *The Third Reich*, 512.

Chapter 5

1 Jasmina Dervisevic-Cesic, *The River Runs Salt, Runs Sweet* (Eugene, OR: Panisphere, 1994, 2003), 49, 51, 121.

2 Dervisevic-Cesic, *The River Runs Salt, Runs Sweet*, 37.

3 Benjamin Lieberman, *Terrible Fate: Ethnic Cleansing in the Making of Modern Europe* (Chicago: Ivan R. Dee, 2006), 308.

4 Roy Gutman, *A Witness to Genocide* (New York: Macmillan, 1993), 44–5.

5 Vulliamy, *Seasons in Hell*, 102.

6 Richard Holbrooke, *To End a War*, revised edition (New York: Modern Library, 1999), 37.

7 András J. Riedlmayer, "Destruction of Cultural Heritage in Bosnia Herzegovina 1992–1996: Postwar Survey of Selected Municipalities," < http://hague.bard.edu/reports/BosHeritageReport-AR.pdf>

8 The *Guardian*, July 29, 1992.

9 Mark Danner, *Stripping Bare the Body: Politics Violence War* (New York: Nation Books, 2009), 145.

10 Rezak Hukanovic, *The Tenth Circle of Hell: A Memoir of Life in the Death Camps of Bosnia* (New York: Basic Books, 1996), 53, 63–63.

11 Ludwig Boltlzmann Institut, "Ethnic Cleansing Operations in the Northeast-Bosnian City of Zvornik from April through June 1992,"

<http://bim.lbg.ac.at/de/stellungnahmen-und-gutachten/ethnic-cleansing-operations-northeastbosnian-city-zvornik-april-through>

12 Hukanovic, *Tenth Circle of Hell*, 52.

13 *Daily Telegraph*, September 19, 1992.

14 Vulliamy, *Seasons in Hell*, 147–8.

15 Greg Procknow, *Recruiting and Training Genocidal Soldiers* (Regina, Canada: Francis & Bernard, 2011).

16 Svetlana Broz, Laurie Kain Hart, and Ellen Elias-Bursać, *Good People in an Evil Time: Portraits of Complicity and Resistance in the Bosnian War* (New York: Other Press, 2004).

17 Martin Shaw, *What is Genocide?* (Cambridge, UK and Malden, MA: Polity Press, 2007), 49–60.

Chapter 6

1 Akcam, *A Shameful Act,* 348.

GLOSSARY

Abdul Hamid II Sultan of the Ottoman Empire from 1876–1909

Aegean Sea Sea within the Mediterranean between Greece and Turkey

Albanian Ethnic group in southeastern Europe—now live mainly in Albania and Kosovo

Anatolia Large peninsula in western Asia that makes up most of modern-day Turkey

Anielewicz, Mordechai Leader of Warsaw Ghetto Uprising of 1943

Arendt, Hannah Philosopher and writer who wrote about the trial of Adolf Eichmann

Arkan (Zeljko Raznatovic) Leader of paramilitary that carried out ethnic cleansing in Bosnia

Arrow Cross Hungarian Fascist movement that toppled Hungary's government in 1944

Ashkenazi Jews with roots in Central and Eastern Europe

Asia Minor Peninsula of Western Asia—older name for region of Anatolia

Assyrians Christians found chiefly in eastern Anatolia and in Iraq

Auschwitz-Birkenau Major death camp in Upper Silesia

Azerbaijan Region to east of Armenia that borders on Caspian Sea

Babi Yar Ravine and site of 1941 massacre outside Kiev in Ukraine

Bach-Zelewski SS leader and anti-partisan commander on Eastern Front in the Second World War

Balakian, Grigoris Armenian Bishop

Balkan Wars Wars of 1912 and 1913 that led to loss of most Ottoman territories in Europe

Balkars Muslim ethnic minority deported by Stalin

Banja Luka Town of northern Bosnia

Belzec Major death camp in eastern Poland

Bergen-Belsen Concentration camp in Germany

Beria, Lavrenty Leader of NKVD during the Second World War

Bessarabia Region adjacent to Black Sea disputed by Romania and USSR

Bolsheviks Communist Party that gained power in Russian Revolution and Civil War

Bosnia Herzegovina Republic of the former Yugoslavia that declared independence in 1992

Bosnian Muslims (Bosniaks) Muslim ethnic group of Bosnia

Bouhler, Philipp Official in Hitler's Chancellery who oversaw forced euthanasia

Brandt, Karl Hitler's attending physician who, along with Bouhler, oversaw forced euthanasia

Buchenwald Concentration camp in Germany

Cambodia Country in Southeast Asia to west of Vietnam

Caucasus Mountain chain between Black and Caspian Seas

Chechens Muslim ethnic minority deported by Stalin

Cheka (OGPU) Soviet state security services

Chelmno Death camp in Poland north of Lodz

Cilicia Region along southeast cost of Asia Minor or Anatolia

Committee of Unity and Progress (CUP) Turkish nationalist political organization

Congo Free State Large region in Central Africa placed under rule of King Leopold of Belgium

Convention on the Prevention and Punishment of the Crime of Genocide—Genocide as defined by United Nations in 1948

Crimean Tatars Muslim ethnic minority of the Crimea deported by Stalin

Croatia A former republic of Yugoslavia that declared independence in 1991

Croats Slavic ethnic group and Catholics

Dachau Concentration camp in Germany located in town of Dachau near Munich

Danube River that flows east from Central Europe to the Black Sea

Dardanelles Strait that connects the Aegean Sea and the Sea of Marmara

Dashnaks Armenian nationalist movement

Dayton Accords Peace between combatants in Bosnia Herzegovina arranged through 1995 negotiations in Dayton, Ohio

Death's Head SS Unit of SS that provided guards in concentration camps

Der Zor Town in Syria on Euphrates River

Dhimmi (Zimmi) Peoples of the Book—for example, Jews and Christians in the Ottoman Empire

Dubrovnik City in Croatia on Adriatic Sea

Edirne City formerly known as Adrianople in eastern Thrace

Eichmann, Adolf SS official who oversaw deportation of Jews

Eicke, Theodore Head of Death's Head SS

Einsatzgruppen Units comprised of SS and others that engaged in mobile killing

Enver Turkish Minister of War during the First World War

Erzurum City in eastern Turkey

Foca Town in southern Bosnia

Frank, Anne Jewish girl who lived in hiding in Amsterdam before being deported and killed—author of diary

Frank, Hans Head of German occupation zone (General Government) in Central Poland

Führer Hitler's title as the Leader

Galen, Bishop Catholic Bishop of Münster in Germany

Galicia Region in eastern Poland and western Ukraine

Gallipoli Peninsula on edge of Turkish Eastern Thrace between Aegean Sea and Dardanelles Strait

General Government (Gouvernment) German occupation zone in Central Poland during the Second World War

German Southwest Africa German colony in area that later became country of Namibia

Gestapo Nazi Secret Police

Ghetto Sealed-off Jewish quarters created under German occupation in Poland and Eastern Europe

Globocnik, Odilo Leader of SS and Police in Lublin under German occupation

Gobineau, Arthur Nineteenth-century author who developed and influenced racist thinking

Goering, Hermann Founder of Gestapo and head of the German Air force (Luftwaffe)

Gokalp, Ziya Turkish nationalist sociologist

Gulag Soviet prison camp system

Harput (Kharpert) Town in central Anatolia

Herero African people targeted for extermination in German Southwest Africa

Heydrich, Rudolf Head of the SD and of the German security policy in Nazi Germany—assassinated 1942

Himmler, Heinrich Head of the SS

Holodomor Term given for genocide of Ukrainians

Horthy, Miklos Head of state of Hungary during the Second World War until 1944

Höss, Rudolf Commandant of Auschwitz

Hunchaks Armenian political party—Social Democrats

Hutus Majority ethnic group in Rwanda

HVO (Croatian Defense Council) Croatian military formed in Croat controlled areas of Herzegovina in Bosnia Herzegovina

Iasi City in northeastern Romania on border with Bessarabia

IDP Internally displaced person or persons

Ingush Muslim ethnic minority deported by Stalin

International Criminal Tribunal for the former Yugoslavia (ICTY) Tribunal for investigating crimes committed in former Yugoslavia

Ittihadists See CUP (Committee of Union and Progress)

JNA Yugoslav National Army

Jehovah's Witnesses A millenarian Christian denomination whose members are pacifists

Jewish Fighting Organization (ZOB) Resistance organization in Warsaw Ghetto

Jews' House Houses into which Jew were concentrated and isolated in Nazi Germany

Kalmyks Buddhist Ethnic minority deported by Stalin

Karachai Ethnic minority deported by Stalin

Karadzic, Radovan President of Republika Srpska

Katzmann, Friedrich SS General and Police Leader in Galicia

Kaunus City in Lithuania

Kemal, Mustafa (Ataturk) Leader of Turkish Nationalists and first President of Republic of Turkey

Keraterm Camp in Bosnia

Khmer Rouge Communist movement that held power in Cambodia from 1975–9

Kiev Chief city of Ukraine

King Leopold King of Belgium who gained the Congo

Kosovo Predominantly Albanian region of the former Yugoslavia contested by Serbs and Kosovar Albanians

Krajina Border region of southern Croatia

Kristallnacht Pogrom attacking Jews on November 9–10 in Nazi Germany

Kulaks Peasants said to be wealthier in Soviet Union

Kurds Ethnic group of eastern Anatolia also found in nearby countries

Lenin First leader of Soviet Union

Lodz City in central Poland

Lublin City in eastern Poland

Lukic, Milan Convicted of crimes against humanity committed in Bosnia

Lviv City in western Ukraine previously in eastern Poland

Majdanek Concentration camp near Lublin

Marmara, Sea of Sea located between Bosporus strait and the Dardanelles Strait

Mauthausen Concentration camp in Austria southeast of Linz

Milosevic, Slobodan President of the former Yugoslavia and of Serbia

Mladic, Ratko Chief of Staff of Military of Republika Srpska

Morgenthau, Henry United States Ambassador to Ottoman Empire

Mostar City on Neretva River in Herzegovina in eastern Bosnia Herzegovina

Nama African people targeted for destruction in German Southwest Africa

NKVD Soviet State Security Force

NSDAP German National Socialists Workers' Party or Nazi Party

Lemkin, Rafael Creator of term genocide

Lepsius, Johannes German Protestant Pastor active in Armenian issues

Levi, Primo Survivor of Auschwitz and author

Lueger, Karl Mayor of Vienna

Operation Barbarossa German invasion of Soviet Union June 1941

Operation Reinhard Extermination of Jews in General Government occupation zone of Poland

Order Police Reserve police in German military

Ottoman Empire Large Empire in southeastern Europe and Western Asia along with parts of North Africa that lost territory in decades before the First World War

Partisans Soviet Anti-German resistance forces in Eastern Europe; also Communist resistance in Yugoslavia

Petliura, Symon Head of independent Ukrainian Government during Russian Civil War

Pogroms Mob attacks on a particular population such as in pogroms against Jews

Pol Pot Leader of Khmer Rouge

Pontic Greeks Greek population that lived along shores of Black Sea

Prijedor Town in northern Bosnia

Pristina Capital of Kosovo

Reich Security Main Office (RSHA) Office linking security police and criminal police

Republic of Armenia Former Republic of Soviet Union that gained independence in 1991

Riga Capital of Latvia

Riggs, Henry American missionary in central Turkish city of Harput during the First World War

Righteous among the Nations Honor awarded to rescuers of Jews by Yad Vashem

Ringelblum, Emmanuel Historian and social worker of Warsaw Ghetto

RKFDV Agency that resettled ethnic Germans in areas slated for Germanization

Roma Ethnic group often referred to as Gypsies

Rumkowski, Chaim Elder and head of Lodz Ghetto

Rwanda Country to east of Congo and site of genocide in 1994

Salonica Greek city and port on Aegean Sea

Sarajevo Capital of Bosnia-Herzegovina

Sarikamis Site of Turkish Russian battle in the First World War

SD Security Service branch of SS

Second Sweep Phase of massacres in occupied Soviet Union that followed the initial killings by Einsatzgruppen

Security Police Gestapo combined with criminal police

Sephardic Jews with Spanish origins

Serbia Former Republic of Yugoslavia

Serbian Volunteer Guard (Tigers) One of the major Serb paramilitary forces in Bosnia

Serbs Slavic ethnic group and Orthodox Christians

Serpska, Republic Created by Serbs in Bosnia Herzegovina

Shark Island Camp in German Southwest Africa

Silesia Region of western Poland—longtime border zone of Poland and Germany

Sinti A gypsy population

Sobibor Death camp in eastern Poland

Solovetsky islands Islands in northern Russia and site of a Gulag camp

Solzhenitsyn, Aleksandr Soviet prisoner, author, and dissident

Spanish Civil War General Franco and rebels overthrew Spanish Republic—1936–9

Special Organization (Teskilat-I Mahsusa) Killing squads in Armenian Genocide

Srebrenica Town in eastern Bosnia and site of massacre

Stalin Leader of Soviet Union from 1920s until death in 1952

Stangl, Franz Commandant of Treblinka and of Sobibor death camps

T4 Forced euthanasia of disabled Germans

Talat Minister of Interior in Turkey during the First World War

Thrace Region in southeastern Europe today divided between Greece and Turkey

Tito (Josip Broz) Leader of Partisans in Yugoslavia during the Second World War and of Yugoslavia

Transcaucasus Region south of main mountain chain of the Caucausus

Treblinka Major death camp located northeast of Warsaw

Tudjman, Franjo Croatian nationalist politician and President of Croatia

Tutsis Minority ethnic group in Rwanda

UNHCR United Nations High Commissioner for Refugees

UNPROFOR A UN peace-keeping force in Bosnia

Ustasha Croatian Fascist movement that gained power in occupied Croatia

Van City in eastern Turkey

Vichy Collaborationist regime created in south of France after French defeat in 1940

Vilna (Vilnius) Lithuanian city

Visegrad Town in eastern Bosnia

Volhynia Region of western Ukraine once divided between Poland and the USSR

Vukovar City in eastern Croatia on the Danube River

Wangenheim German Ambassador to the Ottoman Empire

Wansee Suburb of Berlin and site of 1942 conference

Wegner, Armin German nurse, photographer, and human rights activist

Weimar Republic German Republic from 1918–33

White Rose Resistance movement located in Munich

Wirth, Christian Inspector of Operation Reinhard camps

Yad Vashem Israeli Memorial to the Holocaust and research center

Yagoda NKVD chief until 1936—executed 1938

Yerevan Capital of Republic of Armenia

Yezhov NKVD chief—executed 1940

Yiddish Ashkenazi Jewish language

Young Turks Turkish nationalist movement that emerged in late nineteenth century

Yugoslavia Country of south Slavs originally founded after First War—broke apart 1991–2

Zeks Common prisoners in Gulag

Zepa Town in eastern Bosnia

Zvornik Town in eastern Bosnia

Zyklon B Commercial name for poison used in gas chambers at Auschwitz

BIBLIOGRAPHY

Akçam, Taner. *The Young Turks' Crime against Humanity: The Armenian Genocide and Ethnic Cleansing in the Ottoman Empire*. Princeton, NJ: Princeton University Press, 2012.

—. *A Shameful Act: The Armenian Genocide and the Question of Turkish Responsibility*. New York: Metropolitan, 2006.

Aly, Götz. *Hitler's Beneficiaries: Plunder, Racial War, and the Nazi Welfare State*. New York: Metropolitan, 2007.

Aly, Götz, Belinda Cooper, and Allison Brown. *"Final Solution": Nazi Population Policy and the Murder of the European Jews*. London: Arnold, 1999.

Applebaum, Anne. *Gulag: A History*. New York: Doubleday, 2003.

Arad, Yitzhak. *The Holocaust in the Soviet Union*. Lincoln: University of Nebraska Press, 2009.

Arendt, Hannah. *Eichmann in Jerusalem; A Report on the Banality of Evil*. New York: Viking Press, 1963.

Balakian, Peter. *The Burning Tigris: The Armenian Genocide and America's Response*. New York: HarperCollins, 2003.

Bartov, Omer. *Murder in Our Midst: The Holocaust, Industrial Killing, and Representation*. New York: Oxford University Press, 1996.

—. *Hitler's Army: Soldiers, Nazis, and War in the Third Reich*. New York: Oxford University Press, 1991.

Berkhoff, Karel C. *Harvest of Despair: Life and Death in Ukraine Under Nazi Rule*. Cambridge, MA: Belknap Press of Harvard University Press, 2004.

Bloxham, Donald. *The Final Solution: A Genocide*. Oxford: Oxford University Press, 2009.

—. *Genocide, the World Wars and the Unweaving of Europe*. London: Vallentine Mitchell, 2008.

—. *The Great Game of Genocide: Imperialism, Nationalism, and the Destruction of the Ottoman Armenians*. Oxford: Oxford University Press, 2005.

Breitman, Richard. *Official Secrets: What the Nazis Planned, What the British and Americans Knew*. New York: Hill and Wang, 1998.

—. *The Architect of Genocide: Himmler and the Final Solution*. New York: Knopf, 1991.

Browning, Christopher R. *Ordinary Men: Reserve Police Battalion 101 and the Final Solution in Poland*. New York: HarperCollins, 1992.

Browning, Christopher R. and Jürgen Matthäus. *The Origins of the Final Solution: The Evolution of Nazi Jewish Policy, September 1939-March 1942*. Lincoln: University of Nebraska Press, 2004.

Bugaĭ, Nikolaĭ Fedorovich. *The Deportation of Peoples in the Soviet Union*. New York: Nova Science Publishers, 1996.

Carmichael, Cathie. *Genocide Before the Holocaust*. New Haven: Yale University Press, 2009.

—. *Ethnic Cleansing in the Balkans Nationalism and the Destruction of Tradition*. London: Routledge, 2003.

Cigar, Norman L. *Genocide in Bosnia: The Policy of "Ethnic Cleansing."* College Station: Texas A & M University Press, 1995.

Clark, Wesley K. *Waging Modern War: Bosnia, Kosovo, and the Future of Combat*. New York: Public Affairs, 2001.

Conquest, Robert. *The Harvest of Sorrow: Soviet Collectivization and the Terror-Famine*. New York: Oxford University Press, 1986.

—. *The Great Terror: Stalin's Purge of the Thirties*. New York: Macmillan, 1968.

Curthoys, Ann. "Raphaël Lemkin's 'Tasmania': An Introduction." *Patterns of Prejudice* 39, no. 2 (2005): 162–9. Historical Abstracts, EBSCOhost (accessed July 6, 2012).

Czerniaków, Adam, Raul Hilberg, Stanislaw Staron, and Joseph Kermish. *The Warsaw Diary of Adam Czerniakow: Prelude to Doom*. New York: Stein and Day, 1979.

Dadrian, Vahakn N. *Warrant for Genocide: Key Elements of Turko-Armenian Conflict*. New Brunswick, NJ: Transaction Publishers, 1999.

—. *The History of the Armenian Genocide: Ethnic Conflict from the Balkans to Anatolia to the Caucasus*. Providence, RI: Berghahn Books, 1995.

Davis, Leslie A. and Susan Blair. *The Slaughterhouse Province: An American Diplomat's Report on the Armenian Genocide, 1915–1917*. New Rochelle, NY: A.D. Caratzas, Orpheus Pub, 1989.

Dean, Martin. *Collaboration in the Holocaust: Crimes of the Local Police in Belorussia and Ukraine, 1941–44*. New York: St. Martin's Press, 2000.

Dervisevic-Cesic, Jasmina, Joanna Vogel, and Bruce Holland Rogers. *The River Runs Salt, Runs Sweet: A Memoir of Visegrad, Bosnia*. Eugene, OR: Panisphere, 2003.

Fleming, Gerald. *Hitler and the Final Solution*. Berkeley: University of California Press, 1984.

Friedländer, Saul. *The Years of Extermination: Nazi Germany and the Jews, 1939–1945.* New York, NY: HarperCollins, 2007.

Friedlander, Henry. *The Origins of Nazi Genocide: From Euthanasia to the Final Solution.* Chapel Hill: University of North Carolina Press, 1995.

Gellately, Robert. *Lenin, Stalin, and Hitler: The Age of Social Catastrophe.* New York: Alfred A. Knopf, 2007.

Gerlach, Christian. *Extremely Violent Societies: Mass Violence in the Twentieth-Century World.* Cambridge: Cambridge University Press, 2010.

—. *Krieg, Ernährung, Völkermord: Forschungen zur deutschen Vernichtungspolitik im Zweiten Weltkrieg.* Hamburg: Hamburger Edition, 1998.

—. "The Wannsee Conference, the Fate of German Jews, and Hitler's Decision in Principle to . . ." *Journal of Modern History* 70, no. 4 (December 1998): 759. Historical Abstracts, EBSCOhost (accessed July 6, 2012).

Getty, J. Arch and Oleg V. Naumov. *The Road to Terror: Stalin and the Self-Destruction of the Bolsheviks, 1932–1939.* New Haven, CN: Yale University Press, 1999.

Goldhagen, Daniel Jonah. *Hitler's Willing Executioners: Ordinary Germans and the Holocaust.* New York: Knopf, 1996.

Gross, Jan Tomasz. *Neighbors: The Destruction of the Jewish Community in Jedwabne, Poland.* Princeton: Princeton University Press, 2001.

Grossman, Vasiliĭ Semenovich, Antony Beevor, and Luba Vinogradova. *A Writer at War: Vasily Grossman with the Red Army, 1941–1945.* New York: Pantheon Books, 2005.

Gust, Wolfgang. *Der Völkermord an den Armeniern 1915/16: Dokumente aus dem Politischen Archiv des deutschen Auswärtigen Amts.* Springe: Zu Klampen, 2005.

Gutman, Roy. *A Witness to Genocide: The 1993 Pulitzer Prize-Winning Dispatches on the "Ethnic Cleansing" of Bosnia.* New York: Macmillan Pub. Co, 1993.

Hamerow, Theodore S. *Why We Watched: Europe, America, and the Holocaust.* New York: W.W. Norton & Co, 2008.

Heer, Hannes and Klaus Naumann. *War of Extermination: The German Military in World War II, 1941–1944.* New York: Berghahn Books, 1999.

Helsinki Watch (Organization: US) and Ivana Nizich. *War Crimes in Bosnia-Hercegovina.* New York: Human Rights Watch, 1992.

Herbert, Ulrich. *National Socialist Extermination Policies: Contemporary German Perspectives and Controversies.* New York: Berghahn Books, 2000.

Hilberg, Raul. *The Destruction of the European Jews*. New York: Holmes & Meier, 1985.

Hochschild, Adam. *King Leopold's Ghost: A Story of Greed, Terror, and Heroism in Colonial Africa*. Boston: Houghton Mifflin, 1998.

Holbrooke, Richard C. *To End a War*. New York: Random House, 1998.

Hovannisian, Richard G. *The Armenian Genocide in Perspective*. New Brunswick [NJ] USA: Transaction Books, 1986.

Hukanović, Rezak. *The Tenth Circle of Hell: A Memoir of Life in the Death Camps of Bosnia*. New York: Basic Books, 1996.

Ioanid, Radu. *The Holocaust in Romania: The Destruction of Jews and Gypsies Under the Antonescu Regime, 1940–1944*. Chicago, IL: Ivan R. Dee, 2000.

Judah, Tim. *Kosovo: War and Revenge*. New Haven: Yale University Press, 2000.

—. *The Serbs: History, Myth, and the Destruction of Yugoslavia*. New Haven: Yale University Press, 1997.

Kaplan, Chaim Aron and Abraham Isaac Katsh. *Scroll of Agony; The Warsaw Diary of Chaim A. Kaplan*. New York: Macmillan, 1965.

Kévorkian, Raymond H. *The Armenian Genocide: A Complete History*. London: I. B. Tauris, 2011.

Kiernan, Ben. *Blood and Soil: A World History of Genocide and Extermination from Sparta to Darfur*. New Haven: Yale University Press, 2007.

Kruk, Herman and Benjamin Harshav. *The Last Days of the Jerusalem of Lithuania: Chronicles from the Vilna Ghetto and the Camps, 1939–1944*. New Haven, CT: YIVO Institute for Jewish Research, 2002.

Levi, Primo. *The Drowned and the Saved*. New York: Summit Books, 1988.

Levi, Primo, S. J. Woolf, and Philip Roth. *Survival in Auschwitz: The Nazi Assault on Humanity*. New York: Simon & Schuster, 1996.

Longerich, Peter, Jeremy Noakes, and Lesley Sharpe. *Heinrich Himmler*. Oxford [England]: Oxford University Press, 2012.

Lewin, Abraham and Antony Polonsky. *A Cup of Tears: A Diary of the Warsaw Ghetto*. Oxford, OX, UK: Basil Blackwell in association with the Institute for Polish-Jewish Studies, Oxford, 1988.

Lieberman, Benjamin David. *Terrible Fate: Ethnic Cleansing in the Making of Modern Europe*. Chicago: Ivan R. Dee, 2006.

Longerich, Peter. *Holocaust: The Nazi Persecution and Murder of the Jews*. Oxford: Oxford University Press, 2010.

—. *"Davon haben wir nichts gewusst!": die Deutschen und die Judenverfolgung 1933–1945*. München: Siedler, 2006.

Lower, Wendy. *Nazi Empire-Building and the Holocaust in Ukraine*. Chapel Hill: University of North Carolina Press, 2005.

Maass, Peter. *Love Thy Neighbor: A Story of War*. New York: Alfred A. Knopf, 1996.

Madley, Benjamin. "From Africa to Auschwitz: How German South West Africa Incubated Ideas and Methods Adopted and Developed by the Nazis in Eastern Europe." *European History Quarterly 35*, no. 3 (2005): 429–64. Historical Abstracts, EBSCOhost (accessed July 6, 2012).

—. "Patterns of Frontier Genocide 1803–1910: The Aboriginal Tasmanians, the Yuki of California, and the Herero of Namibia." *Journal of Genocide Research 6*, no. 2 (2004): 167–92. Historical Abstracts, EBSCOhost (accessed July 6, 2012).

Malcolm, Noel. *Kosovo: A Short History*. New York: New York University Press, 1998.

Mcdonnell, Michael and A. Dirk Moses. "Raphael Lemkin as Historian of Genocide in the Americas." *Journal of Genocide Research 7*, no. 4 (2005): 501–29. Historical Abstracts, EBSCOhost (accessed July 6, 2012).

Miedzyrzecki, Feigele Peltel. *On Both Sides of the Wall: Memoirs from the Warsaw Ghetto*. New York: Holocaust Library, 1979.

Moore, Bob. *Victims and Survivors: The Nazi Persecution of the Jews in the Netherlands, 1940–1945*. London: Arnold, 1997.

Morgenthau, Henry and Ara Sarafian. *United States Diplomacy on the Bosphorus: The Diaries of Ambassador Morgenthau, 1913–1916*. Princeton, NJ: Gomidas Institute, 2004.

—. *Ambassador Morgenthau's Story*. Garden City, NY: Doubleday, Page, 1918.

Naimark, Norman M. *Stalin's Genocides*. Princeton, NJ: Princeton University Press, 2010.

—. *Fires of Hatred: Ethnic Cleansing in Twentieth-Century Europe*. Cambridge, MA: Harvard University Press, 2001.

Nekrich, Aleksandr Moiseevich. *The Punished Peoples: The Deportation and Fate of Soviet Minorities at the End of the Second World War*. New York: Norton, 1978.

Neufeld, Michael J. and Michael Berenbaum. *The Bombing of Auschwitz: Should the Allies Have Attempted It?* New York: St. Martin's Press, 2000.

Neuffer, Elizabeth. *The Key to My Neighbor's House: Seeking Justice in Bosnia and Rwanda*. New York: Picador, 2001.

Olusoga, David and Casper W. Erichsen. *The Kaiser's Holocaust: Germany's Forgotten Genocide and the Colonial Roots of Nazism*. London: Faber and Faber, 2010.

Palakéan, Grigoris, Peter Balakian, and Aris G. Sevag. *Armenian Golgotha*. New York: Alfred A. Knopf, 2009.

Paulsson, Gunnar S. *Secret City: The Hidden Jews of Warsaw, 1940–1945*. New Haven: Yale University Press, 2002.

Peterson, Merrill D. *"Starving Armenians": America and the Armenian Genocide, 1915–1930 and After*. Charlottesville: University of Virginia Press, 2004.

Pohl, J. Otto. *Ethnic Cleansing in the USSR, 1937–1949*. Westport, CN: Greenwood Press, 1999.

Power, Samantha. *A Problem from Hell: America and the Age of Genocide*. New York: Basic Books, 2002.

Press, Bernhard. *The Murder of the Jews in Latvia: 1941–1945*. Evanston, IL: Northwestern University Press, 2000.

Riggs, Henry H. *Days of Tragedy in Armenia: Personal Experiences in Harpoot, 1915–1917*. Ann Arbor, MI: Gomidas Institute, 1997.

Ringelblum, Emanuel. *Notes from the Warsaw Ghetto; The Journal of Emmanuel Ringelblum*. New York: Schocken Books, 1974.

Rohde, David. *Endgame: The Betrayal and Fall of Srebrenica, Europe's Worst Massacre Since World War II*. New York: Farrar, Straus and Giroux, 1997.

Sakowicz, Kazimierz and Yitzhak Arad. *Ponary Diary, 1941–1943: A Bystander's Account of a Mass Murder*. New Haven: Yale University Press, 2005.

Schaller, Dominik J. and Jürgen Zimmerer. *Late Ottoman Genocides: The Dissolution of the Ottoman Empire and Young Turkish Population and Extermination Policies*. London: Routledge, 2009.

Sells, Michael Anthony. *The Bridge Betrayed: Religion and Genocide in Bosnia*. Berkeley: University of California Press, 1996.

Sierakowiak, Dawid, Alan Adelson, and Kamil Turowski. *The Diary of Dawid Sierakowiak: Five Notebooks from the Łódź Ghetto*. New York: Oxford University Press, 1996.

Silber, Laura and Allan Little. *The Death of Yugoslavia*. London: Penguin Books, 1995.

Snyder, Timothy. *Bloodlands: Europe between Hitler and Stalin*. New York: Basic Books, 2010.

—. *The Reconstruction of Nations: Poland, Ukraine, Lithuania, Belarus, 1569–1999*. New Haven: Yale University Press, 2003.

Solzhenitsyn, Aleksandr Isaevich. *The Gulag Archipelago, 1918–1956: An Experiment in Literary Investigation*. New York: Harper & Row, 1974.

Steiner, Jean-François. *Treblinka*. New York: Meridian Book, 1994.

Stiglmayer, Alexandra. *Mass Rape: The War against Women in Bosnia-Herzegovina*. Lincoln: University of Nebraska Press, 1994.

Sudetic, Chuck. *Blood and Vengeance: One Family's Story of the War in Bosnia*. New York: W.W. Norton, 1998.

Suny, Ronald Grigor and Terry Martin. *A State of Nations: Empire and Nation-Making in the Age of Lenin and Stalin.* Oxford: Oxford University Press, 2001.

Suny, Ronald Grigor, Fatma Müge Göçek, and Norman M. Naimark. *A Question of Genocide: Armenians and Turks at the End of the Ottoman Empire.* Oxford: Oxford University Press, 2011.

Toynbee, Arnold and James Bryce Bryce. *The Treatment of Armenians in the Ottoman Empire, 1915–16: Documents Presented to Viscount Grey of Fallodon, Secretary of State for Foreign Affairs, by Viscount Bryce.* London: H.M.S.O., 1916.

Üngör, Uğur Ümit. *The Making of Modern Turkey: Nation and State in Eastern Anatolia, 1913–1950.* Oxford: Oxford University Press, 2011.

Valentino, Benjamin A. *Final Solutions: Mass Killing and Genocide in the Twentieth Century.* Ithaca, NY: Cornell University Press, 2004.

Venezia, Shlomo, Béatrice Prasquier, and Jean Mouttapa. *Inside the Gas Chambers: Eight Months in the Sonderkommando of Auschwitz.* Cambridge, UK: Polity, 2009.

Vulliamy, ed. *Seasons in Hell: Understanding Bosnia's War.* New York, NY: St. Martin's Press, 1994.

Weine, Stevan M. *When History Is a Nightmare: Lives and Memories of Ethnic Cleansing in Bosnia-Herzegovina.* New Brunswick, NJ: Rutgers University Press, 1999.

Weiss-wendt, Anton. "Hostage of Politics: Raphael Lemkin on 'Soviet genocide'." *Journal of Genocide Research* 7, no. 4 (2005): 551–9. Historical Abstracts, EBSCOhost (accessed July 6, 2012).

Weitz, Eric D. *A Century of Genocide: Utopias of Race and Nation.* Princeton, NJ: Princeton University Press, 2003.

Williams, Brian Glyn. *The Crimean Tatars: The Diaspora Experience and the Forging of a Nation.* Leiden: Brill, 2001.

Wilmer, Franke. *The Social Construction of Man, the State, and War: Identity, Conflict, and Violence in Former Yugoslavia.* New York: Routledge, 2002.

Winter, J. M. *America and the Armenian Genocide of 1915.* New York: Cambridge University Press, 2003.

Wollenberg, Jörg. *"Niemand war dabei und keiner hat's gewusst": die deutsche Öffentlichkeit und die Judenverfolgung 1933–45.* München: Piper, 1989.

Woodward, Susan L. *Balkan Tragedy: Chaos and Dissolution After the Cold War.* Washington, DC: Brookings Institution, 1995.

Zimmerer, Jürgen. "The Birth of the Ostland Out of the Spirit of Colonialism: A Postcolonial Perspective on the Nazi Policy of Conquest and Extermination." *Patterns of Prejudice* 39, no. 2 (2005): 197–219. Historical Abstracts, EBSCOhost (accessed July 6, 2012).

Zimmerer, Jürgen and Joachim Zeller. *Genocide in German South-West Africa: The Colonial War (1904–1908) in Namibia and Its Aftermath.* Monmouth, Wales: Merlin Press, 2008.

Zuccotti, Susan. *The Holocaust, the French, and the Jews.* New York, NY: Basic Books, 1993.

—. *The Italians and the Holocaust: Persecution, Rescue, and Survival.* New York: Basic Books, 1987.

INDEX